W9-BCV-137

AUTOMATING THE NEWS

AUTOMATING THE NEWS
HOW ALGORITHMS ARE REWRITING THE MEDIA

Nicholas Diakopoulos

Humber College Library
3199 Lakeshore Blvd. West
Toronto, ON   M8V 1K8

Harvard University Press

Cambridge, Massachusetts & London, England   *2019*

Copyright © 2019 by the Presidents and Fellows of Harvard College
All rights reserved
Printed in the United States of America

First printing

Library of Congress Cataloging-in-Publication Data

Names: Diakopoulos, Nicholas, author.
Title: Automating the news : how algorithms are rewriting the media /
    Nicholas Diakopoulos.
Description: Cambridge, Massachusetts : Harvard University Press, 2019. |
    Includes bibliographical references and index.
Identifiers: LCCN 2018046708 | ISBN 9780674976986 (alk. paper)
Subjects: LCSH: Journalism—Technological innovations. | Online journalism. |
    Digital media. | Algorithms. | Multimedia data mining.
Classification: LCC PN4784.T34 D53 2019 | DDC 070.4/3—dc23
LC record available at https://lccn.loc.gov/2018046708

To teachers everywhere

CONTENTS

AUTOMATING THE NEWS

INTRODUCTION:

THE ERA OF NEWS ALGORITHMS

Every fiscal quarter automated writing algorithms dutifully churn out thousands of corporate earnings articles for the Associated Press (AP), a more than 170-year-old newswire service. Drawing on little more than structured data, the stories are short, under 200 words, but disseminated very quickly to the AP wire, where they can then be published by any of the more than 1,700 news organizations that constitute the cooperative. By 2018 the AP was producing more than 3,700 stories this way during every earnings season, covering most US traded stocks down to a market capitalization of $75 million. That's more than ten times the number of stories they wrote without automation, enabling a far greater breadth of coverage. The stories won't be earning Pulitzer prizes any time soon, but they do convey the basics of corporate earnings in a straightforward and easily consumable form, and they do it at scale.

This is the era of news algorithms. Automation and algorithms have reached a point in their maturity where they can do real newswork—contributing to the journalistic endeavor in a variety of ways. But the story is as much about the people designing and working with automation as it is about the computational algorithms themselves. The technology doesn't supplant human practices so much as it changes the nature of the work. Algorithms are not going to replace journalists wholesale. Instead, the era of news algorithms is about designing efficient and effective human-computer systems.

News organizations such as the Associated Press know this—it's part of the strategy. "The difference is that rather than having to rush to write that first 200-word story on what earnings were, they [reporters] can actually take some time to digest an earnings release and focus on if there's news," explained Lisa Gibbs, a business editor who helped with the initial roll-out of the automated earnings stories. The automation frees up valuable time for staff to focus on thematic stories that use earnings as a news hook for deeper analysis—the content human journalists are generally more excited to work on anyway. "They can really focus on adding value and explaining what's going on in a particular industry or with a particular company," Justin Myers, the news automation editor at AP told me. The organization is quick to argue that no jobs have been lost to automation, and that the technology has in fact offloaded an equivalent of about three full-time jobs' worth of effort from business reporters. They are now freed up to pursue other work, including more creative and ambitious stories about corporate trends and business in general.

The business reporters at AP sometimes blend their own efforts with that of the machine, treating the automated earnings reports as a starting point. It's a way to get something out on the wire quickly and cheaply and gives them cover to circle back and write-through an article later on after additional reporting. Maybe they add a quotation from a corporate executive to enrich the story with context and perspective. Other situations call for editorial override. If an experienced reporter thinks that the earnings consensus from the data that feeds the automation is not well calibrated to other sources, he or she might manually write-in additional context and interpretation from an alternative data source. In these cases the signpost at the end of the story updates to reflect the human-machine collaboration: "*Elements* of this story were generated by Automated Insights using data from Zacks Investment Research."

In some edge cases the automation still isn't up to the task, and experienced editors have to step in to get the job done. When it was first automating earnings reports, the AP would not automate bank earnings because banks were still reporting settlements and unique circumstances related to the 2008 financial crisis. "There was just no way we were going to be able to get an accurate, sensible [automatically generated] earnings story as long as that was happening," Gibbs told me. "Everybody else was merrily enjoying the fruits of automated earnings. But my banking reporter was still coming in at 6:30 in the morning to write on Bank of America earnings." Clearly there are limits to what algorithms and automation can do for news production; human journalists will be needed more than ever.

Of course, automated writing technology is just one piece of this new era. Algorithms and automation are suffusing the entire news production chain, whether enhancing investigative journalism with machine-learning and data-mining methods, creating new interactive media such as newsbots that converse with audiences, or optimizing content for various media platforms using data-driven headline testing. There's almost no facet of the news production pipeline, from information gathering to sense-making, storytelling, and distribution that is not increasingly touched by algorithms.

Ebullient mysticism swirls around all of the possibilities algorithms create. Automatically written texts ready to publish without a second glance do have an almost magic air about them. And as I write this, artificial intelligence is at a pinnacle of hype. But my hope is that this book will help to inure you to that seduction, to keep your feet firmly planted on the ground. While full automation sounds tantalizing (sure, what person wouldn't want to let the computers do the hard work, while they themselves take a long lunch), the reality is that the era of news algorithms is more aptly characterized as a human-computer symbiosis. Algorithms and automation will continue to be incorporated into news production in important ways, but in most cases they will act as a complement to human effort, rather than a substitute. Whether to enhance scale, speed, efficiency, and breadth or to create new possibilities through content adaptation, optimization, and personalization, there *are* exciting and seemingly magical things that algorithms make possible. But behind the curtain are designers, editors, reporters, data scientists, and engineers all contributing in direct or indirect ways.

Algorithms have very real limitations. Chiefly, they rely on a quantified version of reality: they must measure the world and use that data in coming to decisions about classifying, ranking, associating, or filtering information. That is a severe handicap when we're talking about the news: the world is highly dynamic in everything that can happen. Without the flexibility to adapt what they measure, and how they measure it, algorithms will always be behind the curve. Anything lying outside the bounds of what is quantified is inaccessible to the algorithm, including information essential to making well-informed ethical decisions. If every decision is reduced to numbers, a lack of context threatens to rob challenging decisions—those that are slightly askew, nonroutine, or out of bounds—of appropriate nuance. These fundamental limitations of algorithms, together with the human ability to mitigate them, contribute to my belief that the era of news algorithms will still have plenty of people around. The jobs, roles, and tasks those people have will just look a bit different.

The Algorithmic Evolution of News Media

How do algorithms and automation change the news media? This book considers three main themes in the professional adoption of algorithms and automation in news production. These include: (1) the reflection of human values (including, but not exclusively journalistic values) in the design and use of these technologies; (2) the change in journalistic practices that arise as algorithms are blended into news routines; and (3) the contribution that algorithms and automation play in enhancing the sustainability of news production.

The first theme takes as the premise that all technologies embed and encode human values. If journalistic designers are able to explicate the ineffable, such as news values and other ethical rules and mandates, they can craft an image of algorithmic media that is more in line with their professional ideology. The role designers and operators play in algorithmic news media is not to be understated: they make key editorial decisions about how algorithms are parameterized, the defaults chosen, what the algorithm pays attention to, and indeed the values baked into the core of the system itself. For the Associated Press, templates and written fragments of text reflect journalistic knowledge and expectations about genre, style, word choice, and tone. The editorial thinking of the organization is inextricably woven into the system via data, knowledge bases, and rules. In this book I will repeatedly make the case that people and their values are embedded throughout the human-algorithm system now constituting the news media. This recognition suggests a strategic opportunity for news organizations to become more cognizant of their ability to embed their own organizational and institutional values into technological advances that then structure news production workflows.

The second theme of the book relates to the many ways in which news production practices are changing in light of new forms of automation and algorithms. The history of journalism is one of adaptation as new technologies—telephony, photography, reproduction, and computerization—changed the nature of roles, tasks, and workflows. This book presents a continuity of this idea, but with an emphasis on how technologies of automation and algorithms lead to shifts in practices. For instance, new tasks for configuring, parameterizing, and template writing to support automated content production are leading to roles for "meta journalists," who think and work in ways to support the technology. To keep those AP earnings reports humming along, new tasks relating to the upkeep of knowledge bases had to be created. Data about whether a company moved, changed names, or merged are important to keep current, which becomes a task that gets divvied up amongst the reporters on the business desk. Future journalists will need to develop computational thinking skills so that they understand the design space for algorithmic tools and are sensitive to the sorts of alien and unfamiliar errors that computer algorithms may produce. Making the most out of increasingly human-machine hybrid systems will require the acquisition of technology-specific skills. New flavors of work will also be necessitated, such as auditing or reverse-engineering algorithms that are increasingly used throughout the public and private sectors in decision-making contexts. Not only will reporters need traditional skills for reviewing documents, unraveling threads, and asking tough questions in interviews, but they will also need to develop new ones for quantitative thinking, designing experiments, and writing computer code to collect, analyze, and present data. Accommodating the increasing use of algorithms and automation in news production will entail labor dislocation—not layoffs necessarily, but certainly shifts in how journalists work and are educated.

Finally, the third theme I explore in the book is how the use of automation and algorithms has implications for the economics and sustainability of news production and public-interest media. Data-mining techniques can create information subsidies for finding stories in masses of documents. Automated content can enhance the scale, speed, breath, and personalization of news. Newsbots can amplify the engagement of audiences. And optimization algorithms can improve the efficiency of attention capture in the distribution of content. These capabilities all stand to add to the bottom line of news organizations. Whether it's a matter of routine tasks that are entirely automated, or nonroutine tasks that are made more efficient for human workers, the economic potential of these technologies is beginning to be realized. Yet economic imperatives must be put into dialogue with editorial ones if ideological values are to be maintained. In light of the first theme, journalists are at a turning point in how they choose to imprint commercial values alongside editorial values in the algorithms and automation they design. Because of its affordances for scale and speed, automation creates a "more, more, more" mentality with respect to content production, but the ethical deployment of these technologies necessitates consideration of when more is less, or when more needs to mean "more quality" rather than "more output." So, while there are important contributions for automation and algorithms to make to the sustainability of media, my goal here is to put those in context.

A Note on Methods

I've spent the better part of a dozen years studying computational journalism, first from the perspective of a computer and information scientist and more recently as a journalism and communication studies scholar. My methodological approach for this book involves first of all an interdisciplinary synthesis of research spanning the relevant disciplines. In that respect my goals are to stimulate an exchange between research literatures that are not often put into dialogue and to develop ways of thinking about computational journalism that reflect the interdisciplinarity of the subject. Second, I've undertaken interviews with key practitioners from news organizations both large and small. In total I spoke to sixty-three individuals, primarily in editorial roles, over the course of 2017 and 2018. My sampling was purposive, based on topics and projects that were known to me through research. I also recruited participants through referrals and out of convenience in the practitioner networks where I circulate in the United States and Europe. Many of my interviewees were male (81 percent), a situation that reflects the skew toward men in many technology-oriented fields (for example, Google's 2018 tech workforce was 79 percent male), as well as highlighting a limitation of relying on a convenience sample. While I do not believe this skew undermines the observations I make in this book, it does underscore a key diversity issue related to who is designing and developing algorithmic media. A semistructured interview guide was tailored to each interviewee with respect to how his or her work touched on a specific topic (or sometimes topics), including data mining, automated content, newsbots, and algorithmic accountability, while probing thematic elements of values, practices, and sustainability. All interviews were audio recorded, transcribed, and then analyzed through a process of iterative qualitative coding of concepts and themes. This data informs many of the observations and syntheses I develop. Finally, on several occasions throughout the book I present data-driven vignettes or anecdotes. These are meant to be illustrations or potentialities, though in a somewhat oxymoronic twist I do not place great emphasis on quantitative evidence in the book.

What to Expect in This Book

In addition to the introduction you're reading, this book consists of six core chapters, plus a forward-looking capstone chapter. Professionals and practitioners should come away with a sharper critical eye toward algorithms and how they impact the media system and society, while gaining knowledge that informs strategic and responsible adoption of such technology in practice. In parallel, researchers and scholars should expect to gain an overview of the state-of-the-art landscape of computational journalism and a synthesis that provides new orientations and opportunities for research in journalism, communication, and information studies.

Chapter 1 develops the idea of hybrid journalism, first by exploring background material about algorithms and journalism and then by drawing out the potentials for intersecting and weaving the two together. Can algorithms do journalism? How can they contribute to the types of value-added information tasks that journalists undertake on a daily basis? And how should human and algorithm be blended together in order to efficiently and effectively produce news information? I examine the limitations of algorithmic approaches to production, highlighting key areas of complex communication and expert thinking where human cognition will be essential. I also introduce how computational thinking may help us design algorithms that continue to advance in capability. Ultimately, I argue for a future in which algorithms, automation, and humans are hybridized in new workflows that expand the scale, scope, and quality of news production in the future.

Data-mining and machine-learning techniques are increasingly being used throughout news organizations. Chapter 2 sets out to answer the question of what these techniques offer to editorial production in journalism. From finding stories to monitoring or predicting events, evaluating content and sources, and helping to curate discussions, data mining is proving to have a range of utility. I argue that the capabilities of data mining can subsidize newsroom activity, creating new economic opportunities for newsrooms by saving time and lowering the cost of story development, by speeding up the monitoring of new information, and by allowing for time reinvestment that results in higher quality and more unique journalism that lends a competitive edge in the marketplace. I then discuss the appropriate deployment and adoption of data-mining techniques into journalistic practice with respect to how it may shape coverage and how knowledge claims are built for public consumption by grappling with the statistical uncertainty often inherent in these techniques.

Chapter 3 turns to the central topic of automation in content production. This includes deployments such as the Associated Press's use of automated writing software for financial earnings, as well as other examples from data-rich domains such as sports, politics, and weather and in different modalities such as video and data visualization. Opportunities afforded by the technology, such as enhanced speed, scale, accuracy, and personalization, are contrasted with limitations such as data contingencies, flexibility, and adaptability to an evolving world, interpretation and explanation, and writing quality. The integration of human and machine is perhaps nowhere more visible than in "automated" content production. I show that from design and development to supervision and maintenance during operation, automated content systems create new demands on human skills as production practices shift to accommodate the technology. Looking to the future, I suggest novel opportunities for applying automated content production in less descriptive genres, and for topics that may benefit from the breadth of content that automation enables.

Newsbots are the subject of Chapter 4. Automated agents that live on social media, newsbots are shaping the ways that news information is delivered, gathered, and monitored, thereby creating possibilities for interaction and engagement with information framed by a closely authored social persona. As a new medium, bots are only just beginning to be explored as useful tools for serious journalism, offering new possibilities for exercising accountability journalism and for expressing opinion and critique in new ways. Yet they also have a dark side. Just as easily as they can enhance the journalistic enterprise if used thoughtfully, they can also be employed for less wholesome purposes— spreading lies and misinformation, overwhelming and distracting attention from what matters, and even attacking and bullying individuals. Vigilance about the misuse of bots on social platforms offers an intriguing possibility for a new beat in which journalists monitor the ebb and flow of automated communicators and their effects on the public sphere.

Chapter 5 focuses on the role that algorithms play in the distribution of news information. Platforms such as Google and Facebook are coming to dominate vast amounts of human attention using curation algorithms. The ways in which these algorithms surface, filter, highlight, and disseminate information can make the difference in whether important civic stories are heard and reach critical mass. News organizations are increasingly optimizing their content to succeed in this algorithmically driven commercial environment. But some are also stepping back to consider how core editorial values can be put into dialogue with commercial metrics of content success, setting the stage for an innovation I refer to as the "journalistic newsfeed."

Chapter 6 considers how the proliferation of algorithmic decision-making in many facets of society—from criminal justice, to education, to dynamic pricing—is impacting journalism practice. New techniques are needed to help hold these decisions accountable to the public. In the face of important or expensive errors and mistakes, discrimination, unfair denials of public services, or censorship, journalists are developing methods to audit and explain such systems to the public in a practice I call "algorithmic accountability reporting." In this chapter I describe the evolving algorithms beat, detailing different types of algorithmic accountability stories and the methods needed to uncover them. Complicating factors include legal access to information about algorithms, the dynamic and shifting nature of sociotechnical systems, and how journalistic skills and teamwork will need to advance to do this type of reporting. At the same time, journalists themselves must grapple with their own use of algorithms in the production and publication of information. I argue that algorithmic transparency can be a productive path for increased accountability of algorithmic media.

The concluding capstone chapter synthesizes previous chapters' content and outlines challenges related to the evolution of algorithmic media and what that evolution means for algorithms, individuals, and society. These challenges call for rigorous new programs of study and institutional investment in how information gathering can be enhanced using automation and algorithms, how advanced interfaces for hybrid newswork can be designed and evaluated, how journalists will need to be educated differently in order to take full advantage of the efficiency gains offered by new computational tools, and how society will need to cope with the undermining of authenticity of media. Addressing these challenges will require an ambitious interdisciplinary approach and increased collaboration between academia, industry, and civil society.

Throughout this book I emphasize new capabilities at the frontier of algorithmic news production while exploring how the relationship and tension between human and computer play out in the context of journalism. This manifests both in terms of how values (and whose values) come to be embedded in the technology driving the news media, as well as how work practices are redesigned to reap economic rewards while balancing the strengths and weaknesses of automation against those of people. I hope you'll find I present an optimistic view of the role algorithms can play in media, while tempering that optimism to seek a responsible and ethically conscientious way forward as algorithms are adopted more widely in news production.

1

HYBRIDIZATION:

COMBINING ALGORITHMS, AUTOMATION,

AND PEOPLE IN NEWSWORK

The Panama Papers was un-
doubtedly the biggest investigative news story of 2016. The Pulitzer
prize–winning project built on a massive trove of 11.5 million
leaked documents—more than 2.6 terabytes of data—concerning
offshore companies and the powerful people behind them.
Buried in those documents were scoops that led to the downfall
of the prime ministers of Iceland and Pakistan, rocked the worlds of
banking and sports, and exposed the shady business dealings of
major companies such as Siemens.[1] The International Consor-
tium of Investigative Journalists (ICIJ) coordinated close to 400
journalists working with the leaked documents as they produced
more than 4,700 news articles based on the data.[2] The scale of
the investigation simply dwarfed anything attempted up to that
time. How did ICIJ and their partners pull it off? (Hint: there
were no fancy artificially intelligent "robots" involved.)

The scale of the Panama Papers leak makes it almost unimagi-
nable to consider *not* using heavy-duty computer power. But
the real trick was to harness computing in a way that enabled the
hundreds of collaborating investigative journalists to contribute
their expertise and ability to contextually interpret what they
were finding. If there were a mantra it would be, "Automate what
computers do best, let people do the rest." On the one hand is
the necessary task of converting the millions of leaked documents

into digital text indexed in databases, something machines excel at using optical character recognition (OCR) algorithms. In the case of the Panama Papers ICIJ delegated the OCR process to about thirty machines operating in parallel in the cloud.[3] This allowed documents to be put into databases that could be searched according to lists of keywords. On the other hand are tasks related to figuring out what companies and people to search for in the first place, and then connecting those entities to find patterns that allude to improprieties, such as tax evasion. These are tasks that still fall heavily on the shoulders of knowledgeable people. ICIJ maintains a collaboration platform that lets reporters post queries, documents, or comments to leverage the collective intelligence of partners.

The Panama Papers illustrates the power of combining human knowledge and expertise with the capabilities of machines to cope with an immense scale of data. Such complementarity between human and machine labor will continue to drive the evolution of newswork in the coming years. Wholesale substitution of reporting and editing jobs with automation is far less likely given the current state-of-the-art in technology. Meticulous estimates by economists suggest that only about 15 percent of reporters' time and 9 percent of editors' time is automatable using currently demonstrated technology.[4] Journalists are in fairly good shape in comparison to occupations like paralegals, who have an estimated 69 percent of their time that could be automated. Journalism jobs as a whole will be stable, though bits and pieces will fall prey to automation and algorithms.

Every job or workflow mixes different types of tasks with different susceptibilities to automation. Some tasks are highly skills-based, while others are contingent on knowing a set of specified rules, and still others rely on a store of knowledge or expertise that's built up over time.[5] An example of a skills-based task is keying in text from a digitized document so that it can be indexed. ICIJ could have trained people to do this work, but we would all be long gone by the time they finished. Algorithms have reached a high degree of reliability for this type of task and so offer a new opportunity for scaling up investigations. Entity recognition is an example of a rules-based task that involves marking a piece of text as referring to a particular corporation or person. This type of task reflects a higher level of cognition and interpretation but can be automated when the rules are well-established (that is, it's clear what constitutes an entity being labeled as a person rather than a corporation) and the data (in this case the output of the OCR process) feeding the task are reliable. Finally, knowledge-based tasks reflect those activities with high uncertainty, such as when data are vague and ambiguous. For an investigation like the Panama Papers, a knowledge-based task might be understanding the relationship between two entities in terms of the intents and obligations of those entities to each other and to the jurisdictions where they reside. Each macro-task will have a different composition of subtasks, some of which may be skills- or rules-based steps that are more amenable to automation. Knowledge-based tasks can be enhanced through complementary algorithms and user interfaces that allow an expert to work more quickly. Most workflows will not be entirely automated. Instead, different levels of automation will be involved at different stages of information production.

As technology advances, however, more and more artificial intelligence and machine-learning techniques will be introduced into investigations like the Panama Papers (as we'll see in Chapter 2). Algorithms are beginning to make headway in cognitive labor involving rule- and knowledge-based tasks, creating new possibilities to expand the scale and quality of investigations. Some of this technology will completely automate tasks, opening up time to reinvest in other activities. Other advances will be symbiotic with core human tasks and will, for instance, make finding entities and interpreting a web of relationships between banks, lawyers, shell companies, and certificate bearers easier and more comprehensive for the next Panama Papers. The challenge is to figure out how to weave algorithms and automation in with human capabilities. How should human and algorithm be blended to-gether in order to expand the scale, scope, and quality of journal-istic news production?

To understand how this blend may come about, it is impor-tant to delineate the capabilities and limitations of our two main actors. What are algorithms, and what is it exactly that they do? And, what is journalism, and what do journalists do? Answering these questions will pave the way toward designing the future of hybridized newswork.

What Do Algorithms Do?

An algorithm is a series of steps that is undertaken in order to solve a particular problem or to accomplish a defined outcome. A cooking recipe is an algorithm—albeit one that is (often) exe-cuted by a human. It consists of a set of inputs (ingredients) and outputs (the cooked dish) as well as instructions for transforming and combining raw ingredients into something appetizing. Here we are concerned with algorithms that run on digital computers and that transform and combine information in different ways—information recipes cooked by computer, if you will.

The singular term that describes algorithms that operate on in-formation is "computing," formally defined as "the systematic study of algorithmic processes that describe and transform infor-mation."[6] A fundamental question of computing concerns what information processes can be effectively automated. Automation in turn has been defined as "a device or system that accomplishes (partially or fully) a function that was previously, or conceivably could be, carried out (partially or fully) by a human operator."[7] A related term is "artificial intelligence" (AI), which can be under-stood as a computer system "able to perform tasks normally requiring human intelligence."[8] The phrase "autonomous tech-nology" entails a version of full automation in which a system operates without human intervention, notwithstanding the human design and maintenance work that all designed systems require.

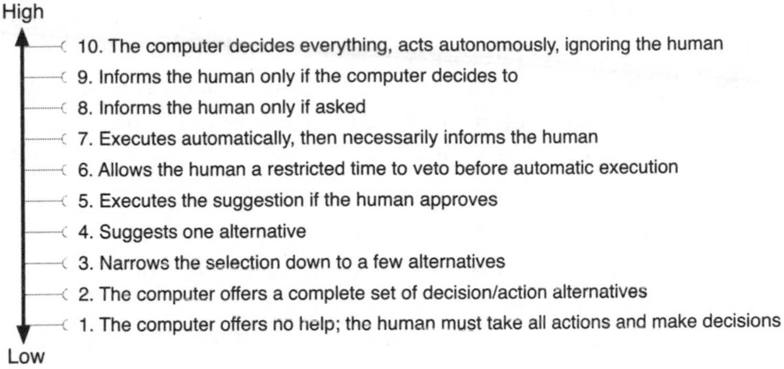

High

↑ ⊰ 10. The computer decides everything, acts autonomously, ignoring the human

⊰ 9. Informs the human only if the computer decides to

⊰ 8. Informs the human only if asked

⊰ 7. Executes automatically, then necessarily informs the human

⊰ 6. Allows the human a restricted time to veto before automatic execution

⊰ 5. Executes the suggestion if the human approves

⊰ 4. Suggests one alternative

⊰ 3. Narrows the selection down to a few alternatives

⊰ 2. The computer offers a complete set of decision/action alternatives

↓ ⊰ 1. The computer offers no help; the human must take all actions and make decisions

Low

Figure 1.1. Levels of automation that blend more or less human and automated effort. *Source:* Figure derived from "A Model for Types and Levels of Human Interaction with Automation," *IEEE Transactions on Systems, Man, and Cybernetics* 30, no. 3 (2001).

Full autonomy is one extreme in a spectrum of options that blend humans and computers (see Figure 1.1).

Much as machines and mechanization transformed the production of material objects in the nineteenth and twentieth centuries, computing is now transforming information work by offloading intellectual and cognitive labor to computers. This has been referred to as the "second machine age" because computers are now doing for mental work what machines did for physical work in the first machine age.[9] This cognitive labor encompasses computing tasks but also crosses into the terrain of AI to capture the idea of analytic information manipulation tasks typically associated with intelligence. Things start to get particularly interesting when algorithms enter into the evaluative phase of cognitive labor, in effect judging and *making decisions*. The quality of those decisions dictates how far we can push automation.

This has been a long time coming. As early as 1958 researchers at IBM described a program that could automatically extract an abstract from a research paper or news article.[10] In order to work, the system had to analyze each sentence and then judge how well it captured a key idea from the article. If it was a representative snippet, then the algorithm would extract and add it to the summary. Fifty-five years later, in 2013, Yahoo! started using summarization technology in its news app to condense information from several news articles into a single briefing. The technology to analyze text by computer has been around for decades. But the automatic judgments needed to summarize an article have only recently reached a level of quality that allows the summaries to have actual value in the media marketplace.

Computer algorithms can do work in a few different ways. Some information tasks involve calculations of noncontroversial mathematical equations. Psychologists would call this an "intellective task," or a task with a demonstrably correct answer.[11] There are plenty of intellective tasks beneficial to information production processes. Digitization is a big one. Arrays of bits from audio or pixels from scanned documents—like the millions analyzed in the Panama Papers leak—need to be converted into recognizable words and symbols that can be further transformed and indexed in databases.[12]

But many tasks don't necessarily have a demonstrably correct answer and instead involve subjective judgment. Judgment tasks are politically interesting because they do not often have a correct answer. Instead, a preferred alternative is chosen based on facts as well as values, beliefs, and attitudes about the alternatives. The judgments that algorithms make are often baked in via explicit rules, definitions, or procedures that designers and coders articulate when creating the algorithm. Algorithms are neither neutral nor objective—though they will apply whatever value-laden rules they encode *consistently*. Machine-learning algorithms learn how to make decisions based on data. The algorithm is provided a set of observations about the world and learns how to make a judgment, such as a classification, by extracting patterns from those observations. The *New York Times* uses a machine-learned classifier to help it moderate comments on its site. Using data about which online comments have been flagged by a moderator as "toxic," an algorithm learns to classify future comments as "toxic" or "non-toxic."

The main value proposition of algorithms is their ability to make high-quality decisions, and to do so very quickly and at scale using automation. There are at least four fundamental judging decisions that algorithms make: prioritizing, classifying, associating, and filtering. Oftentimes these decisions are then composed into higher level information tasks. To take news article summarization as an example, such an algorithm must first *filter*, or select, a subset of representative sentences from an article and then *prioritize* them in terms of importance to a user before presenting them as a summary. Other composite decisions are possible, too. The relevance of a search engine result could be considered a combination of an *association* decision between a search query and a result (that is, whether a particular website is related to a search term) and a *prioritization* decision that directs attention by communicating the magnitude of that association in a ranked list. All of these decisions rely on the calculation of analytic criteria, which themselves may be highly subjective, such as what defines a "representative" sentence or how one determines the "relevance" to a user for a ranking.

Prioritization decisions are perhaps some of the most crucial in the context of news media. A cousin to prioritization is optimization, which considers the top-priority item—the optimum along some dimension of priority. Given the limits of human attention, algorithms that can prioritize or optimize for the most interesting or informative content can select that content and present it first or give it privileged screen real estate so that it captures more attention. For instance, headline variations can be prioritized to pick the one that will optimize the click-through rate to an article. Designed into every prioritization decision are criteria that may be computed or derived and then used to sort items. These sorting criteria determine what gets pushed to the top and reflect editorial choices and value propositions that embed the design decisions of the algorithm's human creators.

Classification decisions also pervade newswork. For instance, organizations such as the Associated Press and the *New York Times* use algorithms to classify and standardize their vast content archives, allowing them to organize, store, transmit, or further process content in well-defined ways. Classification is highly political, involving decisions that range from what deserves to be a category to begin with to how categories are defined and operationalized quantitatively for computers.[13] Such algorithms can also be imbued with bias based on the input data they've been trained on. Human influence is woven into the process of defining, rating, and sampling the data to train the algorithm. Consider the toxic comment classifier again. The people who rate and grade comments to create training data end up having their biases built into the algorithm. Research has shown that men and women rate toxicity of comments in subtly different ways. So if men produce the majority of training data, as is the case for some commercially operational systems, then we can expect this bias to be refracted through the subsequent decisions the classifier makes.[14]

Association decisions denote relationships between entities. One example of an associative relationship between two datasets is correlation, which indicates that as a value in one dataset increases or decreases, the corresponding number in another dataset also increases or decreases in step. Such a relationship implies a statistical connection between the two datasets. Of course, there are many other types of—and semantics for—associations that algorithms can help to identify, but they are always built on some criteria that define the association and a measure of similarity that dictates how precisely two things must match to be considered to have the association. For instance, in an investigation like the Panama Papers an association algorithm might be defined between two entities in order to link a person or company to another person or company in order to uncover or trace the flow of money. Such an association could be indicative of fraud, corruption, or a criminal scheme that is of interest to an investigative journalist.

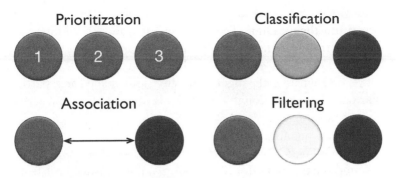

Figure 1.2. A schematic diagram of four fundamental information decisions. These can be composed into higher-level decisions such as summarization or relevance and are undergirded by calculations of analytic criteria.

Finally, algorithms can make decisions and take actions about what to selectively show, filter out, emphasize, or diminish, based on rules or criteria. Newsfeeds like Facebook's, news reading apps, recommendation widgets, and even news homepages make use of algorithms that dictate what to show or hide. This gets at a core function of what news organizations do: deciding what to publish or not publish. Filtering algorithms are increasingly used to help moderate social media by hiding offensive or uncivil posts that might disturb users. A news organization might deploy a toxic comment classifier by using the toxicity rating as scored by the classification algorithm to filter from view those comments with a score above some preset threshold.

In summary, algorithms can do intellective tasks such as calculating things based on equations or transforming digital bits into words and symbols really fast, as well as make a range of decisions related to prioritization, classification, association, filtering, and compositions of these basic decisions (see Figure 1.2). Both calculating and decision-making algorithms have an immense potential to change the nature of information production. Yet automatic decisions are suffused with human judgments and values that undergird the various definitions and choices that constitute their design. The question of how far automation can penetrate into news and information production tasks depends on the types of decisions that need to be made in those tasks, and whether the algorithmic decisions made for a particular task are high enough quality to be accepted by end-users of that information.

What Is Journalism, and What Do Journalists Do?

A sound starting point for the function of journalism comes from sociologist Michael Schudson, who defines it as "the business or practice of regularly producing and disseminating information about contemporary affairs of public interest and importance."[15] In this sense journalism is about a relatively narrowly scoped production of information for society. But the concept of journalism can also be construed via an array of other activities and perspectives. To name just a few possibilities, journalism can be considered a practice, a profession, a business, an institution, a social field, or an ideology.[16] And the boundaries of what is and is not considered journalism are in constant flux: it is "a constantly shifting denotation applied differently depending on context."[17] Here I make use of the ideological view, which identifies shared beliefs in journalism about the importance of public service, objectivity, autonomy, immediacy, and ethics.[18] The ideology reflects a set of constitutive commitments—beliefs and codes—that journalists use to rationalize practices that are within the purview of journalism and that shape modes of thinking within the discipline.[19] Practitioners of journalism depict it as concerned with truth and verification, loyalty to the public, and independence and autonomy from those they cover, as well as being produced with an eye toward building community and fostering deliberative conversation.[20] Aspirational codes of practice, such as those from the Society for Professional Journalists, largely reflect and reinforce the ideological view.[21] Taking both the practices and the ideological commitments into account, I consider journalism as a practice of news information and knowledge production that is filtered through a particular value system.

In the summer of 2009 I was a science reporting fellow at the *Sacramento Bee* newspaper, where I quickly got into a routine of calling sources for information, looking for datasets, reading scientific documents, and talking to editors as I scanned for my next story. As I made sense of the information collected, I would figure out an angle to frame the story and hook a reader's attention. Then there was the presentation of the story: perhaps I would just do a straightforward written article, but sometimes an intermingled data visualization or photograph would help illustrate a point. When it was all composed, it would of course get edited and finally published to the website and oftentimes in the printed newspaper the next day. My brief experience as a reporter made it easy to see the whole news production pipeline as information was transformed: from reporting and gathering of information to organizing and making sense of it, presenting and communicating it in a variety of media, and finally disseminating it to an intended audience.[22] Much of what journalists do on a day-to-day basis is taking raw observations of the world, including talking to sources or examining documents, and then transforming those observations into information and knowledge that they communicate to their audiences. In the process they make a variety of value-laden information judgments such as how to frame a story, what angle to focus on, and what is newsworthy—what is "of public interest and importance" in Schudson's words.

Journalists practice well-honed communication skills as they gather and then convey information. In so doing, they add a lot of value to information in transforming it from a "raw" state into a final easily consumed form of media. Information scientist Robert Taylor developed a helpful model for understanding how value is added during information production (value here is meant in the utilitarian sense rather than the ideological one).[23] Taylor suggests that as data is associated, related, and enriched, it becomes information. And as information is then validated, synthesized, and put into context, it becomes knowledge, which is in turn helpful for making decisions. As data becomes information and then knowledge, value is added. This is exactly what journalists do: increase the value of information for news consumers and for society.

Consider the Panama Papers investigation. The initial trove of leaked data contained thousands of documents for offshore companies: certificates of incorporation, copies of passports, lists of board members, and emails, among others. That data was transformed into information and given greater meaning when journalists began to find connections between companies, transfers of money, and the people behind the operations. But it was only when those connections were validated and understood within the appropriate legal contexts that we could say the information had been transformed into knowledge, which in this case might be the certitude of malfeasance, for example, by a prime minister or major company. But this is just one specific example of value-adding in journalism. Taylor's model identifies at least four dimensions of value relevant to what journalists add to information in their daily practice: quality, usability, noise reduction, and adaptability.

Quality is of the utmost importance if the information and knowledge produced by journalists are going to be useful for making sound decisions in society. Quality can in turn be considered according to dimensions of accuracy (freedom from error), comprehensiveness (completeness of coverage), currency (up-to-date), reliability (consistent and dependable), and validity (well-grounded, justifiable, and logically correct). Journalists engage in quality control at many stages of information production in order to ensure that they produce trustworthy content. This involves everything from copy editing to remove errors from a text to triangulating sources when trying to verify and assess the reliability and validity of an image found on social media.

Journalists also add to the value of information by making it more usable. This could involve designing and presenting information in a way that is easy to consume on a user's device or that highlights the most relevant piece of information for a particular user. It could also entail making information more searchable or browsable to support goal- or non-goal-directed information access, or it could mean ordering or ranking content along some dimension of interest to make information easier to scan. The usability of information displays such as news apps, data visualizations, and video are increasingly important to news organizations seeking to enhance the value of their news offerings to end users. Even in terms of writing, the most routine journalistic activity, we can think about how a well-told story can enhance the usability of news information by making it more memorable, salient, and engaging.

Noise reduction is a result of decisions about inclusion and exclusion of information while maintaining focus and precision in the information that's delivered. In news production, noise reduction can involve clarifying and editing information about a major event to summarize what's known or curating and editing a collection of social media posts to focus on a topic of interest. Selection and filtering decisions often serve to help clarify information with respect to quality, brevity, topicality, relevance, time spent, or really any other dimensions of editorial interest. Because of the paucity of human attention and immense competition for that attention, being able to reduce noise by focusing on the most important and relevant bits for news consumers is essential.

Adaptability captures the idea that information is used in particular contexts for making sense of particular problems or for making particular decisions. Two journalists could produce a story on exactly the same topic, such as corporate earnings, but one may present it for the sake of investors looking to make a trade decision, while another might cover it as an instance of a larger economic trend. News producers add value to information by aligning that information with how people will actually use it and by understanding what it is exactly that their audience hopes to glean from the content. For example, audience engagement editors routinely think about how content can be adapted or framed for different audiences so as to capture their attention.

At the end of the day, journalism is about ideology and values, and journalists are about increasing the value of information for their audiences. Together with commercial imperatives, the ideology of journalism drives journalists to add value to information across the news production pipeline whether by increasing quality, usability, and adaptability or by reducing noise. Beyond the strictly utilitarian, journalists produce value by helping people figure out where they fit in the world and by offering opportunities to identify with others or just find some entertainment.[24] At their best journalists do all of this in a responsible and ethical fashion that creates social value by supporting public understanding and democratic participation.

Can Algorithms Do Journalism?

As I've just outlined, journalism describes a set of practices for news information and knowledge production that are aligned with a particular journalistic ideology. Can that ideology be reflected in news production algorithms?

Yes!

At their core both journalism and computing share a focus on transforming and adding value to information. Computing approaches information from an algorithmic perspective whereas journalism focuses on information production practices that are informed by particular ideological commitments. Because algorithms can act to produce information and knowledge, and do so in light of values that are imbued through their design, algorithms can indeed do journalism. Of course they need not. Alternative values, such as those of noneditorial stakeholders in news media, people dominant in other fields or in society at large, or end users interactively tweaking and tuning, may infuse algorithms instead.[25]

With this as background, I define computational journalism as *information and knowledge production with, by, and about algorithms that embraces journalistic values.* While others, including myself, have proffered other characterizations in the past,[26] here I wish to emphasize that computational journalism involves exploring the relationship between the underlying values of journalism and the ways in which algorithms are both designed and incorporated into news information production practices. Given the affordances of computation itself, computational journalism will not just mimic the value propositions of journalism (though it could), but will rather blend the ideology of journalism with the inherent affordances and values of computing, including, for example, an emphasis on scale, speed, and abstract problem-solving while relying on a quantified version of reality.[27] This book focuses on "computational journalism" rather than related terms such as "data journalism," "computer-assisted reporting," "interactive journalism," "algorithmic journalism," or "automated journalism" because "computational journalism" hews most closely to the idea of algorithmic information production that incorporates journalistic values.[28]

Technology has coevolved with the tasks of journalism throughout history, changing both the pace and structure of work, while shaping the content and industry too.[29] Each technology has its own values that may subtly permeate how information meets the public. These embedded values may offer opportunities for continuity in professional practices, but may just as well offer affordances that create tension with traditional journalism values.[30] As a technically oriented domain, however, computational journalism need not adopt the technologies others create and imbued with their own values.[31] With a distinct focus on designing "practices or services built around computational tools in the service of journalistic ends,"[32] the field is oriented toward designing and building technologies and algorithms to reflect the journalistic ideology. A stalwart computational journalist might declare a need for independence from the biases and values inherent in tools built by nonjournalists. Algorithm design will become the new way of exercising journalism so that the ethical responsibilities of the profession are met in the implementation and expression of journalistic values via code.[33]

A side effect of deliberately designing value-laden technology is that in order to articulate the set of steps in an algorithm, designers should be able to explicate and justify those steps in advance instead of after the fact (as is typical of justifications of journalistic activity[34]). For example, in order for a data-mining algorithm to detect a story lead in a large dataset, it must embody some clearly articulated and mathematically precise notion of "newsworthiness." In effect, practicing journalism using algorithms prompts an explicit consideration of an information selection process and its justification ahead of time. But explication of the factors built into a system has the benefit of allowing for discussion, debate, and deliberate adjustment.[35] Algorithms can and do express the values embodied in their design, and so by adopting more cognizant and reflective practices, value-sensitive designers can develop algorithms intended to operate within the ideological framework of journalism.[36] Value-driven modes of design thinking can help create technologies and algorithms that reflect journalistic priorities—something news organizations should consider if they want to ensure their values are present in the algorithms that drive the future of the media.

Can Algorithms Do What Journalists Do?

Algorithms can produce information while enacting the values of journalism and therefore they can do journalism. But can they execute a range of tasks and practices that are recognizable or analogous to what journalists do? Not entirely. Just as journalists add value to data and information, so too can algorithms. But they are oftentimes still limited in their capacities to do so.

Let's take the value-added journalistic practice of adaptability and consider a specific algorithmic application of adaptability: providing personalized content recommendations. Based on the topical interests of a user, an algorithm can *associate* content with an individual based on a *classification* of the content's topic. Using the magnitude of that association, the algorithm can then *prioritize* and *filter* content, surfacing a set of personalized recommendations for each person. The quality of algorithms to add this type of value to information is quite advanced and allows them to operate in the high end of the autonomy spectrum (see Figure 1.1). But what if we want to design this recommendation algorithm so that it balances personal interests with the importance of content to a local community deliberation, thereby better fulfilling the ideological goal of building community awareness. How should an algorithm know that a story should be shown to everyone regardless of their personal interest? Algorithms are not yet up to the task of calculating something like the social, political, economic, or deliberative significance of a piece of content. Assessing those kinds of factors is better left to a person who has deep contextual knowledge of the community and an understanding of the myriad routes through which the news item could impact an issue in that community. So while a content recommendation algorithm can operate autonomously, in some situations we might still need it to be augmented with human capabilities if we want it to reach its full journalistic potential.

The effective and ethical design of news production algorithms will entail partitioning information and knowledge tasks: which should a person be making, and which can be reliably delegated to an algorithm?[37] To decide this, we need to understand both the decision-making capabilities of algorithms and the mental acuities and advantages of humans. The frontier of what types of cognitive labor algorithms are capable of is constantly shifting, but in *The New Division of Labor* Frank Levy and Richard Murnane posit that there are two key domains where humans have an edge over computers, and may still for some time: complex communication and expert thinking.[38]

Complex communication involves the two-way exchange of information and includes activities such as listening, negotiating, persuading, and explaining across both verbal and nonverbal channels. This sounds a lot like reporting, the bread and butter of journalistic information gathering, but it also includes tasks such as interpreting information to present an angle in a written news story, adapting information for different storytelling technologies and media, incorporating the current zeitgeist and public agenda, and putting information into context to meet particular audience needs.[39] Because journalism is so reliant on gathering information from people, complex communication also encompasses the social intelligence needed to engage empathetically or emotionally in a range of situations. Collecting information can involve undertaking difficult interviews with sources unmotivated to share information, perhaps even deceptive or antagonistic in their interactions. Developing trust with sources so they feel comfortable sharing sensitive information that might paint themselves or their organizations in a negative light is no easy task. Negotiating for information involves a push and pull of knowing when and how to convince an individual or organization to open up. And asking a source the "right" questions involves intent listening and reacting in the moment to a conversation that may be unfolding in unpredictable ways. While not highly automatable, many complex communication tasks can still be enhanced by technologies that complement human practices, such as a voice recorder that offloads a memory burden from a reporter or a spell-checker that improves the quality of copy a reporter produces.

Expert thinking, on the other hand, involves the ability to solve problems effectively using domain knowledge. Some of this knowledge may be tacit or difficult to express formally. Complex problems often require some out-of-the-box thinking to know what's working and what's not, and to apply metacognition to identify when a problem-solving strategy needs to be switched out because it no longer seems promising. Oftentimes expert thinkers apply pattern matching based on detailed knowledge of a domain, using analogies to intuitively map new problems into more familiar ones. While not every task in news production entails expert thinking, investigative journalism of the Panama Papers variety certainly does. Investigation can include analyzing documents, data, and other sources for relationships and associations that may not be known ahead of time and whose significance and verity may become clear only through the interpretation of an expert with deep domain knowledge.

Human abilities in complex communication and expert thinking exhibit particular value in nonroutine situations. While algorithms excel at encoding and executing rule-based tasks, consistently and tirelessly responding to expected events at great speed, performing repetitive actions reliably, and detecting anticipated patterns, their downside is their inflexibility and inability to cope with unanticipated scenarios.[40] This is a key weakness in applying algorithms to newswork. Algorithms also lack the human capacity for creativity. By combining many different pieces, they may at times appear to produce novelty, but they are currently extremely limited in their ability to operate in new situations or conceptual spaces.[41] Rare is the algorithm that can surprise and delight in entirely unanticipated ways. The inflexibility limitation extends to complex communication abilities, too. As storytelling formats, technologies, and modes of interaction with audiences evolve, human adaptation of content presentation will be essential. Furthermore, algorithms and, in particular machine-learning approaches, are simply unsuitable in some scenarios, particularly those involving complex chains of reasoning, diverse background knowledge, and common sense, as well as those in which there isn't at least a modicum of tolerance for statistical error.[42]

Yet there may still be ways to transform some aspects of expert thinking and complex communication into more structured, systematized, and routinized tasks in which algorithms can be brought to bear. One approach to designing the frontier of what algorithms are able to accomplish for news production is to adopt a computational thinking mindset. Computational thinking is defined as "the thought processes involved in formulating problems and their solutions so that the solutions are represented in a form that can be effectively carried out by an information-processing agent."[43] It is important to emphasize that computational thinking is *not* about getting people (journalists in this case) to think more like a computer. It's also not about writing computer programs per se. It's really a way of thinking about how to best use a computer to solve a problem, oftentimes at scale. In a way computational thinking is a reflection of the value system of computer scientists, who are trained to formulate and solve problems using computers. Computational thinkers will ultimately be more effective at exploiting the capabilities of automation when they see ways to structure and routinize processes to be executed by computer. While perhaps not a universally necessary skill for journalists, computational thinking capabilities will be essential for those wishing to be at the forefront of future algorithmic news production processes.[44]

A key tenet of computational thinking is abstraction. Seeing a specific problem and recognizing that it is an instance of a more general problem allows computational thinkers to recognize opportunities for applying computers to solve the larger-scale general problem. The algorithm can then solve the problem over and over again, thereby allowing for the benefits of computational scale to be realized. Abstraction is evident in the various chart-, map-, meme-, or quiz-making tools that have proliferated at news organizations such as *Vox, Quartz*, and the *New York Times*.[45] Each tool creates an abstract template that encodes a specific and particular form and style of content. For instance, the Mr. Chartmaker tool from the *New York Times* streamlines chart creation, while also making the output charts look more consistent.[46] Systematizing the authoring process and outputs allows news organizations to create more content, more quickly on deadline, and with less skilled content creators.

An important aspect of abstraction is parameterization, a process for creating procedures that can apply to a range of cases or contexts via parameter substitutions. Let's look at parameterization in terms of an analog algorithm for baking a cake. Suppose one of the ingredients called for by the recipe is eggs, but we want to adapt the recipe to make a vegan cake. What are eggs to the recipe really? Eggs are something to keep the other ingredients adhered together in the batter, a binding agent. For a vegan version of the recipe we can use a different binding agent, such as ground flax meal. By abstracting the binding agent as a parameter for the recipe we can use a parameter of "eggs" for the regular cake and a parameter of "ground flax meal" for the vegan cake. Parameters enable a combinatorial explosion of options for abstracted algorithms, allowing them to achieve many different outcomes and suit a much wider range of contexts.

Modeling is a process closely related to abstraction. Models encode simplified representations of the world to describe objects and their relationships. Models can also be statistical in nature, articulating mathematical associations between variables of interest and allowing for prediction based on new data. Modeling is largely an editorial process of systematically deciding what is included, excluded, or emphasized by a particular representation of the world. For example, user models are often used by news organizations to articulate an abstracted view of their audience. Dimensions in the model might include a user's age, interests, income level, geography, occupation, education level, marital status, or other factors. Although such a model is a limited approximation to any given individual visiting a site, it does enable some useful outcomes. For instance, article recommendations can be made systematically according to interests, and advertisements can be targeted based on geography.

The final component of computational thinking is decomposition. Many processes or tasks entailed in producing the news are composed of smaller actions. Decomposition is about pulling apart the steps of a process to get at those smaller actions and tasks. Upon examining a big gnarly process and breaking it into simpler subtasks, the computational thinker will be able to identify which of those smaller tasks might be reliably solved by a computer. Decomposition provides a lens for process re-engineering using automation and algorithms. Of course, some subtasks may still need human attention and thus can't be automated. But by disaggregating a process, we can see what components are suited for a machine and what components are suited for a person, and then recombine these subtasks to more efficiently solve the larger problem.

Whether algorithms can do what journalists do is a moving target that will ultimately depend on whether the practices of journalists can be abstracted, parameterized, modeled, and decomposed in a manner that enables designers to see how to systematize processes and insert automation as a means of substituting or complementing human activity in constructive ways. The pieces of the work that can be routinized may be automated (such as OCR or entity recognition in something like the Panama Papers investigation), but in very few cases does such routine work constitute the entirety of a job in journalism. Human tasks will still account for the nonroutine exigencies of covering news events that emerge from a messy and unpredictable world. Despite strong routines in journalistic work, there are still creative and improvisational scenarios demanded by news events that break with expectations.[47] Not all journalistic decision-making will be amenable to algorithms: this includes ethical judgments in particular, but really any judgments for which quantifications are not available or feasible. Still, computational thinking will help point the way to where algorithms can be effectively deployed.

Toward Hybrid Journalism

I've argued in the previous sections that algorithms can do journalism, and that they're advancing onto the turf of what journalists do, but that there are fundamental tasks of complex communication and expert thinking that will be complemented rather than replaced by algorithms. The future of computational journalism is in finding ways to harness computational thinking skills to invent new methods for combining human and computer capabilities that reinforce each other and allow the appropriate delegation of work. Stated more simply: How do we design and build an effective hybrid journalism? The role of algorithms is unavoidable in the future of journalism, but so too is the role of people.

Designing hybrid journalism won't be easy; there's no cookbook, no algorithm here. Yet production processes will need to be reinvented to take full advantage of technical capabilities. This reinvention is complicated by a sociotechnical gap: the divide between what we know we need to support some sophisticated human activity (such as complex communication) and what we know can feasibly be supported.[48] The allocation of tasks between humans and computers will emerge from a design process that entails iterative prototyping, development, and testing by a variety of entrepreneurs, established organizations, and research labs.[49] Processes will need to be carefully designed to take into account what computers and humans do well and to make the outputs of what each produces seamless, usable, and interoperable with what the other produces. Difficult design questions such as how to cope with nuance and uncertainty in algorithmically driven journalism will need to be grappled with and surmounted. Innovation will be needed to re-engineer processes and practices around information production while ensuring those new processes meet stakeholder expectations, including the quality and accuracy of content for audiences, the autonomy and satisfaction of journalists, and the bottom line of news organizations. Ideally hybrid workflows will both lower costs and enable an entirely new echelon of breadth, comprehensiveness, adaptability, speed, and quality of content, which will unlock new possibilities for original, unique, and exclusive material that will be valuable to organizations seeking to compete in a largely commodity information market.[50]

Journalism studies scholars have begun to set the stage for this future by examining the decomposability of journalistic work through the theoretical lens of actor network theory (ANT). ANT considers behavior as emerging from an assemblage of humans (actors), objects and technologies (actants), and their relationships. For computational journalism it is essential to recognize the range of the actors and actants—both human and nonhuman, and inside or outside the newsroom—and examine the associations they engage in as news information is produced.[51] We must ask not only "who" does journalism, but also "what" does journalism, and that "what" includes technical artifacts and algorithms.[52] Understanding how to design assemblages of actors and actants to organize the work of producing news is a fundamental question for the future of computational journalism. As economists Erik Brynjolfsson and Tom McAfee argue, "Effective uses of the new technologies of the second machine age almost invariably require changes in the organization of work."[53] The relevant question here is then: Which actors and actants need to be put together, and in what ways, in order to accomplish some particular information or knowledge transformation task?

Studies of crowdsourcing offer instructive lessons. Crowdsourcing is fundamentally concerned with how tasks are accomplished in a distributed fashion by a set of people connected via a computer network. It often involves decomposing tasks into smaller tasks that are then completed and recomposed or synthesized into a final work output. Various news production tasks are already being reimagined so they can feasibly be carried out with crowdsourcing, including tasks such as copy editing, article writing, and reporting and information gathering.[54] Crowdsourcing has also been studied with respect to broader processes in news production, such as using crowds to check documents during investigations, verify locations and context for social media content, serve as a source of distributed knowledge, and co-develop ideas or brainstorm topics.[55] Examining how work is decomposed for crowdsourcing workflows suggests ways, as well as challenges, for the completion of work by assemblages of novices, experts, and algorithms.[56]

Much research remains to be done in developing a design science to grapple with the challenges of creating feasible human-computer workflows for news information and knowledge production. For instance, workflow design must ensure that tasks can be decomposed and also recomposed without loss of information, and while ensuring a high-quality output on par with legacy modes of production. The human workers in hybrid workflows typically serve to maintain quality, either by preprocessing data fed into algorithms or by postprocessing algorithmic results.[57] Particularly in the news domain, workflows should not be restrictive or rigid, given that this could inhibit the ability to deal with contingencies present in work that is complex and unpredictable, has dynamic interdependencies, or is heavily time-constrained.[58] In order for some subtasks to be automated, fragments of those workflows will need to be parameterized, while leaving open opportunities for collaborating humans to adapt the algorithm to unforeseen circumstances. Humans integrated into the workflow may help to lubricate the automation, allowing it to flex and adapt as needed.

The humble chat system offers an important interface between people and algorithms working together. For many years now, chat systems have allowed groups of people to organize workflows without necessarily making all roles or information explicit.[59] The muddiness of an unstructured chat interface allows people to coordinate behavior in flexible ways. This may to some extent explain the rise of the use of the Slack messaging platform within newsrooms.[60] Not only does it support flexible and relatively unstructured coordination, but it also enables the integration of automated scripts or bots that can interject or help when tasks can sensibly be delegated to a machine. An intermediary platform like Slack functions as a glue for coordinating human and automated workers as workflows evolve.

To fully realize hybrid systems, there are key challenges that need to be resolved relating to task dependency. A Microsoft Research project ran into dependency issues when it developed a crowdsourcing process to write articles about local events.[61] Work was decomposed across four roles: reporter, curator, writer, and workforce manager, whose tasks were coordinated via email or Twitter. One of the difficulties for workers in the reporter role was that they lacked context and found it difficult to know how to cover an event without appropriate background knowledge or indeed training in how to approach individuals for interview purposes. "Breaking down the task into component pieces, as well as distributing it to several people, created fragmentation that led to context loss," the researchers wrote.[62] In effect, for this model of task decomposition to function effectively, work must be broken up into small and independent pieces of effort in which dependencies between pieces are understood and managed. Otherwise the decomposition and recomposition of work can end up introducing more overhead and trouble than they're worth.

Another factor to consider is the economic viability, or total cost and effort, involved in a hybrid workflow. This will depend heavily on both the complexity of the task and its prevalence. The greater the complexity of the task, the higher the fixed costs of designing and programming an automated solution and the higher the costs of recomposition of work from subtasks. The costs of the initial programming of an automated solution can of course be amortized depending on the prevalence of the task, thus modulating the cost per unit output. Ideally, the additional costs associated with recomposing work outputs from automation and from other human actors are less than simply having an individual undertake the macrotask on his or her own.

Designing hybrid systems demands a degree of creativity to understand how human and machine work can amplify each other. Steven Rich, a database editor at the *Washington Post*, provides a good illustration of workflow innovation by journalists who code. In the course of developing the *Post*'s Fatal Police Shooting

Database he found himself needing to file around fifteen Freedom of Information (FOI) requests every week in order to get the necessary details from individual police jurisdictions. But he realized he could delegate this task to machines, so he programmed a script to feed information from a database into a form letter that could be automatically sent as a FOI request. This allowed him to offload the routine aspect of the work to a computer program, saving him from having to perform a repetitive task every week.[63] Of course, after the records requests were fulfilled, a person still had to read through the documents and key in and validate the data.

Trial and error will be required as different alternatives are prototyped and tested. The design of workflows themselves is, however, likely to remain a human endeavor. In instances where algorithms do substitute directly for humans in completing subtasks, interesting questions about management will arise: human workers will need to flag exceptions as well as have agency to stop and start processes in light of evolving conditions.[64] One could even imagine cases in which an algorithm becomes manager, delegating subtasks to human workers and managing the reconstitution of the work. Who, then, will have the authority to override an automated component, and under what circumstances?

Difficult questions remain as responsible and ethical approaches to hybrid news production emerge. But as I'll show again and again throughout this book, the adoption of hybrid workflows in practice is already well underway. As of 2018, roughly a quarter of Bloomberg News content already incorporates some degree of automation, a proportion that will only grow as news producers get better at blending human and computer capabilities.[65]

In this chapter I've articulated the central value proposition of algorithms: more effective and efficient decision-making. They calculate. They judge. They offload cognitive labor from people and make information jobs easier. Computational journalism, in turn, is the study of information production using algorithms operating within the value system of journalism. As the frontiers of what is possible to accomplish with automation, algorithms, and hybrid systems continue to expand, human journalists will still have a lot to add when it comes to complex communication, expert thinking, and ethical judgment—essential elements at the core of journalism that will resist the application of algorithms. In the following chapters we'll see these ideas play out in various different contexts: data mining (Chapter 2), automated writing systems (Chapter 3), newsbots (Chapter 4), and distribution algorithms (Chapter 5). Clever hybridization of algorithmic and editorial thinking will be the key throughout.

2

JOURNALISTIC DATA MINING

If there's one person you should be able to trust—whom you have to be able to trust with your body—it's your doctor. That's why it was such a startling revelation when the *Atlanta Journal Constitution* newspaper published an investigative report uncovering more than 2,400 doctors across the United States who had betrayed that trust. These doctors had been disciplined for sexual misconduct in their practice, but about half of them still had licenses and were seeing patients.[1]

The story began to come to light after reporter Danny Robbins, who had been doing other investigations into doctors in the state of Georgia, noticed a pattern of doctors continuing to practice after being accused of sexually violating patients. He compiled those cases and found about seventy in the state of Georgia alone. To see how big the issue was nationally, his team then tried to use public records requests, but "nearly all [states] said they didn't keep such data, and only a few provided other information addressing our requests."[2] Instead they had to turn to scraping—collecting medical board documents using automated scripts written by data journalist Jeff Ernsthausen so that they could crawl each state's website and download the documents about disciplinary actions against doctors. The scraping was productive, yielding more than 100,000 documents in which those 2,400 disturbed doctors were buried. But reading 100,000 documents would take thousands of hours. How could the team possibly realize their ambition of a national look at the issue?

To cope with the scale of documents, the team turned to a data-mining technique. They used a logistic regression classifier on the text of those documents to score each for its likelihood of containing a case that was relevant to the investigation. Ernsthausen iteratively built the model by reading documents and noting key terms that were both indicative and not indicative of sexual misconduct. For instance, a document mentioning "breast" could be referring to negligence in a case of "breast cancer," rather than sexual misconduct. He and other reporters tagged hundreds of documents as "interesting" or "not interesting" based on their close readings. From the set of tagged documents the model then learned to weight the selected terms and score a document based on their presence. With 84 percent accuracy the statistical model could tell the journalists whether a document was likely to yield a substantive case for their investigation.[3] And, all of a sudden, the classifier melted the 100,000 documents down to a tenth the size— still formidable, but also surmountable by the team in the given timeframe allotted for the project. From there it was still months of effort to review documents, report out hundreds of cases, and flesh out the overall story. Without the data-mining technique the investigation would have needed to scale back: "There's a chance we would have made it a regional story," explained Ernsthausen.

Advanced data-mining and machine-learning techniques are now used throughout the news industry to extract business and editorial value from massive stores of data. Beyond the investigative scenario developed by the *Atlanta Journal Constitution*, there is a growing array of journalistic uses in which algorithms can be employed for editorial purposes. In this chapter I detail five use cases that demonstrate how data mining enables editorial orientation and evaluation of information. These include discovering stories, detecting and monitoring events, making predictions, finding the truth, and curating content. I then look across these use cases to examine the larger economic rewards, subsidies, and ways in which data-mining algorithms may shape coverage and the production of journalistic knowledge. But before all that, it will be useful to understand what the capabilities of data mining really are. What can data mining do for journalism?

What Data Mining Can Do

Data mining describes a process for discovering new, valuable, and nontrivial knowledge from data.[4] With roots in statistics, machine learning, and databases, it has come to describe the entire process of knowledge production from data, including data collection, data cleaning, statistical model learning, and interpretation and application of those models. Data mining broadens data journalism by incorporating the idea that some aspects of the data-analysis phase of news production can be automated. There are six primary data-mining capabilities that enable different types of knowledge to be produced. These include: classification, regression, clustering, summarization, dependency modeling, and change and deviation detection.[5] Oftentimes these are coupled to interactive visual analytic interfaces that augment human analysis of data.

Classification involves assigning a data item to a set of predefined classes, such as "newsworthy" or "not-newsworthy," as the investigative journalists at the *Atlanta Journal Constitution* did. Regression entails mapping a data item into a predicted numerical variable, such as a veracity score for an image found on social media. Clustering is a process that seeks to divide data into a set of emergent categories. Tweets can be clustered into groups that represent events of interest, for example. Summarization entails the description of a set of data in a more compact form. This includes something as simple as taking the mean to represent the average value of a set of numbers, as well as more complex operations such as curating a representative set of comments to reflect debate around a news issue. Dependency modeling describes the process of finding associations (both their existence and their strength) between variables of interest. In news investigations, knowing that there is an association between two people could imply something

predictions, finding the truth, and curating content. Various specific journalistic uses, along with the enabling data-mining capability, and specific illustrative examples are shown in Table 2.1.

Discovering Stories: Finding the News in Data

A lot happens in the world. Most of it is unremarkable, but some of it includes events that lots of people want to know about. For a journalist confronted with an overwhelming array and scale of information, an important question then becomes how to surface the things that are interesting and newsworthy to a wide variety of people, or at least to a subset of people in a particular audience. The question "What is news?" is a difficult one to answer because it is contingent on a range of individual, organizational, social, ideological, cultural, economic, and technical forces.[11] Certain news values have, however, been repeatedly observed in journalistic news selection and are manifest in the types of stories journalists report and publish.

A recent review of news values for contemporary news practices presented a typology of fifteen possibilities including exclusivity, conflict, surprise, bad news, good news, audio-visuals, shareability, entertainment, drama, follow-up, the power elite, relevance, magnitude, celebrity, and news organization's agenda.[12] Other newsworthiness factors include proximity, novelty, salience, and societal significance (whether it be political, economic, cultural, or scientific).[13] Different domains of reporting, such as investigative or breaking news, may weigh the importance of these values in the selection of stories differently. Moreover, a story needs to fit with a publication's editorial focus, agenda, or other organizational constraints, as well as with audience expectations. Newsworthiness is not intrinsic to an event. It arises out of a judgment process that humans, and increasingly algorithms, contribute to.

The six data-mining capabilities noted earlier—classification, regression, clustering, summarization, dependency modeling, and change and deviation detection—offer new possibilities for helping to detect and discover what's newsworthy within data and documents. But each data-mining capability varies in the affordances and utilities it offers for finding different types of stories. Depending on what dimension of newsworthiness a journalist is going after, he or she might want to draw on data mining in different ways. So, for instance, dependency modeling, which entails finding associations in data, can inform investigative journalism oriented toward stories concerning connections or influence among people and organizations. Clustering, on the other hand, can be useful for collapsing the many social media posts about a particular event to find the one that has the greatest magnitude of participation. Classification can orient attention to documents likely to have salient individual stories to exemplify a broader trend. And change and deviation detection can detect anomalies and outliers that are surprising. In general, data mining enables the news value of "exclusivity" because it permits journalists to find and reveal news stories in ways that would not otherwise have been possible. It also amplifies the news value of "magnitude" as it expands the ability to find stories that are greater in scope. In the following subsections I consider specific approaches to finding stories with data mining.

Detecting Surprises, Anomalies, Changes, and Deviations
Stories often emerge where there's a mismatch between the expectation of a reporter and a measurement of the world provided by data—a surprise. There's a lot of statistical machinery available to help find surprises in data. In science expectations are called "hypotheses," and statistical hypothesis testing can be used to answer the question of whether what the data shows is a valid, reliable, and nonspurious reflection of there being a surprise (or not) in expectations. While not widely practiced, this form of lead generation has contributed to recent investigative journalism projects such as "The Tennis Racket" published by BuzzFeed News in 2016.[14] The investigation examined the issue of fraud in professional tennis, specifically as it relates to the potential for a player to intentionally lose a match and therefore enrich

people who had bet against the player. By analyzing betting odds at both the beginning and ending of a match, journalists were able to identify instances where there was an unlikely large swing (in other words, a violation of expectation, or surprise). BuzzFeed's analysis provided statistical evidence that some deviations in betting odds were anomalous. One way to think about these statistical aberrations is as leads deserving of further investigation.

Change and deviation detection techniques can also help find story leads in the routine monitoring of streams of information or data. For instance, the British Broadcasting Corporation's (BBC) research and development lab developed a prototype called "Data Stringer" that monitors numerical datasets and triggers alerts when various rules are matched.[15] Journalists could set a rule, for instance, for whether the crime rate in a particular neighborhood saw a substantial increase in comparison to last month—an interesting local story. In addition to rule-based methods, statistical anomaly detection can be used to trigger alerts. The Newsworthy project (previously called "Marple" in its prototype phase) from Journalism++ Stockholm detects statistical anomalies, or outliers, as well as trends in numerical data streams localized to different municipalities.[16] It monitors dynamic Swedish and European datasets such as employment numbers, crime reports, real-estate prices, and asylum applicants with the goal of increasing the ability of local reporters to develop news articles about any of the anomalies detected. (See Figure 2.1 for a news lead produced by the system.) In its pilot deployment the prototype system distributed thirty to one hundred news leads per dataset per month to journalists who were part of the partner network in Sweden. According to Jens Finnäs, who runs the project, anywhere from 10 to 50 percent of the leads result in some form of published story, though this conversion rate depends on factors such as the topic of the data, the day of the week, the time of year (such as summer when it's a slower news cycle), and the availability of a local journalist's time to chase the lead.

The number of asylum applicants from Turkey to Germany reach highest level since 2008

Published: 2017-11-03

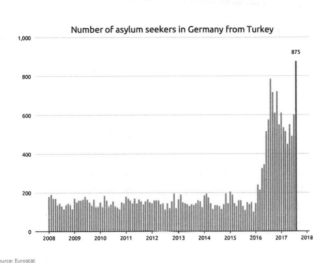

Number of asylum seekers in Germany from Turkey

Source: Eurostat
Prepared and analyzed by Newsworthy.se

At the end of August 875 citizens from Turkey had pending asylum applications in Germany, according to new data from Eurostat. That is more than any month since 2008.

On average Germany has seen 213 asylum applications from Turkey per month since 2008.

In the whole European Union Germany received the most asylum applications from Turkey, 875 in August, while Bulgaria, Denmark, Hungary, and Slovakia received fewest (0 applications).

None

Get the chart

As png (web)   As svg (web/print)   As eps (print)

📊 Make chart with Localfocus

Get the data

📄 As excel file   📄 As csv file

The data has been gathered from Eurostat. Get the original data here.

Figure 2.1. A news lead produced by the Newsworthy system using data from Euro Stat about asylum seekers to Germany. The system detected a spike in November 2017. Note the combination of headline, descriptive text, and annotated graph, as well as links to high resolution or interactive versions of the graph, and to the original data source. *Source:* Newsworthy (https://www.newsworthy.se/en/).

Swiss media company Tamedia sees document and data monitoring as a competitive advantage and is investing $1.5 million over three years in its Tadam project.[17] The system monitors and ingests data from social media, scraped websites, press releases, or document dumps, and triggers alerts when something newsworthy shows up. The system accepts a range of documents that it first puts through optical character recognition (OCR) in order to digitize and make them indexable for textual searches. According to Titus Plattner, who helps manage the project, it supports about twenty journalists on a regular basis and perhaps one hundred of the organization's more than one thousand journalists use it on a more ad hoc basis. Because the system must support journalists working throughout Switzerland, it automatically translates documents (and can thus trigger alerts according to language rules) into German, French, and English. This leads to interesting new capabilities for monitoring. For instance, reporter Hans-Ulrich Schaad configured the system to scrape the twenty to seventy Swiss federal court decisions posted online at noon every day and get alerts within minutes for the handful that impact the local canton he reports on. In Switzerland the language of court proceedings can vary depending on the preferred language of the defendant. Because of the automatic translation, the system was able to alert Schaad to a locally relevant decision that he could then report on for his German-speaking canton, even though the original court proceeding was in French.

Monitoring software allows journalists to expand the scope of their surveillance for potentially interesting stories. The Marshall Project, which covers criminal justice issues in the United States, developed an open-source web-monitoring tool called "Klaxon," which they use to monitor the web sites of Departments of Correction and Supreme Courts in all fifty states. Tom Meagher, the deputy managing editor, says it allows him to cover a lot more terrain than he would otherwise be able to. "It's just easier for me to sort of be aware of what's going on and to then determine where to target my energy," he explained. The

monitoring capability of Klaxon has directed attention to newsworthy material that the Marshall Project has then been able to
share as leads with partner organizations. But Meagher is careful
to note that they really use the tool just for orienting attention—
any final decisions about editorial significance are reserved for
reporters and editors.

Derek Willis takes a similar approach to monitoring election
information for ProPublica's Election DataBot news app, which
tracks campaign finance contributions as well as other sources of
election data.[18] "You cannot report on presidential campaigns, on
the campaign finance aspect of it, without software. . . . The filings
are too large. You'll miss things. You won't understand things.
You won't even get the numbers right," explained Willis. At any
given time he runs eight to ten data-driven rules, or simple classification algorithms, that send an alert when something of interest
in the stream of campaign finance disclosures pops up. The rules
are set to trigger on patterns of activity that deviate in some way
from Willis's expectations; a few even lead directly to stories.[19]

Filtering for Known Patterns

Once a journalist is aware of a newsworthy pattern in a dataset,
that journalist can write rules or train classifiers to scale up their
ability to monitor or search for that pattern. At the LA Times reporters use an email monitoring system to track police reports of
who was arrested the previous day. The system parses the email
attachments sent from the local police departments every day and
reconciles them in a database. Some simple newsworthiness rules
are then run across the database to identify potential news leads,
such as by sorting by the biggest bail amount or highlighting if
anyone with certain occupations such as teacher or judge was arrested. Another version of this idea is the Local News Engine,
which scans civic data from courts, housing developments, and
business licenses in several London boroughs.[20] If it detects any
newsworthy people, places, or companies, these get sent as leads
to local news media.

Beyond simple rules or triggers (which can be quite effective), ML techniques can also be employed for finding patterns in large datasets. BuzzFeed News used this approach to sift through the flight data of 20,000 planes it had collected in order to identify planes exhibiting patterns of movement resembling those of FBI or DHS planes involved in surveillance (hint: they fly in circles). Using a machine-learned classifier, they were able to uncover a host of aircraft involved in suspect surveillance activities buried in the data.[21] In Ukraine ML was applied to satellite imagery to identify areas where illegal amber mining was taking place.[22] Amber mining produces a characteristic pockmarked appearance in the images that makes them relatively easy for an algorithm to distinguish from ordinary natural or urban terrain.

The Associated Press (AP) used an unsupervised data-mining technique to help find additional instances of unintentional child shootings within the Gun Violence Archive (GVA) dataset.[23] The GVA is full of data entry errors such as misspelled names, incorrect ages, or missing tags, which made it difficult to comprehensively find the cases the reporters were interested in for the story. Using the principal components analysis (PCA) technique for dimensionality reduction on the tags data, reporters were able to see how incident entries with messy data aligned with the patterns in the data associated with child shootings. "Incidents with less detail in them could thus be fit into the more generalized patterns," Francesco Marconi of the AP told me. "After the PCA was computed, every incident was either determined to be 'definitely in our scope,' 'could be, but errors/incomplete information put it on the fence,' or 'definitely not in our scope.' Deeper analysis could proceed immediately on incidents that were definitely in our interest, while vetting and research efforts could be targeted to incidents that were on the fence."

Establishing Associations and Connections
Data-mining capabilities have also proven valuable to journalists looking to find connections and associations in large document

and data sets. For instance, the "follow the money" style of journalism practiced by the Organized Crime and Corruption Reporting Project (OCCRP) hinges on an ability to link one person or company to another in order to trace the influence of money in politics or to track it across borders. This allows journalists to detect fraud, corruption, or other criminal schemes. Such investigations often need to synthesize across many data sets to find connections between people of interest and other leaked documents or databases. Journalists can then leverage graph databases to query relationships by type, such as finding an individual's connections to corporations.[24] In some cases networks of relationships can be further mined using network centrality metrics to help identify and prioritize the most important figures for investigation.[25]

The challenge with these techniques is that the same people or corporations mentioned in one database might not be referred to in the same way in another database. There's lots of noise from missing data or typos that confound journalists' ability to easily match one record or document to another. Friedrich Lindenberg, a software developer with OCCRP, has been working on several data-mining solutions to cope with these challenges. Using their Linkage tool, reporters can upload a set of companies that are then matched to all of the various international databases that OCCRP curates, which then yields a list of potential associations between companies and other actors. The tool helped find a company that was smuggling US electronics components to Russian defense technology firms and was paid using laundered Russian money. The company had already been put on an international sanctions list for electronics smuggling, and so the Linkage tool could match it to OCCRP's investigation on Russian money laundering.[26] Another OCCRP tool enriches an uploaded dataset of companies or people by connecting information about ownership, control, or other relationships.[27] The tool spits out a network diagram that the journalist can visualize to see tentative links and similarity scores between entities.

Record linkage is prevalent throughout document- and data-heavy investigative journalism. Chase Davis, the former head of interactive news at the *New York Times,* explained how they built a custom data-mining system to make the task of campaign finance reporting more tractable. Although campaign finance contributions must be filed and are open to journalists to analyze, the Federal Elections Commission (FEC) does not link the records from multiple donations by the same donor. The data is really messy. One record might list a donation by "Robert L. Mercer," while another omits a middle initial and lists "Robert Mercer," and a third abbreviates a first name and transposes characters in a last name as "R. Mrecer." In order to understand the story of how money influences politics, it's necessary to be able to add up all of the contributions from a single donor. Doing this requires linking the variations on a name to a single unique identifier for that donor. As Chase told me, the *New York Times* uses an algorithm that can "discern with some probability whether this Robert Mercer, at this address or that, lives in this city, with this stated occupation, and employer . . . is the same as this other Robert Mercer who you know has maybe something slightly similar or slightly different listed in all of those fields."

The software development time and expertise needed to use tools developed by OCCRP and the *New York Times* is still fairly high, but record linkage is slowly becoming more accessible. MaryJo Webster at the *Minneapolis Star Tribune* told me about her use of Dedupe.io, a commercial tool that has a straightforward interface that journalists can use to train an ML classifier to find record matches across messy datasets.[28] After interactively training it on her specific data, she felt confident it was finding matches she would not have found with other techniques. To be sure, each of those matches was then reported out and verified to ensure accuracy and also to flesh out the stories for each person in the dataset.

Data mining can also uncover associations that allow journalists to find and tell entirely new types of stories. Turning back to campaign finance, Nikolas Iubel and Derek Willis wanted to better characterize the different types of relationships between donors and recipients based on patterns of donations. To do so, they built a tool called "Bedfellows," which includes a set of six association metrics that connect legislators with political action committee (PAC) donors along different dimensions such as exclusivity or duration of the donor-recipient relationship.[29] The tool led to at least one story showing that donors to Republican leaders like Paul Ryan are more similar to donors to Democratic leaders than to some other Republican members of Congress.[30] The only limit to the development of new stories and angles like this is the creativity of computational journalists and their ability to write code that can measure the existence and strength of some meaningful relationship of interest.

Counting

Counting things is a tried and true way for data journalists to find a story. Whether it's the number of serious crimes committed, a statistic about unemployed workers, or the count of votes cast in an election, the absolute and relative rates of occurrence of various quantities in the world can trigger newsworthy observations about the magnitude or distribution of counts, or more generally about deviations and anomalies based on prior expectations.

Classification algorithms can help count items into different categories, which then provides interesting new angles on large document sets. For instance, the *LA Times* uses a classifier to tabulate the rate of campaign finance contributions from different sectors, such as "unions" or "entertainment," and this sometimes triggers follow-on reporting if investigators notice breaks in expectations for those counts. Classification was also used to help inform the story in "The Echo Chamber," an investigation into the nature and characteristics of US Supreme Court petitions that were ultimately heard by the court.[31] The story looked at both the type of petitioner (such as business or individual) and the topic of each petition to understand trends and patterns between type of petitioner and topic. The distribution of topics in the petitions was tabulated using a data-mining technique called "Latent Dirichlet Allocation" (LDA), which identified words most

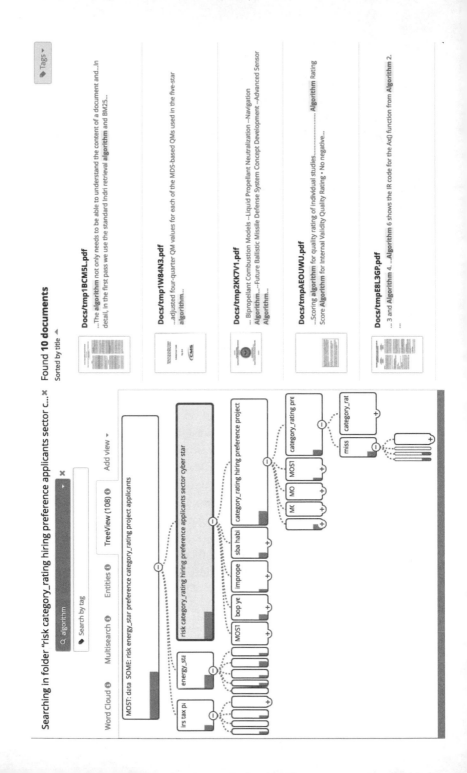

associated with any of forty different topics. This allowed the journalists to count the types of petitions that different lawyers typically submitted and to find, for example, that large firms tend to take cases pro bono only when they relate to criminal law or social issues such as same-sex marriage.

Interactive Exploration

Leads from data-mining techniques provide a form of information subsidy to reporters looking for stories—they orient attention to something *potentially* interesting. If a reporter is convinced there may be something newsworthy to write about, then he or she can do additional research and reporting or engage in a variety of verification tasks before moving toward publication. This is precisely how the *Atlanta Journal Constitution* used classification to save time in its investigation of doctors and sex abuse. But pure data mining can often provide only the most basic of starting points: "look here." Story selection is an iterative and contingent process that can benefit from interactivity. Coupling human perceptual abilities in a tight feedback loop with data-mining capabilities can help move the process from "looking" for stories to interactively selecting them.[32] Interactive exploration of data using visualizations integrated with automated data-analysis capabilities is known as *visual analytics*, a growing field of research that is also increasingly being used to find news stories.

Overview is a visual analytic tool that incorporates document clustering to help investigative journalists hone in on stories of interest.[33] As of 2017, journalists had found and published about two dozen stories as a direct result of using the tool's interactive data-mining and visualization capabilities.[34] The visual clustering interface allows journalists to see groups of documents that are

Figure 2.2. The Overview tool visual analytic interface showing a hierarchical tree view of clustered PDF documents. When the user searches within the document set the tree is highlighted and excerpts of documents are extracted and highlighted in the reading pane. *Source:* Overview (https://www.overviewdocs.com/).

related based on their contents (see Figure 2.2). These groups may correspond to document subsets of interest to an investigation. RevEx (for "Review Explorer") is another example of a visual analytic interface successfully used to enable journalism. New York University and ProPublica developed it in collaboration in order to investigate more than 1.3 million Yelp reviews of healthcare providers.[35] A similar academic-plus-industry collaboration between Technische Universität Darmstadt and *Der Spiegel* developed the new/s/leak tool, which focuses on the visualization of networks of entities.[36] The goal was to help answer the question "Who does what to whom?" for investigative journalists examining large document sets. Interactive tools like Overview, RevEx, and new/s/leak acknowledge that making sense of huge document sets requires iterative slicing, dicing, and visual representation of data, exploration of what the data might contain that the analyst may not have initially considered, and an ability to iteratively question and hypothesize about what the story may really be.

Detecting and Monitoring Events

Twitter, Facebook, YouTube, and other platforms produce an immense scale and velocity of social media content. Eyewitnesses upload photos and videos and share real-time observations of events, creating an opportunity for journalists to monitor the platforms for newsworthy material. Twitter can even act as a sort of distributed social sensor system that feeds algorithms to detect physical events such as earthquakes within minutes after they occur.[37] A growing number of algorithmically augmented social media listening tools are now commercially available and are used extensively by newsrooms.[38]

Monitoring Social Platforms

Reuters is big enough that they decided to build their own social monitoring tool. The tool, called "Tracer," knits together many of the six core data-mining capabilities to help journalists keep track of social media at scale.[39] Tracer provides a set of data-

mining algorithms that feed an interactive user interface for journalists. The algorithm monitors and filters a sample of tweets from
Twitter, clusters and detects events by grouping tweets likely to be
about the same thing, labels those clusters using text summarization, scores events based on a newsworthiness prediction, and
then rates the veracity of the event. Professional journalists can
then interactively adjust event curation according to search terms
and automatically generated facets relating to location, recency,
and magnitude of impact.[40] For instance, a journalist could set up
the tool to monitor for "disaster" events related to the topic of
"oil" along the Gulf Coast, and it would alert them if an explosion
happens at an oil refinery there. The journalist can then independently verify the event through his or her own contacts and
sources before deciding to publish.

Tracer enables a whole new scale of social media monitoring
that simply wouldn't be possible without data-mining algorithms. The tool churns through huge piles of tweets—filtering
through about 12 million per day, clustering those down to about
16,000 events, and then winnowing further down to about 6,600
based on the newsworthiness prediction. The tool provides a
competitive advantage when it comes to speed: it detected the
2016 Brussels airport bombing two minutes before local media,
eight minutes before the standard Reuters alert was sent, and ten
minutes before the BBC reported it. An evaluation of thirty-one
events found that the tool would accelerate the speed of Reuters'
news alerts in 84 percent of cases.[41] The tool orients Reuters
journalists to breaking news events, often giving them a head
start in their reporting and providing welcome hints about the
veracity of the event.

The increased scale and speed Tracer affords to Reuters' journalists comes at a cost though. Machine-learned classifiers for
evaluating events according to newsworthiness and veracity are
far from perfect. In an evaluation, researchers used a test set
of 300 events in which 63 were newsworthy according to journalists. Ranking those 300 events by their newsworthiness score

and then looking at only the top 50 resulted in finding 36 events deemed newsworthy by journalists (and 14 non-newsworthy events). Such a benchmark is fairly impressive given that an idea like newsworthiness depends on reporting context and is subjective and difficult for many journalists to articulate. A corpus of more than 800 test events evenly split between true and false events was used to evaluate the veracity scoring algorithm. The method could debunk "75% of rumors earlier than news media with at least 80% accuracy."[42] The accuracy improves over time, reaching 83 percent after twelve hours and almost 88 percent after seventy-two hours. These evaluations point out the main trade-off involved in employing a system like Tracer: it helps with scale, but introduces potential for errors. Predicted newsworthiness and veracity scores have uncertainty associated with them.

On the academic side of research on social media monitoring, the City Beat project at Cornell Tech used geotagged Instagram posts to locate neighborhood-level events in New York City.[43] Deployment of the tool to four local newsrooms led to several key insights about the design of such monitoring tools for journalists. For one, journalists are aware that popularity can be a red herring: just because a lot of people are sharing information about an event doesn't make it important news. Newsworthiness is a construct whose definition varies from newsroom to newsroom, so tools like City Beat also need to have configurable definitions of newsworthiness detection algorithms in order to meet those different needs. Also, because Instagram was the source of media used by City Beat, many of the events detected were conferences, concerts, festivals, gallery openings, sports events, and so on, as well as a few emergencies such as fires. Most of these (with the exception of fires) are planned events, which are almost always announced via other channels in advance, limiting the utility of the tool.

Monitoring News Media
Other forms of media, such as photos or videos from the news media itself, can also be monitored automatically using data-

mining techniques.[44] For instance, Global Data on Events, Location, and Tone (GDELT) monitors the world's media in over one hundred languages and can detect three hundred different categories of events such as protests or acts of aggression.[45] Such systems are typically bootstrapped using linguistic rules, but can then be refined using statistical techniques to classify an event type and associate a source and target of the event.[46] So the sentence "Postal service workers stage protest over cutbacks by federal government" could be classified as representing a protest event with a source of "postal service workers" and a target of "federal government." Extracting typed events from media reports using data-mining techniques has the potential to allow journalists to go beyond the initial alert about the existence of the event to learn about who might be involved, which could in turn inform decisions about newsworthiness.

Media monitoring can also be useful for building datasets that enable tracking of events over time. The Documenting Hate News Index, produced by ProPublica, uses a machine learned classifier to identify instances of hate crimes reported in the news media; in effect, it acts as a type of aggregator on the topic.[47] Another recurring issue warranting the development of ongoing monitoring has been the use of fatal force by police. News organizations such as the *Guardian* and the *Washington Post* create datasets to track the issue by, for instance, submitting public records requests to learn more about each case. Research in data mining is also making progress in tabulating such events automatically. A recently published algorithm was able to detect thirty-nine cases of fatal police shootings missed by a manually created police fatality database.[48] Yet overall accuracy benchmarks are still lackluster. False alarms, incorrectly associated actors (such as a police officer being fatally shot rather than doing the fatal shooting), and events that may happen in the future or are hypothetical all confound such techniques. But complete automation is the wrong way to think about the application of these techniques in journalism practice. The results of automated event detection can be coupled to human knowledge and intellect. The algorithm can detect fatal shooting events that are moderately to highly likely and highlight why that may be the case, and then a human can verify each instance.

Making Predictions

While detecting or extracting events based on vast troves of media can help journalists stay on top of breaking events and tabulate events of interest over time, the frontier of data mining online media is in predicting events in the future. US intelligence services are already deploying the technology to get a jump on geopolitical events. For instance, the Early Model Based Event Recognition Using Surrogates (EMBERS) project funded by the Intelligence Advanced Research Projects Activity (IARPA) has the goal of predicting events such as protests, offering alerts that provide advanced warning for planning event responses. By monitoring an array of information from news sites, blogs, and other social media the system can forecast when a protest will happen, in what city it will happen, which subgroups of the population will be protesting, and why they're protesting. And it provides these forecasts an average of almost nine days in advance with an accuracy of 69 percent. It successfully forecast the June 2013 protests in Brazil and the February 2014 protests in Venezuela.

Although news organizations have not yet deployed such event prediction systems, it's not hard to envision their utility. If a news organization were to know ahead of time that a major protest was likely to happen in a particular city, they could deploy reporters or video equipment ahead of time in order to be ready for any breaking news. This is not entirely unlike how forecasts for extreme weather events such as hurricanes work. At the same time, predicting social events is quite different from predicting weather events. Social events are composed of individuals who have agency and can affect outcomes, whereas weather is a physical process. The adoption of prediction for socially oriented events faces interesting ethical questions given that a news organization's own behavior and actions could influence how the predicted events unfold. By publishing a prediction that a protest event is likely to happen, does it send a signal to potential participants that makes it *even more* likely to take place? For social events, the act of publication may create a feedback loop that amplifies (or dampens) the likelihood of the event. Could a news organization truly represent its actions as independent in such cases, given that it may be co-constructing the event?

News organizations are not yet publishing predictions of social unrest, but they are deploying prediction in other editorial scenarios. FiveThirtyEight has become well-known for its forecasts in the domain of sports, including for American football, basketball, and tennis.[49] Other news organizations such as the *New York Times* also publish predictions about sports. Predictions range from how likely a football team is to make it to or even win the Super Bowl to whether a team should punt or go for a goal, to how good an NBA player will be (and how much that player will be worth) several years from now. Data-driven sports coverage is a genre that attracts a lot of attention, and die-hard sports fans may appreciate the rankings such predictions create. Sports has the advantage of being a relatively low-stakes environment where published predictions have limited potential to influence the system they're predicting.

Politics is another domain where news organizations have started to employ prediction. For several years now, the *Atlanta Journal Constitution* has integrated a score into its online news app, the Georgia Legislative Navigator, which reflects a prediction of whether a state bill is likely to pass or not. The model uses features such as which party sponsored the bill, how many co-sponsors it had, and a range of content-related features based on keywords and phrases. It achieves a respectable prediction accuracy that updates over the course of the legislative session.[50] The predictions offer an interesting signal to audience members following at arm's length, although a diligent reporter might produce more accurate predictions by making a few phone calls to gather nonquantified social knowledge about a bill's chances. In one case the predictions led to some community controversy. A bill proposing the creation of a new town got some people in favor of it hopeful and others opposed to it angry when they saw the relatively high predicted probability of the legislation passing. At the end of the day the bill didn't pass—people, pro and con, had gotten excited for nothing. This example raises questions about how to make the uncertainty of predictions more clearly understood, particularly to people who may themselves have limited statistical knowledge.[51] More broadly, new ethical treatments may be needed to grapple with feedback loops and the potential for predictions to impact social behavior and reactions, particularly around high-stakes election predictions.[52]

For several years now FiveThirtyEight, as well as other news outlets, have been active in publishing predictions relating to electoral politics in the United States. The founder of FiveThirty-Eight, Nate Silver, made a name for himself by using statistical models to accurately predict the presidential vote outcome in forty-nine out of fifty states in 2008 and for all fifty states in 2012. But in 2016 Silver's (and others') predictions turned out differently. Their models indicated that Hillary Clinton had a greater chance of winning the election than Donald Trump (she did win the popular vote, but not the Electoral College). The methods Silver uses are complex and extremely wonky—the 2016 forecast was accompanied by a link to an almost 5,000-word "user guide" to understanding the model.[53] The failure of the predictive model (or perhaps of the attempt to convey an apt interpretation of that model) prompted an eleven-part post mortem on "The Real Story of 2016," which unpacked some of the contributing factors, including overhyped early voting, "invisible" undecided voters, electoral college weakness due to concentration of liberal voters in cities, and the impact of then–FBI Director James Comey's letter to Congress suggesting new evidence had surfaced in a case related to Hillary Clinton's private email server.[54] Predictive models may be able to capture some of these aspects of the world in future iterations, but nonquantified events will still impact outcomes—a fundamental weakness of relying too heavily on data-driven prediction.

Finding the Truth

Journalistic reports not only need to be newsworthy, they also need to be true. Editorial evaluations of newsworthiness are pervasive throughout the process of finding and selecting stories, but evaluations of veracity are just as important, and are tightly integrated into the overall workflow as journalists find and select stories.[55] In an interview study of twenty-two journalists, support for helping to verify content was ranked as the number two desired feature for a social media tool, just behind alerts for breaking news.[56] As journalists follow a lead to assess its newsworthiness, they need to ensure that their information sources—whether social media contacts, documents, or databases—are trustworthy. In other journalistic scenarios, such as in fact-checking the statements and claims of politicians or other powerful elites, veracity assessment is an end in and of itself. Data mining can help journalists make more effective decisions about the trustworthiness and utility of information sources as they produce news.

Source and Content Verification

Data journalism relies on data as a source. But as with any other source, journalists need to evaluate its credibility and veracity: Who produced the data, and is it complete, timely, and accurate? Given that government data can be prone to mistakes and errors, sometimes data quality itself is the story. A good example comes from the *LA Times* where reporter Anthony Pesce built a machine-learned classifier to evaluate data received from a public records request to the Los Angeles Police Department (LAPD) about crimes in the city. The classifier allowed Pesce to extend the manual evaluation of a smaller slice of city data he had undertaken as part of a previous investigation. The story showed that the LAPD had misclassified an estimated 14,000 serious assaults as minor offenses, thus artificially lowering the city's crime rate.[57] To arrive at this conclusion the classifier learned which keywords in the crime description data were associated with serious versus minor assaults and then compared this to how the crime had been officially categorized. Despite the classifier itself having an error rate, the technique was able to identify errors in the LAPD's data and to quickly show reporters that the misclassification rate was stable over time.[58] Most likely there hadn't been a blatant attempt to manipulate the crime rate; otherwise the errors would have changed over time.

Evaluating sources is increasingly important on social media, too. Platforms like Twitter make it possible to expand the set of sources available to journalists to include more nonofficial and alternative sources while reducing reliance on mainstream or institutional elite sources.[59] Yet relying on more nonofficial (and perhaps unfamiliar) sources poses challenges to source verification. Journalists need to quickly vet sources for credibility and trustworthiness while coping with the often overwhelming scale of social media content and the time pressure of unfolding events. Journalists need to be able to quickly assess whether any particular Twitter user could be a valuable source for additional information. Different events may demand different evaluations of credibility. The data-mining capability of summarization can help with the scale of this problem by crunching data about account activity and history into scores.[60] But ultimately credibility is a construct that relies heavily on contextual information that may not be available to algorithms. Some stories may call for identifying experts who can speak reliably to a topic or issue, so-called cognitive authorities. In other situations, such as in breaking news, which involve readily perceivable information (fires, crimes, storms, bombings, and the like), cognitive authorities are less useful, at least initially, than eyewitnesses. By nature of their proximity and their ability to report on an event using their own perceptions of the world, eyewitnesses have increased credibility in such situations.

It was against this backdrop that, with collaborators at Rutgers University, I designed a tool called "Seriously Rapid Source Review" (SRSR) in 2011 to integrate data-mined signals about sources on Twitter into an interactive interface journalists could use to search, filter, and evaluate potential sources during a breaking news event.[61] The prototype provided interface cues gleaned from various data-mining routines to show additional source context such as their likely location, their social network connections, and their user type (such as institution, journalist, or other), as well as whether they were identified as a probable eyewitness. Our evaluations with professional journalists looking at data from both a tornado and a riot event demonstrated that these contextual cues could help journalists make quicker and more effective judgments about potential sources.

The eyewitness classification algorithm we developed was built with the understanding that people who see, hear, or know by personal experience and perception are coveted sources for journalists covering breaking news events. The algorithm was simple, relying on a dictionary-based technique to analyze the content of tweets and look for the presence of any of 741 different words that related to categories of perception such as seeing or hearing. The classifier would mark someone as a likely eyewitness if the user had used any of these words in tweets about the event. In evaluating the technique against manually tagged accounts, we found that the classifier had a high precision, where 89 percent of the time if it said someone was an eyewitness then that person was, and a lower recall indicating it only found about 32 percent of eyewitnesses overall (it missed quite a few). More sophisticated ML techniques can classify event witnesses with an overall accuracy of close to 90 percent.[62] Such techniques rely on additional textual features relating to crisis-sensitive language such as "near me" and expressions of time awareness such as "all of a sudden."

Finding credible sources is just a small slice of the search for truth on social media. In the wake of the 2016 US presidential elections the topic of "fake news" reached a fever pitch as media scholars struggled to understand the impacts of misleading or manipulated information, false context, rumors, or even completely fabricated media circulating on social platforms.[63] The key evaluations journalists need to make are whether a piece of content is authentic (that is, it is what it says it is) and that what it claims is true. Those aren't easy tasks with social media. A study of rumor propagation on Twitter quantified the difference between the amount of time it takes to resolve a true rumor (two hours) versus a false one (fourteen hours) and concluded that "proving a fact is not accurate is far more difficult than proving it is true."[64] Data mining is not a silver bullet for automatic content verification or rumor debunking, but it can provide additional signals that human evaluators might take into consideration, such as cues about information provenance or credibility.[65] Such a hybrid approach is what Reuters' Tracer system implemented.

Evaluating content for credibility and veracity is a tall order for data-mining techniques, but initial results have been promising. Research has demonstrated machine-learned classifiers that can rate whether a tweet is credible or not using text from the post as well as features such as sentiment and the use of links and question marks.[66] Accuracy was 86 percent across 608 test cases. More recent research in the InVid project ("In Video Veritas") has developed automated techniques to aid with debunking fake images and videos online, reaching an accuracy of 92 percent with sophisticated ML processes.[67] Users can interactively access the algorithm's results on video content using Chrome or Firefox browser plugins.[68] From year to year international competitions with names like MediaEval and RumourEval promulgate structured tasks, evaluation metrics, and open data sets that challenge researchers to try different approaches for advancing the accuracy of automated content verification.[69]

Fact-Checking
Fact-checking is another type of verification task that tackles the evaluation of statements and claims made by information sources.

Traditionally publishers would check facts before publication, subjecting all the names, stats, and other claims in a story to a rigorous internal verification process.[70] More recently sites such as PolitiFact, FactCheck.org, and FullFact have made a name for themselves by pursuing fact-checking as a public activity, which produces its own form of coverage and content. National Public Radio (NPR) published a near real-time fact-checked transcript of the 2016 presidential debates drawing on the expertise of more than thirty newsroom staffers and attracting record traffic to the website on the day of the first debate.[71] Journalists for these organizations tirelessly research and assess the accuracy of all kinds of statements and claims from politicians, think tanks, and other sources. Drawing on background knowledge, context, and a healthy understanding of how trained communicators try to spin, hype, or reframe facts,[72] the task of parsing out the real facts from the opinions, the matters of taste, and the ambiguously misleading is a painstaking one.

A 2016 white paper from FullFact, a UK-based fact-checking organization, outlined several ideas for computational tools to aid with monitoring claims, spotting claims to check, doing the check, and then publishing the check.[73] Claim-spotting is one of the initial areas of focus since it's more computationally tractable. Claim-spotting can be broken down further into tasks such as detecting claims in new text that have already been checked, identifying new claims that have not yet been checked, prioritizing claims editorially so that human fact-checkers can attend to the more important first, and coping with different phrasings of the same claims. There are a number of challenging data-mining problems here, but FullFact frames the solution as a hybrid that takes advantage of computing to spot claims and surface relevant context while humans take on the sometimes nuanced interpretation and arbitration of statements whose truth values span shades of gray and can be evaluated only with access to nonquantified context and the synthesis of information from multiple sources. Computer-assisted fact-checking appears to be the most productive course of action for scaling up fact-checking activities.[74]

One of the earliest research systems for claim spotting, called ClaimBuster, monitors live interviews, speeches, debates, and social media to identify factual claims that a person might look at more closely.[75] Its classifier can distinguish between nonfactual sentences, unimportant factual sentences, and so-called check-worthy factual sentences. Check-worthy sentences tend to use numbers more often and are written using the past tense of a verb. Trained on more than 20,000 hand-labeled sentences from past US presidential debates, the system rates each sentence it sees on a scale from 0 to 1, with a 1 being more check-worthy. For instance, the last sentence has a score of 0.72, likely due to its use of numbers. (See Figure 2.3 for further examples.)[76] In general, 96 of the top 100 sentences that received a check-worthy score were claims that human raters also agreed should be checked. The score also correlated well with claims that CNN and PolitiFact checked, thus showing good external validity in terms of ability to rank statements that professional fact-checkers find important to assess. News organizations are already making use of automation to help spot claims for human fact-checkers to focus on. Duke University's Reporters' Lab uses the ClaimBuster scores to monitor CNN transcripts for checkable claims on a daily basis. The claims are automatically sent to newsrooms such as the *Washington Post* and PolitiFact, where professional fact-checkers decide if they want to actually check a claim.[77] In the first eight months of 2018 at least eleven fact checks were published as a result of these alerts. FullFact has developed a claim spotting algorithm that they use to highlight checkable claims for fact-checkers in real time during television broadcasts. By using more sophisticated representations of language their algorithm achieves a 5 percent relative performance improvement in comparison to ClaimBuster, in particular by missing fewer checkable claims in the texts it scans.[78]

Another aspect of claim-spotting is the identification of textual claims that have already been checked.[79] Politicians tend to

ClaimBuster: Automated Live Fact-checking

2016 Third Presidential Debate Live. Oct. 19, 2016, 9 p.m. EST

Venue: University of Nevada, Las Vegas, Nevada. Broadcasted by: C-SPAN.

Moderators: Chris Wallace

Participants: Donald Trump, Hillary Clinton

Least Check-worthy `>=0.1` `>=0.2` `>=0.3` `>=0.4` `>=0.5` `>=0.6` `>=0.7` `>=0.8` `>=0.9` `>=1.0` Most Check-worthy

> 0.28 Mr. Trump, you go first in this segment.
> 0.18 You have two minutes.
> 0.29 Mr. Trump: First of all, she wants to give amnesty which is a disaster and very unfair to all of the people waiting in line for many, many years.
> 0.17 We need strong borders.
> 0.57 In the audience tonight we have four mothers of -- i mean, these are unbelievable people that i've gotten to know over a period of years, whose children have been killed, brutally killed, by people that came into the country illegally.
> 0.52 You have thousands of mothers and fathers and relatives all over the country, they're coming in illegally, drugs are pouring in through the border.
> 0.36 We have no country if we have no border.
> 0.19 Hillary wants to give amnesty.
> 0.19 She wants to have open borders.
> 0.47 The border -- as you know, the border patrol agent, 16,500 plus i.C.E.
> 0.31 Last week endorsed me.
> 0.33 First time they've ever endorsed a candidate.
> 0.17 It means their job is tougher.

Figure 2.3. ClaimBuster scores for an excerpt of the 2016 third presidential debate. *Source:* Claimbuster: http://idir-server2.uta.edu/claimbuster/

repeat their talking points all the time, so why repeat a fact-check if you've already got a database of checks that simply need to be associated to the various versions of the statement coming across the wire? Matching a checked statement to a new statement is actually harder to automate than you might think. There are a lot of different ways of saying the same thing, which confounds natural language understanding by algorithms. Moreover, the tiniest change in context could alter the meaning of a statement and make it difficult to assess the equivalence of statements. A statement such as "The employment rate in New York rose to record levels last year" depends on what year the statement was written; the truth might be different depending on whether we're talking about 2017 or 2018 as "last year." Instead of trying to do this whole process automatically FullFact's tool surfaces context for each claim it matches to its database, giving the fact-checker a chance to verify the match before publishing.

Nascent research efforts are also developing algorithms that can not only identify claims to check, but also automatically assess the truth value of the claim itself. For instance, one effort has focused on assessing the factuality of simple numerical claims by using a knowledge base that can corroborate or refute the claims.[80] So the statement "Germany has about 80 million inhabitants" could be compared against a knowledge-based entry <Germany; Population; 2017; 82,670,000> and show that the statement is quite close to being true. The algorithm first matches entities in a sentence to the knowledge-base entries, then these candidates are filtered using a machine-learned classifier that assesses the relevance of each entry to the claim, and finally the value in the statement is compared to the value in the knowledge base in order to label the claim as true or not. The approach is limited by the coverage of the knowledge base and is also unable to deal with sentences with more than one property, such as comparisons. Such scores could be productively woven into the workflow of human fact-checkers to make them more efficient and effective. But for now, fully automated claim-checking remains quite challenging, with systems able to deal only with simple statements that lack implied claims, comparisons, or any real degree of linguistic complexity.

Curating Content

A 2013 survey found that 100 percent of top national news outlets and more than 90 percent of local news outlets in the United States allowed for users to write comments published below news articles.[81] While extremely prevalent online, such comments can be both a boon and a bane to news organizations. At their best they offer a space for users to exchange additional information, develop opinions through debate, and interact socially while building loyalty for the news brand. But they also raise concerns over the potential for vitriol and off-putting interactions that could push people away.[82] Some journalists see it as within their purview to act as conversational shepherds, shaping these online spaces to develop positive experiences for participants.

Moderating online news comments is a particularly challenging task due to the overwhelming volume of content. A recent visit to washingtonpost.com revealed articles like "Republicans Fear Political Risk in Senate Races as House Moves to Extend Tax Cuts" which had more than 2,300 comments. The challenge of scale is combined with the nuance and finesse moderators sometimes need in order to make effective decisions without stifling discussion. A variety of editorial decisions confront moderators, but perhaps most significant are those that reflect the exclusion of damaging, hateful, harassing, trolling, or otherwise toxic comments that could easily derail a debate, mislead people's perceptions, or erupt into a war of words.[83] Here we see a problem suited to the deployment of automation to cope with the scale of content moderation. Rule-based auto-moderation has been in use for some years on sites such as Reddit,[84] but 2017 saw the emergence of data-mining-based classifiers to distinguish acceptable from unacceptable news comments. Almost simultaneously both the *Washington Post* and the *New York Times* deployed machine-learned models to help them automatically make moderation decisions about individual comments.

The *Post* has been collecting data for years on the actions of their moderators: as of late-2018 it was receiving somewhere on the order of about 1.5 million comments every month, of which about 70,000 received some form of attention from moderators. This data provides the raw material that the *Post* mined for signals, such as what types of words tend to reflect a comment flagged by the community as inappropriate. The system, called "ModBot," was then further trained by the comments editor, who provided feedback on cases in which the classifier disagreed with human moderation decisions. ModBot's classifier provides both a threshold and a certainty score for each comment it reads.[85] "When ModBot is extremely certain that comments should be deleted, we allow it to automatically delete those comments. When it's very certain that a comment should be approved, we allow ModBot to approve those comments. And then for anything in between we send comments on to the moderators," Greg Barber, the director of newsroom product, told me. A performance test on a sample of 3,796 comments demonstrated an accuracy rate of 88 percent. The classifier was initially deployed mainly in the "new user" queue for first-time comments made by newly registered users, which require moderation before appearing on the site. According to Barber, a good chunk of the comments in that queue are fine and don't violate any rules or norms, and so, he says, "We can rely on ModBot more heavily there [because] it requires less human decision-making skill." In the initial roll-out the *Post* has seen the amount of time that moderators spend in the new users' queue drop significantly, allowing them to redirect attention to comments that have been flagged as problematic by the community, or to pay closer attention to strategically important or controversial stories.

Much like the *Post*, the *New York Times* was sitting on years' worth of tagged comments data—more than 16 million of them. But unlike the *Post*, the *Times* has historically employed comment moderators to read each and every comment *before* it's published to the website. A staff of fourteen people makes this possible. Because of the heavy reliance on human labor, the *Times* could never allow commenting on more than about 10 percent of articles, otherwise staff would be totally overwhelmed. As of mid-2017, that figure had increased to 25 percent of articles, while using the same or even slightly less staff time, due to the *Times'* decision to partner with Alphabet's subsidiary company Jigsaw to develop an aptly named system called "Moderator." This system uses machine-learned classifiers to predict the tags human moderators would have applied. The algorithm grades each sentence of each comment with a score for each tag, such as "inflamma-tory," "obscene," or "off-topic," plus a score Jigsaw developed called "toxicity," and an overall summary score that aggregates the reject likelihood, obscenity, and toxicity scores. The worst scoring sentence for a comment becomes the overall score for the comment. When I spoke to *New York Times* Community Desk Editor Bassey Etim, he told me that his desk currently uses the scores only to make automated comment approval decisions. Re-jection decisions are still made by people, although moderators' work is greatly accelerated because the user interface highlights low-scoring sentences, which allows for quick scanning and re-jection by human eyes. The interjection of human oversight miti-gates concerns over technical limitations, such as an inability to discern profanity from harmful ideas dressed in the trappings of civil language.[86] Etim is aware that the algorithm isn't perfect—there are at least a few dozen falsely approved comments each day—but also thinks it's a fair trade-off and not terribly different from the types of mistakes human moderators have always made.

Sifting out the dreck addresses only one side of the online dis-cussion quality issue. Top publishers are also interested in se-lecting and highlighting high-quality comments that set the tone for the site. The *New York Times* calls these "NYT Picks," and they are meant to represent the "most interesting and thoughtful" comments on the site. The *Times* is still struggling to implement a data-mining solution to help automatically identify comments likely to be NYT Picks, but research I have conducted shows that there are a variety of quality-related scores that could enable this capability. For instance, there is a strong correlation between the rate at which a comment is selected as a NYT Pick and that com-ment's relevance to the article or to the rest of the conversation.[87] Other dimensions of comment quality discernable in NYT Picks comments include argument quality, criticality, internal coherence, personal experience, readability, and thoughtfulness.[88] Scores such as readability, personal experience, and relevance were benefi-cial to journalists when presented in a prototype visual analytic

Table 2.1. Journalistic uses of data mining, with supporting capabilities, and specific examples.*

Journalistic Uses	Data-Mining Capability	Examples
Find story lead via statistical surprise, anomaly, change, or deviation	Change and deviation detection (e.g., anomaly detection)	BuzzFeed Tennis Racket; Newsworthy Project; *Data Stringer;* Tadam; Klaxon; Election DataBot
Find or expand story via filtering for known patterns	Classification (e.g., interesting vs. not interesting)	Atlanta Journal Constitution Doctors & Sex Abuse; LA Times police reports; Local News Engine; BuzzFeed Spy Planes; Ukrainian Amber Mining; AP Gun Violence
Find story via connections between entities	Dependency modeling (e.g. find associations); clustering (e.g., find groups of related records)	Linkage; Dedupe; Bedfellows
Find story by counting	Classification (e.g., item to be counted or not)	LA Times campaign finance; The Echo Chamber
Find story via interactive exploration of data and documents	Clustering (e.g., grouping related documents); summarizing (e.g., labeling groups); dependency modeling (e.g., visualizing networks)	Overview; RevEx; */new/s/leak*
Event detection in social media	Clustering (e.g., grouping related posts); summarizing (e.g., labeling groups); prediction (e.g., of newsworthiness, credibility)	Tracer; *City Beat*
Media monitoring	Classification (e.g., count instances via text)	Documenting Hate; *Police Shootings*

(continued)

Table 2.1.   (continued)

Journalistic Uses	Data Mining Capability	Examples
Event Prediction	Regression (e.g., predicted score)	Georgia Legislative Navigator; 538 U.S. Elections
Evaluate Source Data	Classification (e.g., compare predicted data category to official data category)	LA Crime Rates
Evaluate Source Credibility	Classification (e.g., type of source such as eyewitnesses); Regression (e.g., predicted credibility score)	*Seriously Rapid Source Review (SRSR);* Tracer
Evaluate Content Verity	Classification (e.g., of manipulated image or video)	InVid
Claim Spotting	Classification (e.g., identify claims worth fact-checking); Dependency modeling (e.g., find related claims that were already checked)	FullFact; ClaimBuster
Claim Checking	Regression (e.g., predict likelihood a claim is true)	*Knowledge base comparison* (see note 80, Chapter 2)
Comment Curation	Classification (e.g., appropriate vs. inappropriate)	ModBot; Moderator; *CommentIQ*

* Examples shown in italics are prototypes that could inform practice, while other examples are already in use in journalism practice.

interface called "CommentIQ," which was designed to assess the metrics' utility in interactively finding high-quality comments.[89] An ongoing challenge for computational linguists is to develop reliable data-mining techniques for numerically scoring a comment by a broader set of high-quality indicators.

Making Data-Mining Work for Journalism

Understanding the opportunities that data mining offer for story finding, event detection, prediction, verification, and curation is essential background for drilling into the consequences of data mining for the practice of journalism and for the broader provision of content by the news media. Four areas warranting further reflection on how to harness data mining for journalism include: the economics of content provision via automated analysis, the interface between journalists and data mining, gatekeeping and the role data mining plays in shaping coverage, and how journalistic routines absorb the evidence derived from data mining. I consider each of these in turn, as they relate in particular to core themes of sustainability, changes to practices, and journalistic values.

Ironing Out Economics

The deployment of data mining and automated analysis technologies in editorial tasks raises questions about the economics and sustainability of content provision. How is labor redistributed across human and algorithmic actors? What is the cost structure of story discovery? And how can news organizations use data mining to gain a competitive advantage in increasingly commodified news markets? The utility data mining provides can act both to complement human labor, which can increase the scope and quality of content, as well as to substitute human labor, which can speed production up or decrease overall human time spent.

Data mining can expand the ambition, scope, and quality of stories, and thus amplify the potential impact of journalism. At the *LA Times*, for example, campaign finance coverage was able to move beyond city elections to include more ambitious federal campaign finance stories, in ways that, given the volume of campaign contributions, would not have been possible without automation. Similarly, the crime classification algorithm at the *LA Times* allowed reporters to expand a manual pilot analysis back in time to cover almost a decade's worth of data. The *Atlanta Journal Constitution*'s "Doctors & Sex Abuse" story might have remained a state-level or perhaps regional story without the help of the attention-orienting classifier that allowed reporters to expand the story nationally. Here we see the value of deploying data mining to increase the geographic scope and ambition of stories, as well as to improve the quality of journalistic output, particularly in investigative scenarios where it can enhance the comprehensiveness of the investigation. For instance, the *New York Times*'s and the *Minneapolis Star Tribune*'s use of machine-learned algorithms to do record linkage resulted in more robust and complete investigations. In such complementary deployments of data mining, the level of human effort is more or less constant, but the scope and quality of output are enhanced, which in turn could lead to greater impact and more unique stories. Data mining can offer a competitive advantage to news organizations seeking to develop original and unique content—a valuable asset for building a brand in a crowded marketplace.[90] Chase Davis underscored this utility, "These techniques enable us to look at data in ways that get us stories we just couldn't otherwise get."

On the other hand, substituting human effort with data mining can speed things up faster than a person could ever go, as well as save the effort of people having to continuously monitor information sources. Again, Reuters' Tracer sped up its news alerts in about 84 percent of cases, which is valuable given that it competes on breaking news information. In other cases, such as the Marshall Project or Tamedia's monitoring of government websites, journalists can have information pushed at them via notifications rather than spending time every day looking at information sources and finding that there's nothing new to see. The news leads sent by Newsworthy every month save time by identifying interesting patterns for follow-up. In some cases outlets might simply copy and paste the text from leads directly into stories. Labor substitution can also compress the timeframe for completing investigative projects. "It makes it quicker on something we probably would have done already," noted Anthony Pesce at the *LA Times,* while also turning "a task that before we were using these techniques would have taken a year and ten people and a bunch of interns" into "three or six months with a handful of people and no interns." An interesting question for future research will be whether the average amount of time it takes to complete an investigation decreases as data-mining tools become more widespread.[91] Rigorous evaluations of the tradeoffs in efficiency and accuracy between automated and manual or crowd-sourced workflows will also be needed.[92] Depending on the specifics of an investigation, it may not always make sense to use a data-mining approach.

In curating comments, the *Washington Post* deliberately deployed ModBot to optimize for labor saving and, since moderators were spending most of their time looking at relatively benign comments in the "new user" queue, rolled out the technology there first. As a result of saving effort, moderator time was reallocated to comments that had been flagged by the community on the site or on stories that were considered strategic. In other words moderator attention could be shifted to where it was more needed and more valuable. Ideally, the *Post* would like to reallocate moderator attention to highlight quality comments on the site. "If we would somehow find the magic bullet that took care of all of the comments that we needed to get off the site, I would still want to spend exactly the same amount of time and money finding good stuff," explained Greg Barber. At the *New York Times*, Bassey Etim explained that as a result of rolling out their Moderator tool, "We've lost a few hours to some other efforts that got redirected, so we've probably got a little bit less staffing." He estimates the amount of staff time being siphoned into other projects at about 10 percent but notes this may continue to fluctuate. A key question that should concern media management is how human effort is reallocated in light of tasks that may be substituted by automation.

Whether the combined human-computer system allows for human time to be invested in increasing scope or quality of current tasks or to be saved and reallocated to other tasks, it's important to acknowledge that new costs and forms of labor also accrue in creating such systems. A full accounting of costs must take into consideration the time to develop or adapt data-mining techniques, learn how to use them, maintain them, and assure the accuracy of their output. Development costs are amortizable, but it's not always clear up front how long a system will be useful or how large a scale in output it will enable. Development often entails doing a trial project, which may be costly in terms of human effort. "If it turns out to be useful in a more general way then we basically try to productize it," explained Friedrich Lindenberg. For the Newsworthy lead generation service, Jens Finnäs noted that each new data domain where they want to provide news leads demands an upfront investment of time in order to do topic-specific analysis. Otherwise the leads won't be meaningful or useful. Productizing data mining takes a substantial amount of effort because it involves generalizing and parameterizing techniques so that they can be used across various stories. News organizations that are able to build data-mining capabilities into products that are applicable to different scenarios will be able to amortize the cost of development of these tools across many stories.

Costs are also introduced as other forms of labor that emerge. Datasets must be labeled in order to train algorithms such as classifiers—tedious work that also requires careful consideration and rigorous application of classification definitions and criteria. In some cases datasets may be categorized as part of ongoing data journalism efforts and these sunk costs can be leveraged into other stories by applying data mining to the labeled dataset. Anthony Pesce notes that this labor is often spread around, so that "when other reporters pitch ideas they're asked to pitch in on some of the manual classification work." But these are also prime tasks for lower-skilled workers, such as interns, who are overseen by experienced reporters and editors.

Building Smart Interfaces

Reaping the rewards of data mining will require the adaptation of news production practices. In order to integrate data mining effectively into human processes, designers and developers need to create interfaces to support journalists in their various workflows. Relevant user interface issues include how to signal whether a news lead is worth the time and energy to pursue; how to filter for the most relevant leads; how to engender appropriate trust, reliance, and provide context to enable expert editorial decision-making based on the lead; and how to ameliorate information overload and alert fatigue while encouraging autonomy of human workers in their interactions with such systems.

News leads should enable journalists to make an informed decision about whether a given lead is worth their time and energy to pursue. They must be salient, credible, and framed in a way that highlights their potential value and impact while including essential context. The data-mining algorithm is essentially pitching a story to an editor, much as a freelancer would. A typical pitch might quickly communicate what the story is about, why it's significant, what the take-away might be, and what the sources are. An important aspect of story discovery tool interfaces is the degree to which they enable configurability in terms of what data and documents are monitored as well as how leads are filtered according to interests, topics, aspects of newsworthiness, or domain-specific concerns. For instance, one issue for journalists using the fact-checking leads provided by the Duke Reporters' Lab is that the system doesn't allow users to filter leads based on the type or identity of the speaker of the claim. For fact-checkers, *who* made a claim is an important modulator of newsworthiness that could be made more salient or filterable in the interface.

Some lead generation systems have begun to grapple with the challenge of presentation by developing multimodal and interactive interfaces. Leads from Newsworthy, for example, include several summary sentences of text about the anomaly, plus a line chart to provide visual evidence and context, and perhaps most importantly the data so that reporters can interpret results for themselves (see Figure 2.1). For the fact-checking leads from Reporters' Lab, a link provides easy access to the source material including a transcript which allows reporters to assess the context of a statement before pursuing it further. Lead presentation is not only scenario dependent, but it can also be topic-dependent: the relevant context could change if a reporter is looking at crime, unemployment, or education data. The Stacked Up project, for example, embeds specific domain knowledge about the appropriate provision of educational textbooks in the city of Philadelphia in order to suggest mismatches between an expectation based on regulation and a reality as conveyed through public data. It produces and presents leads as interactive data visualizations "designed to answer the most common questions a reporter might ask in order to assess whether a story might be found at a particular school."[93] What's clear from all of these early efforts is that ongoing research will be needed to design and evaluate effective information displays and user interfaces for automatically produced news leads in different journalistic contexts.

Another challenge related to the interface between data mining and journalists has to do with information overload and alert fatigue. Friedrich Lindenberg cuts right to the chase: "A lot of our reporters are already incredibly busy. And if we now give them 10,000 possible cases of corruption they're just going to tell us to fuck off." It's clear that there's value to having a data-mining algorithm identify a potential case of corruption, but a balance is required in how many leads to offer, and of course how to present them so they don't feel overwhelming but rather enabling. If there are too many false positive leads, reporters might even be habit-uated to ignore them. One recipient of the Newsworthy leads ex-plained that their newsroom could probably only handle one good lead per month. Even one or two leads per week felt like too many, since each could take up to a week's worth of effort from a reporter to mature into a story. The leads are really just statistical observations, and so time is needed to do the reporting and local sourcing necessary to find impacted individuals and turn the lead into something compelling that people would want to read about. The appropriate volume of leads to provide may be some function of how much human effort it takes to chase a lead in relation to how much human effort is available, which itself can vary according to the news cycle.

The Newsworthy project is experimenting with ways to ame-liorate story fatigue by using additional editorial logic to ensure news leads are sufficiently novel. As Finnäs explained, "If there's the same story happening multiple months in a row, we won't deliver it for several months in a row, but wait at least three months before we send it out again." He says it would be easy to create one news lead per municipality per month, but the service intentionally doesn't do that in order to avoid alert fatigue. In-stead there's roughly a 10 to 30 percent chance of a news lead for any particular municipality turning up in a given month, and so if a journalist is monitoring ten municipalities, then he or she would get no more than a handful of story ideas per month. An-other way to cope with the eventuality of too many leads could be to lower the amount of skill it takes for a human journalist to assess a lead as worthy of pursuit. In other words, if less skilled workers can evaluate news leads as a first step, the most prom-ising leads could then be passed on to seasoned journalists for further investigation.

Shaping News Coverage Algorithmically

Gatekeeping describes the idea that some bits of information make it into the news, while others don't. Different forces impact the flow of information to end-consumers including influences at the level of individuals (cognition or background), routines (patterns of work), organizations (media ownership), social institutions (forces outside an organization), and social systems (cultural or ideological factors).[94] These are the "enduring features of the social, physical, and digital worlds" that shape the gatekeeping function.[95] Gatekeeping theorists acknowledge that "any technological innovation, once adopted, offers routine paths for news organizations to select and shape the news."[96] How will newsroom adoption of data-mining technologies, in particular, shape coverage in significant ways?

By orienting attention and reducing the costs of finding certain types of events or stories, data-mining algorithms provide information subsidies that can influence how journalists end up covering various topics and beats, which in turn will shape the news available for public consumption. Journalists should remain cognizant of how the design and development of data-mining algorithms may affect coverage and consider how journalistic news values and, ideally, public interest values may or may not be reflected in those algorithms. Because algorithms will shape the attention of journalists and ultimately of coverage, society should also be vigilant with regard to the ownership concentration and diversity of editorial perspectives exuded through those algorithms. One hundred or one thousand variations of story-discovery algorithms will be preferable to having "one algorithm to rule them all."[97]

The ClaimBuster system provides an illustration of how data mining could impact coverage. The system was evaluated by comparing the topic of claims identified for fact-checking by the algorithm to claims manually selected for fact-checking by CNN and PolitiFact. Findings showed that ClaimBuster identified more claims about the economy and fewer claims about social issues (see Figure 2.4). If reporters were to solely rely on ClaimBuster to identify and guide attention toward check-worthy factual claims, this could decrease the attention fact-checkers

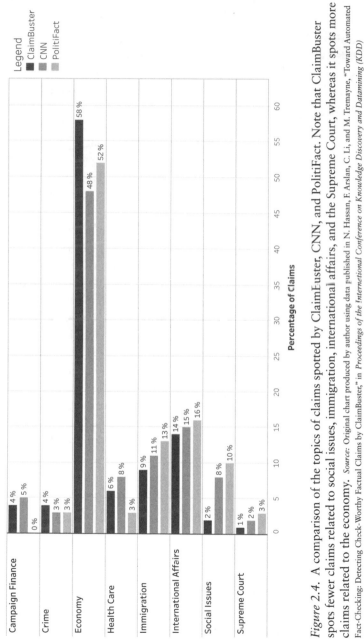

Figure 2.4. A comparison of the topics of claims spotted by ClaimBuster, CNN, and PolitiFact. Note that ClaimBuster spots fewer claims related to social issues, immigration, international affairs, and the Supreme Court, whereas it spots more claims related to the economy. *Source:* Original chart produced by author using data published in N. Hassan, F. Arslan, C. Li, and M. Tremayne, "Toward Automated Fact-Checking: Detecting Check-Worthy Factual Claims by ClaimBuster," in *Proceedings of the International Conference on Knowledge Discovery and Datamining (KDD)* (New York:, ACM, 2017).

give to social issues—an outcome that may not be desirable from a public interest standpoint. One possible solution is to train claim-spotting algorithms on data from different news organizations, allowing them to more easily align results to the predilections of various editorial outlets.[98] Another ClaimBuster evaluation on the twenty-one transcripts of US presidential debates in 2016 showed that Donald Trump had fewer check-worthy factual claims than Hillary Clinton. Combined with the observation that the ClaimBuster system heavily weights the presence of numbers and figures in its selection of claims, this suggests that Trump's rhetoric and mode of communication may have made his statements less susceptible to being highlighted by the algorithm. As automated fact-spotting techniques become adopted in practice, it will be important to assess how they impact the coverage of various types of stories, claims, events, and modes of political rhetoric. Journalists will need to become more cognizant of the ways such algorithms orient (or divert) attention in characteristic ways and be able to fill in the gaps as needed.

Definitions and their computational operationalization are important factors in how data mining influences attention and ultimately the shape of coverage. Redefining a metric could lead to a system surfacing entirely different facts.[99] Defining what sources an event monitoring system tracks leads to sourcing biases. The Social Sensor project, for instance, found an inclination toward male or mainstream sources based on the algorithm that had been defined for finding sources to track.[100] Definitions can also shift from use-case to use-case. The Newsworthy lead generator varies the definition of newsworthiness by topic because the semantics of the data impact whether, for instance, a peak is more interesting (as for crime) than a trend (as for unemployment). Geographic context can also impact newsworthiness—a trend in one city might not become interesting until it's put into contrast with the trend in a neighboring city.[101] Often an appropriate definition of newsworthiness requires a good bit of domain knowledge. "A lot of it depends . . . [on] my experience and knowledge of what political fundraising is like at the federal level," explained Derek Willis. Definitions can limit the adoption of a data-mining system if the definition embedded in the system by its designer does not align with the definition of someone who wants to use the system.

All too often we measure what is easy to measure rather than what we really want to (or should) measure. As prototypes such as City Beat have shown, simply defining newsworthiness according to popularity may be straightforward to do computationally, but isn't so popular with journalists.[102] Definitions other than popularity may be preferable, but if they are not technically feasible to encode into an algorithm, then simpler definitions may prevail. Consider for a moment the challenging proposition of trying to monitor government for stories that are newsworthy by investigative standards. Investigative journalists are typically oriented to a range of problems related to the breakdown of delegated decision-making.[103] These include issues of effort (waste, mismanagement, neglect), money (bribery, embezzlement, theft, corruption), advantage (nepotism, patronage, conflict of interest, rent seeking, influence peddling, favoritism), power (abuse, harassment, misconduct, discrimination, misuse), and information (fraud, deception, and misleading). In some cases, such as fraud, statistical and machine-learning techniques can and have been used to help detect and alert investigators to the issue.[104] But other issues such as political patronage (that is, using state resources to reward people for their political support) might present a greater challenge to a classification algorithm. The information needed to detect something like patronage may simply not be quantified or straightforward to represent in such a way that an algorithm can detect it. Some types of newsworthy stories may ultimately be harder to define in ways that can be written into code, with the result that those types of stories might receive less coverage because algorithms can't pick them up.

Creating Journalistic Knowledge

Epistemology refers to the philosophical understanding of how knowledge is produced by combining evidence and justification to arrive at claims about the world.[105] More simply: How do journalists know what they know? Traditionally journalists have created knowledge by drawing on sources such as eyewitness accounts, interviews with experts, and document inspection. These sources play into a sort of credibility calculus as journalists piece together evidence and seek justifications for what they eventually report as the news. Data-mining algorithms provide a new source of evidence—tips, leads, relationships, and predictions—for journalists to incorporate into their epistemological practices of seeking the truth. But just as with other sources, the knowledge provided by algorithms needs to be evaluated and appropriately weighed in relation to other modes of evidence. While some scholarship has explored the epistemological implications of the use of "Big Data" in journalism, the focus here is more squarely on the role that algorithms play.[106] In particular, how do data-mining algorithms change knowledge production practices for journalists?

Coping with Uncertainty

For many of the projects surveyed in this chapter, the journalists I spoke to expressed the need for ongoing skepticism and verification of the outputs of data mining. A data-mining algorithm is a source like any other, and reliance on it can increase over time as journalists gain familiarity. Jeff Ernsthausen explained how he used a continuous quality assurance (Q/A) process applied to the output of the *Atlanta Journal Constitution*'s sexual-misconduct document classifier by periodically sampling one hundred documents with low "interestingness" scores and reading them manually to make sure the classifier wasn't systematically missing important leads. Evaluating the reliability of results was a challenging aspect of the process: "The hard part is understanding how to generate the things that tell you whether it's working well or not," explained Ernsthausen. Anthony Pesce concurred: "We spent probably a couple weeks looking at the code, going back and forth tweaking the model making sure it was working right, re-testing it on our test and our training data. And then went back through and just looked at a huge sample of them." For their campaign finance project, which they have been pursuing on an ongoing basis, the *LA Times* put in a lot of time upfront to build confidence in the system, but "now that we've used it so much, we're very comfortable with it," explained Pesce. The *Washington Post* does periodic "spot checks" on the output of ModBot to manually examine the comments it has deleted or approved. In other words, substantive effort must be applied toward evaluating evidence to convince editors that model results are reliable. Journalists must be convinced that the outputs of a system are reliable and in line with their own goals. This effort can, however, be amortized if the software is reused by different newsrooms or the same newsroom over time.

In other cases, data mining is presented to journalists not for their acceptance per se but instead to continually remind them that it should be treated with uncertainty. At the *New York Times,* the campaign finance disclosure record-linkage algorithm presents its results in a sorted list. The user interface provides an initial set of matches that have high match certainty, but less certain matches can only be accessed via a link. "We don't want reporters to look at the output of this and assume that it's correct. We want to use it as a tool where they can kind of like get a little bit more information but the interface also makes clear that this is not vetted," explained Chase Davis. "The role of the algorithm . . . is essentially to make the vetting easier," he added.

Journalists acknowledge that data-mining algorithms make mistakes and have inherent statistical uncertainty, but that there are conditions in which that is tolerable or can be overcome. An acceptance of false negatives—documents that should have been classified as sexual misconduct but weren't—meant that the team at the *Atlanta Journal Constitution* knew there would be cases that they missed. This in turn meant that whatever claims they reported publicly about the magnitude and scope of the problem would be a lower bound in terms of the actual number of sexual misconduct cases in the country. At the same time, they also knew that the effectiveness of the classifier varied from state to state based on the quality and verbosity of documents produced by different states. This put limits on their ability to make certain types of claims, such as comparing the rate of sexual misconduct cases between different states. Davis explained the idea with respect to the *Times*' campaign finance project: "It's very unlikely that no matter how fastidious you are that you're going to catch absolutely every last thing. . . . Whenever stories like this are written, there's always some amount of hedging just understanding how messy the data is and how hard it is to be able to get absolute certainty out of it." Uncertainty from data mining can also subtly steer the editorial focus of an investigation. Ernsthausen described a real estate investigation where the focus shifted to larger entities that were less sensitive to geocoding errors. Accepting the limitations of data-mining techniques means modulating the nature, strength, and presentation of claims pursued and ultimately published.

Contingencies on Claims

In their book *Custodians of Conscience* James Ettema and Theodore Glasser note the contextual variability of what constitutes an adequate justification for knowing within the epistemology of journalism: "The criteria for adequate justification may vary from one context to another" and "What counts as sufficient grounds for a knowledge claim varies from one domain of inquiry to another."[107] How then do variations in journalistic context impact the uptake of information produced via data mining? Relevant variations in context include whether a knowledge claim from data mining is made publicly or is used only internally in a newsroom, whether it's possible to corroborate a piece of predicted information, and what the implications and consequences are for individuals or other stakeholders if a particular fact is published.

There are greater demands on justification and verification the closer an algorithm is to direct publication of information. Public claims must be justifiable as judgments that are fair and accurate. "It gets a bit tougher the closer the . . . data mining technique or the algorithm is to a publishable product, the more I think you have to understand about it," explained Davis. In comparison, claims that are used internally in a newsroom or are leads that will not be directly published can be assessed by other reporters or an editor before any claim is made in public. If the data mining is wrong or produces a high degree of uncertainty, but the public doesn't see it, then at worst it wastes some internal newsroom effort. Certain types of ML are easier to justify to editors or the public—often referred to as "explainable models." An example of an explainable model is a decision tree: its classification decisions can be expressed in terms of simple rules that apply to each dimension of data.[108] Davis related some of the benefits of explainability in justifying a model: "I'd use things like decision trees if I was modeling something out and where you can actually at the end of the day if you really really wanted to you can print the decision tree on paper and see exactly how it works. And I could walk an editor through that in human terms." Explainable models can be useful aids for communicating and building credibility for knowledge claims stemming from the model.

In some cases journalists can justify the output of data mining by corroborating it with evidence from other reporting methods. At the *LA Times* they contacted the LAPD about the result of their model—that serious assaults had been systematically underreported in Los Angeles—and got confirmation that the model was correct. "We felt pretty good about it at that point. If they're saying, 'We're not going to contest this, . . . that's pretty much all we needed," explained Pesce. The LAPD had just finished an internal audit of its data and had found the misclassification error was even higher than the *LA Times'* model suggested. The fact that the result of the model was corroborated helped justify its use as evidence in the story.

However, sometimes it's simply not possible to confirm, corroborate, or deny evidence from data mining prior to publication. Take, for instance, the various predictions relating to outcomes of elections or legislative activities. These predictions, by definition, cannot be confirmed until the predicted event takes place. In these types of cases, transparency of the data-mining method is often provided, offering descriptions of how the method works, what data it operates from, how constructs are operationalized, what the performance and error rates are on test data, and sometimes even including open source code repositories to facilitate reproducibility.[109] For instance, for the *Atlanta Journal Constitution*'s Legislative Navigator App, a series of blog posts described in great detail how the predictive model performed on past data. In attempts to reflect the provisional nature of predicted information, some journalists are experimenting with communicating uncertainty directly to the audience. The *New York Times* took this approach in its 2016 US election prediction. As voting results were tallied on election day, a dynamic prediction was depicted as a dial showing the chance that either candidate would win. To convey the uncertainty in the underlying statistical prediction, the dial's needle jittered, especially early in the evening when every new precinct reporting could cause a swing in the model's prediction of the close race.[110]

In the BuzzFeed investigation into professional tennis cheats, the statistical anomalies could likewise not be corroborated through other forms of evidence. As a result the story did not include the names of the players identified. In essence, the evidence from the statistical tests was only suggestive, justified through an open-source code release and anonymized data, but ultimately deemed not solid enough to publicly label any particular players as cheaters. As this case illustrates, the potential consequences of public claims also factors into how journalists come to rely on information produced by data mining. When publishing a claim that impacts an individual in a negative way, it must be clearly justified based on the available evidence. If a classifier indicates that a politician is 80 percent likely to be engaged in banking fraud, that may not be a high enough level of confidence to move forward with a public statement, given that such an indictment could have severe consequences for the individual. When "we're talking about people getting in trouble, it's more important for us to ensure that the 500 people we're putting in there are legit," explained MaryJo Webster, underscoring the additional consideration given to validity and justifiability when publication could negatively impact individuals. This starkly contrasts with typical scientific knowledge claims, which often result in empirically developed theories describing central tendencies of a sample rather than assertions about individuals that can produce negative social consequences. On the other hand, if a model is being used to produce information for entertainment purposes, as is the case in FiveThirtyEight's sports predictions, the consequences of being wrong are far less onerous. Chase Davis contrasts these two situations: "For the really hard investigative stuff that some of this [data mining] is occasionally being applied to . . . you've got a different standard that you're trying to meet."

When journalists have low tolerance for statistical error and need absolute certainty because of the import of claims, they mostly fall back on the manual verification of data-mined results. A "no false positives" mantra is actualized by applying a manual check to any evidence or claim supplied by data mining. In investigative journalism, "The reporters are ultimately going to want to vet everything themselves by hand to ensure that it's correct [and] to ensure that they understand it," noted Davis. For cases that their campaign finance model couldn't classify, or where the classifier had low confidence, the LA Times went back through each of them one by one to see if they could be classified by hand. By manually checking each outcome, journalists are able to catch errors, such as if a person with a common name was accidentally associated with the wrong person in another database. The reli-

ance on manual methods to justify making socially consequential claims in public also has an impact on the way data-mining
models are parameterized. "We can essentially tune so that it
would give us either more false positives or more false negatives
just depending on the threshold of confidence that we're searching
for," explained Davis. "Knowing that we are going to be reviewing
things anyway we essentially wanted the algorithm to be a little
bit overzealous." Algorithms can be tuned to minimize false negatives, increasing confidence in the comprehensiveness of an investigation, while knowing there will be a manual step at the end
to catch any false positives.

Data mining offers a whole host of opportunities that are only
just beginning to be explored and exploited for editorial purposes.
From finding stories to monitoring or predicting events, evaluating content and sources, and helping to curate discussions, the
editorial utility of data mining is gaining increasing purchase in
newsrooms. Data mining has the potential to transform how leads
are developed, to alter the economics of content production, and
to change how knowledge itself is produced. As it becomes more
woven into practice, data mining will ultimately shape coverage,
reflecting whatever values of newsworthiness its designers have
thought to include. Data mining is still just a part of the equa-
tion for automated news production though. Algorithmic analysis
may be helpful for finding the story, but algorithmic content production will be needed for telling it.

3

AUTOMATED CONTENT PRODUCTION

The Swedes love their soccer. So much so that in mid-2016 the Swedish local media company Östgöta Media decided to launch a new site called "Klackspark" to cover every local soccer game in the eastern province of Östergötland. "It's like the national sport of Sweden and you play it even if you're not that good at it," Nils Olauson, the publisher of Klackspark, told me. "I played in Division 6, one of the lower leagues, maybe until I was thirty-four just because it's fun and there's still a lot of prestige in the game. You want to be the best in your neighborhood, you want to be the best in your part of the town, and you get your rivals even in that kind of low league." The sport has a high cultural significance. And when practically every neighborhood has its own team, spanning six divisions of local men's soccer and four divisions of local women's soccer, not to mention the major national and international leagues, that's a lot of games. To reach that breadth of coverage, Klackspark strategically employs automated software writing algorithms, which take structured data about each local game and automatically write and publish a short, roughly one-hundred-word factual summary of what happened in the game. It's not too fancy really. Any given story might recount who scored the goals in addition to the history and league standing of the teams that played. But the automation provides a foundational *breadth* to the coverage—

anyone looking for the quick facts about a local match can find that story on the site.

Olauson described how Klackspark's automated stories are orchestrated with fourteen sports reporters who then add a bit of "spice," layering on details and human interest to the stories on the site. The reporters receive alerts when the software detects something newsworthy or unique in a lower-league game. "When a girl had ten goals in the same game, we had one of our reporters call her up and talk to her. He wrote an article about it, and that article was one of the most read pieces on Klackspark that week." The automation is serving a dual purpose: writing straight factual stories that are directly published and, as detailed in Chapter 2, alerting human reporters to what could be a juicy story if only they did some additional reporting, got some quotes, and fleshed it out. Straight automation provides breadth of coverage, and automation plus professional reporters adds depth to coverage. The automation does the routine work, and the reporters get to focus on more interesting stories. No jobs lost either, at least not yet.

This type of hybrid scenario was the norm for the news organizations I spoke to about their use of content automation. Newsrooms see content automation as being largely complementary to journalists' work.[1] Yes, there are instances in content production where there is complete automation, and if you squint, you might even say there is artificial intelligence operating in narrow targeted areas. But the state of the art is still far from autonomously operating in the unbounded environment of the world and from doing the contextualized interpretation and nuanced communication required of journalists.

This chapter focuses on the content creation phase of editorial production. As various content creation tasks are delegated to automation and algorithms, new opportunities emerge for reinventing editorial processes and practices. I first examine the technical capabilities and potential of automated content production algorithms. Then I detail how algorithms enable faster, larger scale, more accurate, and more personalized journalism, which creates new business opportunities for news organizations. At the same time, this chapter also points out that automated content production has some very real limitations, such as data contingencies and difficulties matching human flexibility and quality in reporting on a dynamic world. This leads to the next topic, a consideration of how people and automation will work together, both in the design and operation of these systems, as well as in how this collaboration will impact the evolution of human tasks and roles. This chapter concludes by exploring what might be next for automated content production.

How Automated Text Writing Works

The basic premise of automated text production is to take structured data, as one might find in a database or spreadsheet, and have an algorithm translate that data into written text. This process is referred to as "natural language generation" (NLG). At the simpler end of NLG are rule-based techniques that work like "Mad Libs"—that is, there are prewritten templates with gaps where numbers are dynamically inserted from a dataset according to manually crafted rules (see Figure 3.1). More advanced template approaches are imbued with rule-sets that incorporate linguistic knowledge and facilitate more sophisticated and dynamic text production. Such techniques can conjugate verbs in different tenses or decline nouns to make them grammatical. Sophisticated templates can be blended in with simpler ones. For instance, a simple template could be used for a headline so that it's more attention getting, but then a dynamic template could drive more heavily descriptive parts of the story.[2] Many rule-based NLG systems are built according to a standard model that includes three distinct stages: document planning, microplanning, and document realization.[3]

The document planning stage consists of determining and selecting *what* to communicate and then *how* to structure that information in paragraphs and sentences. Deciding what to commu-

10 point lead for Clinton in latest NBC/WSJ poll

NBC/WSJ released the results of a new national poll, in which respondents were asked for whom they will vote: Democrat Hillary Clinton or Republican Donald Trump.

Of those who replied, 50.0% said that they plan to vote for former First Lady Hillary Clinton, whereas 40.0% declared that they would give their vote to businessman Donald Trump.

The poll was conducted from October 8 to October 10 via phone. A total of 806 likely voters responded. If one takes into account the poll's error margin of +/-3.5 percentage points, the spread in voter support is statistically significant.

Key

———————— Data taken from raw data

——————— Calculations from raw data

- - - - - - - - Sample synonyms

Figure 3.1. An excerpt of an automatically generated article on PollyVote.com reporting on the results of a US election poll from 2016. Underline style indicates different types of dynamic text.
Source: Andreas Graefe, "Computational Campaign Coverage, *Columbia Journalism Review,* July 5, 2017 (used with permission of the author).

nicate is impacted by what the reader is interested in, what the writer is trying to accomplish (for example, explain or persuade), and by constraints such as the available space and data. Document structure reflects the editorial priority and importance of information as well as higher-level discourse objectives such as telling a story versus explaining a timeline. In the domain of weather a document plan might prioritize the salience or ordering of information related to warnings, winds, visibility, and temperature, among other factors.[4] In election result articles it may take into account the "interestingness" of particular candidates or municipalities, as well as whether a win or loss is a statistical aberration.[5] Document planning works to enumerate all the things the data *could* say and then prioritizes those facts according to newsworthiness criteria.[6] More sophisticated systems may identify "angles" for stories in order to help structure the narrative based on rare events or domain-specific metrics.[7] Depending on what the data indicates, example angles for a sports story might be "back-and-forth horserace," "heroic individual performance," "strong team effort," or "came out of a slump."[8]

The next stage, microplanning, consists of making word and syntax choices at the level of sentences and phrases. This phase of text generation is important because it impacts the variability and complexity of the language output, as well as how publication or genre-specific style guides, tones, or reading levels are produced. Microplanning entails nuanced choices, such as deciding among different templates for conveying the same information or among referring expressions, which specify different ways of mentioning the same person or company in an article. The first time a player is mentioned in a soccer article, their whole name might be used, the second time just the last name might suffice, and if there is a third time, it might be more interesting to use an attribute of the person such as "the 25 year-old."[9] Additional variability can be injected into output texts by integrating synonym selections from word ontologies, which define structured relationships between different words (see an example in figure 3.1). Careful word choice can steer the text away from monotony by blocking the use of certain verbs or phrases if they've already been included in a text. In the case of rule-based systems microplanning decisions reflect editorial choices deliberately coded into the algorithm.

Finally, the realization stage of NLG walks through a linguistic specification for the planned document to generate the actual text. This stage satisfies grammatical constraints, such as making a subject and verb agree, declining an adjective, making sure a noun is pluralized correctly, or rendering a question with a question mark. The realization stage is the most robust and well-studied aspect of NLG, with mature toolkits such as SimpleNLG being used by news organizations to generate text.[10] Many of the decisions at the level of text realization relate to grammar and so there is less potential for journalists to imbue editorial values in the algorithms driving this stage.

An alternative to the standard approach to NLG involves data-driven statistical techniques that learn patterns of language use from large corpora of examples. For instance, machine learning can automatically classify which points of data to include in an American football recap article. This contributes to the document planning stage by considering the context of data points and how that affects inclusion decisions.[11] Such techniques require a high degree of engineering to produce output in closely constrained scenarios. Moreover, rich datasets of content and data need to be available. In one case, a wind forecast statistical NLG system required a parallel corpus of manually written wind forecast texts as well as the aligned source data for each text.[12] News organizations with large corpora of articles could potentially utilize those texts as inputs to train statistical NLG systems.

Purely statistical approaches may, however, come up against barriers to adoption because they can introduce unpredictable errors. In the shorter term, a fruitful path forward appears to be the marriage of template- and statistically based techniques. In 2013 Thomson-Reuters demonstrated a research system that could extract and cluster templates from a corpus of examples, creating a template database.[13] Then the system could generate a new text by iteratively selecting the best template given the available data for each successive sentence. The text production quality was competitive with the original texts, and had the additional benefit of introducing more variability into the output texts, which addressed a weakness of purely template-based approaches.

Beyond Automated Writing

Automated content production is not limited to writing texts, and can work with different inputs besides structured data, including the full range of unstructured texts, photos, and videos proliferating online. To be useful, however, these media must often first be converted into more structured data. Algorithms extract semantics, tags, or annotations that are then used to structure and guide content production. For text this involves natural language understanding (NLU) and for images or video this involves computer vision to detect or classify visual properties of interest. For instance, Wibbitz, a system that semi-automates the production of videos, uses computer vision to identify faces in input photos and videos so it can appropriately frame and crop the visual output.

Another type of content automation is summarization. Given the inundation of social media content, there's a lot of potential value to using algorithms to crunch things down into output summaries that people can skim. Algorithms can summarize events as diverse as the Facebook initial public offering, the British Petroleum oil spill in 2010, or a World Cup match by curating sets of representative media, such as tweets or photos.[14] Summarization can also generate a headline to share on social media, a compact presentation for a news browsing app, or a set of important take-aways from the story.[15] Summarization approaches can be either extractive or abstractive.[16] Extractive summarization corresponds to the task of finding the most representative sentences or text fragments from a document or set of documents, whereas abstractive summarization can synthesize entirely new sentences and words that didn't exist in the original text. Summarization algorithms embed a range of meaningful editorial decisions, such as prioritizing information from inputs and then selecting informative, readable, and diverse visual content. While summarization technology is advancing, it's sometimes hard to tell whether one summary is much better than another. Wibbitz uses summarization algorithms to reduce an input text into a set of points to be illustrated in video, but as Neville Mehta from Law Street Media explained, "Sometimes you get something that's shorter but it's not doing the original piece justice. . . . There is quite a bit of hand editing that goes into it just to maintain the level of quality that we want."

Video generation is considerably more challenging than text because it entails automatically tailoring the style, cropping, motion, and cuts of the visual, while also considering aspects such as the timing between the visual and textual overlays to the video. A system like Wibbitz must curate visual material from a database (such as Getty Images) and then edit that material together coherently. Early research systems capable of editing and synthesizing video stories began to emerge towards the late 2000s,[17] but only in the last few years has the technology been commercialized by the likes of Wibbitz and its competitor, Wochit. Wibbitz is further advancing the field by integrating machine learning that can learn editorial importance from user interactions with the tool. As human editors tune rough cuts, the system learns which content is most interesting to include for other videos on similar topics.

Another output medium for automated content production is data visualization. Visualizations are increasingly used in the news media for storytelling and involve mapping data to visual representations such as charts, maps, timelines, or networks to help convey narratives and engage an audience.[18] Data visualizations are also quite multimodal and often require incorporating a healthy dose of text to aid interpretation.[19] Weaving text and graphics together raises new challenges about which medium to use to convey which types of information, how to refer back and forth between the visualization and the text, and decide which aspects are most important to visualize for the overall story.[20] Automatically generating captions or other descriptive text goes hand in hand with automating data visualization.[21] For instance, systems can automatically produce annotated stock visualizations or annotated maps to augment news articles (see Figure 3.2).[22]

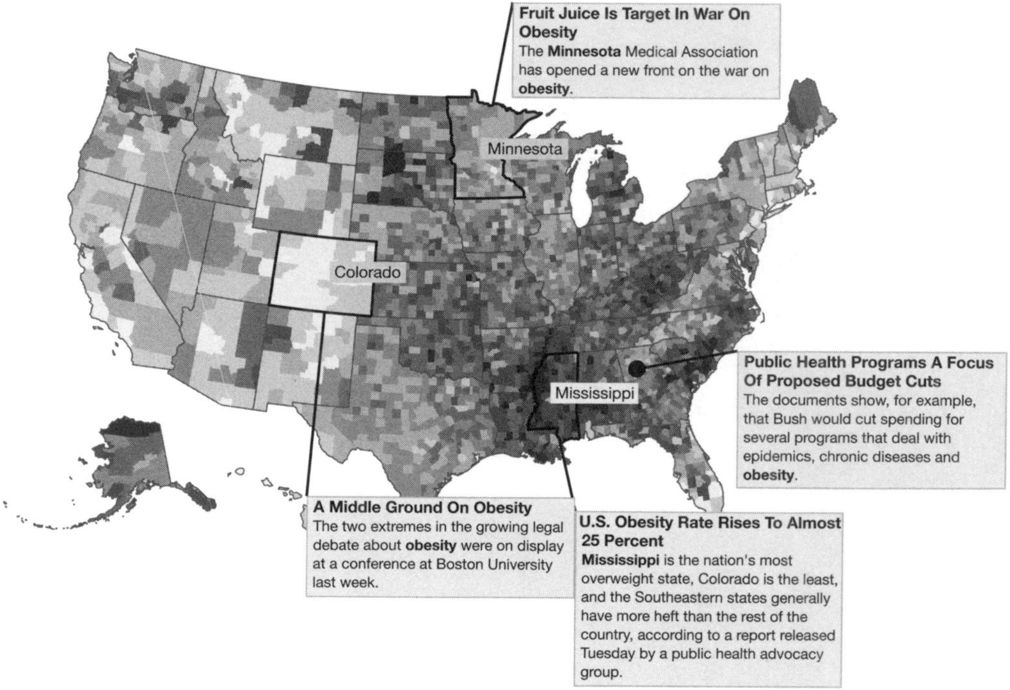

Figure 3.2. A map visualization of obesity rates in the United States, including annotations of various areas of interest. The map was automatically generated based on an input article on obesity and diabetes. The NewsViews tool was originally described in T. Gao, J. Hullman, E. Adar, B. Hecht, and N. Diakopoulos, "NewsViews: An Automated Pipeline for Creating Custom Geovisualizations for News," *Proceedings of the Conference on Human Factors in Computing Systems (CHI)* (New York: ACM, 2014).

Fruit Juice Is Target In War On Obesity
The **Minnesota** Medical Association has opened a new front on the war on **obesity**.

Public Health Programs A Focus Of Proposed Budget Cuts
The documents show, for example, that Bush would cut spending for several programs that deal with epidemics, chronic diseases and **obesity**.

U.S. Obesity Rate Rises To Almost 25 Percent
Mississippi is the nation's most overweight state, Colorado is the least, and the Southeastern states generally have more heft than the rest of the country, according to a report released Tuesday by a public health advocacy group.

A Middle Ground On Obesity
The two extremes in the growing legal debate about **obesity** were on display at a conference at Boston University last week.

Minnesota

Colorado

Mississippi

The editorial decisions encoded into these algorithms are not only in selecting what to show, but also how to show it, and what to make most visually salient through labeling, highlighting, or additional annotation. The Associated Press (AP) produces automatically generated graphics on topics such as the Olympics, finance, and box office numbers, which are then distributed on the wire. Other publishers such as *Der Spiegel* and Reuters are beginning to experiment with automated data visualizations that can augment or even anchor articles.[23]

Machine learning is opening up fascinating new possibilities for automated content, including the wholesale synthesis of new images, videos, or texts on the basis of training data. Research prototypes have generated video using other videos or audio, as well as synthesized images based on photographic corpora, voices using audio of potentially important sources such as politicians, and text to mimic user-generated comments.[24] One prototype demonstrated a system that can take ordinary video footage of a person's face from a webcam, understand the facial expressions made, and then map those onto another video's face in real time. The demo is provocative: videos show the face of Putin or Trump mimicking the same facial movements as an actor's.[25] Faces can now be swapped from one body to another, creating what are popularly known as "deepfakes."[26] Other systems take in an audio clip and synthesize photo-realistic interview video that synchronizes the audio to the mouth shape of the speaker based on training footage.[27] Photos can also be synthesized entirely from data. A machine-learning model trained on a database of 30,000 high resolution photographs of celebrities can output photos of faces for people who don't exist.[28] The photos have the look and feel of celebrity headshots and are striking in their quality (see Figure 3.3). In terms of text, neural networks can generate Yelp reviews that are rated just as "useful" as reviews from real people—essentially going unnoticed.[29]

Figure 3.3. Automatically synthesized faces of people who do not exist created using a neural network model trained on celebrity photos.

Source: T. Karras, T. Aila, S. Laine, J. Lehtinen, "Progressive Growing of GANs for Improved Quality, Stability, and Variation," *presented at the International Conference on Learning Representations,* Vancouver, Canada, 2018, https://arxiv.org/abs/1710.10196, licensed via Creative Commons Attribution-NonCommercial 4.0 International, https://creativecommons.org/licenses/by-nc/4.0/.

Algorithms that synthesize entirely new images, videos, and texts challenge the veracity of visual media and the authenticity of written media. The creation of fake videos showing sources saying something they did not could wreak havoc on the use of visual documentary evidence in journalism.[30] Photoshop has been undermining trust in visual media for years, but these new technologies create a whole new potential for scale and personalization. The output of these systems is rapidly advancing in believability, though to a trained eye there may be subtle signs that the videos aren't quite right, such as the flicker of an imperfectly synthesized mouth or a glazed look in the eyes. As the synthesis technology moves ahead quickly, forensics technology that can identify synthesized facial imagery or synthesized texts is also being developed.[31] Even if synthesized content might sometimes fool the human eye, the forensic algorithm's statistical eye will know it's faked. Still, an arms race is taking shape in which journalists will need to be equipped with sophisticated forensics tools in order to evaluate the authenticity of potentially synthesized media.

Automated Content in Use

The news industry is still actively exploring different domains and use-cases where there is the most strategic potential for content automation. Automated text writing has been used for more than two decades to produce weather forecasts.[32] In finance and markets, Bloomberg has been automatically generating written news alerts for its terminal for more than a decade, and Reuters currently uses automation to facilitate the writing of market recap reports on a daily basis. In 2011, Forbes rolled out automated corporate earnings previews and reports using technology from Narrative Science, and in 2014, the AP began publishing automated earnings reports as well. *Le Monde* deployed automated writing to help report French election results in 2015, and in 2017 in Finland the public broadcaster Yle as well as the newspaper *Helsingin Sanomat* and academic project Valtteri reported the results of the Finnish municipal elections using automation.[33] In the run up to the 2016 US election, automation was used by election forecasting site PollyVote to render written stories about the nearly daily election polls that were coming out.[34]

A mid-2017 survey of fourteen news agencies found that eleven were already using automation or were actively developing it, mostly in the domains of finance and sports.[35] Various publishers have pursued use-cases in specific sports such as soccer, ice hockey, and baseball.[36] The *Washington Post* has used the technology to cover events ranging from the 2016 Olympics to local football games, as well as to cover the 2016 US elections.[37] ProPublica and the *LA Times* have dabbled in generating automatic content in domains such as education, crime, and earthquake reporting.[38] MittMedia in Sweden writes articles about local real-estate transactions automatically.[39] Beyond articles, the *Washington Post* and other publications have explored automated headline writing,[40] and McClatchy has used the technique to convey information from a database as part of a larger investigative story.[41] Some outlets, including the UK Press Association in collaboration with Urbs Media, are exploring the coverage of topics such as road conditions, public safety, crime, and health using open municipal data.

Automation's Advantages

Over time innovators are expanding the scope of content genres and domains where automation offers a benefit. In some cases automation enables a new activity that people simply would not be capable of, whereas in other cases it offloads repetitive tasks from journalists or allows new scenarios of coverage that while possible for people to perform would be cost prohibitive. Automation affords one or more of several advantages in content creation by enabling speed, scale, accuracy, and personalization.[42]

Being the first to break a news story is often a competitive strategy for news organizations. They see speed as a way to drive traffic and enhance authority, despite there not necessarily being the same demand or urgency for speed from the audience.[43] But in some scenarios, and for some end users of news information, speed really is *the* defining factor. At Reuters as well as Bloomberg, which both sell specialized information terminals to stock traders, automation parses text documents, such as earnings releases, and almost instantaneously generates and publishes a headline to the terminal interface that reflects whether the company beat or missed earnings expectations. It's simple stuff written to specific standardized text templates, such as "IBM missed expectations by 0.12: 3.02 versus 3.14." But when new financial information can move a stock, being the first to have access to information can mean profit—and so speed is essential for traders. Finance appears to be the sole domain where full automation—complete autonomy across the entire production pipeline—has gained traction. To interject a human in the loop would diminish the value of the information to traders by slowing it down. Even a non-zero margin of error is outweighed by the sheer demand for speed. Automation for speed in this case is about providing a service that simply would not be possible to provide using human labor.

The domain of finance itself is not necessarily the defining factor in making speed critical, however. The importance of speed is more a reflection of the information needs of particular end users. Take for instance the AP's implementation of quarterly earnings reports described in the introduction to this book. Unlike the headlines pushed to the Reuters and Bloomberg terminals, AP's reports are not published within milliseconds of a corporate earnings release, but instead may be pushed to the wire anywhere from five to ten minutes or even an hour after an earnings release. Thereafter, they may be published by local AP-affiliated newspapers for the sake of local retail investors or individuals who are interested in a particular company. In determining whether speed will be an advantage in a particular automated content scenario, designers should look to how end users will actually use the information. For instance, the *LA Times'* Quake Bot, which reports on earthquakes automatically, generates and publishes story stubs very quickly because this can serve to alert readers to potential risks or safety issues for themselves or loved ones who may be within the earthquake zone. For both prescheduled events (such as earnings releases) and unscheduled ones (such as earthquakes) automation for speed depends on the needs of the audience for the information.[44]

The potential for scale, of increasing coverage and breadth, is another driving factor in the adoption of automated content. A computer algorithm can churn out hundreds or thousands of variations of a story quite easily once set up, parameterized, and fed with a stream of data. Automated content use cases are emerging in areas such as weather, sports, and elections, where the cost of developing an automated system can be amortized over a high volume of output with a long tail that might not otherwise attract dedicated attention from journalists. For instance, instead of covering only 15 percent of congressional races as it had in the past, in the 2016 US elections the *Washington Post* was able to cover elections in all states, including 435 house races, 34 senate seats, and 12 gubernatorial races. That's a dramatic expansion of coverage. And although the *Post* could have reached that scale of coverage using human reporters in prior elections, the costs would have been prohibitive. Automation offers the possibility to create content for ever smaller audiences, relieving the pressure to make editorial decisions that balance labor availability with newsworthiness judgments about things like the magnitude of the event.[45] What constitutes "newsworthy" changes when it's cheap and easy to cover basically everything.[46]

Increased breadth of coverage can allow for more widespread access to information which can in turn impact other societal processes. For instance, one study showed that the earnings reports rolled out by the AP have affected stock-trading behavior. The research examined 2,433 companies on the US exchanges that didn't have any financial earnings coverage by AP prior to the introduction of automation in October 2014.[47] By the end of the sample period, in October 2015, about two-thirds of the companies tracked had received some automated coverage and exhibited higher liquidity and trading volume in comparison to those that didn't receive automated coverage. The relative increase in volume was about 11 percent.

Scale can be considered across different dimensions, including categorical units such as sports teams (for instance, Klackspark's soccer coverage), geographic units (such as the *Washington Post*'s elections coverage), or temporal units (such as periodic polls in politics). The idea of scaling over time has an additional benefit: rather than widening coverage over a conceptual or spatial domain, it allows for consistent and uniform coverage of the same type of events over time. The *LA Times*' Quake Bot, which automatically writes stories about earthquakes using data provided by the United States Geological Survey (USGS), demonstrates this idea.[48] Earthquakes are always happening in California, and while there was audience demand to know when they happened, the *LA Times*' coverage was inconsistent. No reporter really wants to have to write a repetitive pro forma story about a local, relatively minor earthquake. Automation allowed the paper to offload the tedium of writing those basic articles while increasing the consistency of coverage, since basic rules about the magnitude of quakes that warranted a story were baked into code. Ben Welsh, the head of the data team at the *LA Times,* remarked that the reporter who had been tasked to write those stories in the past was now able to focus on more important investigations, such as what buildings in the city were unsafe for the next big earthquake. Scaling over time can contribute to time savings and potentially to labor reallocation that can buttress more substantive coverage of a topic.

Accuracy of text can be another advantage of automated content production. As Andreas Graefe writes in the *Guide to Automated Journalism,* "Algorithms do not get tired or distracted, and—assuming that they are programed correctly and the underlying data are accurate—they do not make simple mistakes like misspellings, calculation errors, or overlooking facts." The remaining errors are usually attributable to issues with the underlying data.[49] Lisa Gibbs, the business editor at the AP who helped with the roll-out of the automated earnings reports, concurred: "The error rate is lower than it was with human reporters. . . . Robots do not make typos and they do not make math errors." And if an error is detected in the output, the software needs to be fixed only once and then it can go back to operating accurately across its thousands of outputs. So once the systems are set up and debugged, they're consistent in their application of a procedure. But that doesn't always translate into more accuracy per se. Yes, automated content production can mitigate the clerical errors related to typos and math mistakes, but different types of errors and accuracy issues can crop up. The different accuracy profile of automated content in turn creates new demands on editors to recognize not the errors of sloppy fingers, but of missing data, unaccounted for context, or other algorithmic limitations.[50]

Speed, scale, and accuracy are all possible reasons for adopting automated content, but there's another affordance of the technology that is still nascent: personalization. A variety of avenues have been explored for news personalization, such as adaptive navigation, dynamic recommendations, geo-targeted editions, or just reordering of content on a page to match an individual's interests.[51] The idea of news personalization has been around almost as long as the World Wide Web,[52] and many modern reading interfaces, from apps, to newsfeeds and homepages, routinely make use of these strategies.

Here I want to focus on personalization at the level of the content itself. This might, for instance, entail automatically rewriting the words of an article to appeal best to an individual's interests or to the characteristics of a particular publication's audience. For instance, financial content can be written quite differently for a general purpose audience consuming the AP's earnings reports as compared to the expert audience reading a niche financial news site. Personalization in this context means any adaptation of a communication to a user. More specifically, content personalization is "an automated change to a set of facts that appear in an article's content based on properties of the reader."[53] Adaptations occur with respect to some model of the user, which could include age, gender, education level, location, political affiliation, topical interests, or other attributes of the individual. When a user sets his or her own model, this is often referred to as "customization," whereas when the model is implicitly determined (such as by observing behavior), this is referred to as "personalization."[54] Oftentimes there is some combination of customization and personalization whereby media is adapted somewhat through personalization and then the user can make further adjustments to customize it. Research on baseball stories that can be interactively customized by end users to focus on particular players or parts of the game showed that such adaptive articles were rated as more informative, interesting, and pleasant to read than nonadaptive articles.[55] It's unclear whether such results hold for implicitly personalized articles, but if they do, this could improve the user experience of news consumption.

Localization is a more narrow type of personalization reflecting adaptations based specifically on geography or language. For instance, localized weather reports are produced for thousands of locations throughout the world.[56] In their pilot, Urbs Media localized articles for the thirty-three boroughs of London using open data to write an article about the diabetes incidence in each borough. In a project together with the U.K. Press Association called "RADAR" (Reporters and Data and Robots), Urbs is expanding this approach to provide localized reports for a range of topics including health, education, crime, transportation, housing, and the environment.[57] A staff of four writers can produce fifteen story templates each week, each of which can in turn generate 250 localized versions.[58] Similarly, Hoodline, a local outlet in San Francisco, is experimenting with automatically localized stories about new or stand-out neighborhood restaurants using Yelp data.[59] Meanwhile, the Norwegian News Agency is considering localizing its automated soccer articles by creating different versions and angles on a story depending on which team a locale typically cheers for. So a home team loss might be framed in a softer way than when that same team crushes a crosstown rival. Another aspect of coverage localization relates to adapting content to a desired language of consumption. This has advantages for global organizations that publish content in multiple languages around the world.

Many of these applications of personalized content generation are in a nascent or developing stage. There are, however, already examples of personalized or customized content integrated into larger data-driven articles from the *New York Times,* the *Washington Post,* and *Vox.*[60] For example, a *Post* article entitled "America's Great Housing Divide: Are You a Winner or Loser?" maps and explains how real-estate prices have shifted over the last decade, showing the dip and uneven recovery after the 2008 financial crisis on a zip-code by zip-code basis. The article highlights several nationally interesting locations such as the San Francisco Bay Area, but it also presents a map and some text showing the locality of the viewer of the article. Using the location information modern web browsers infer based on a user's internet protocol (IP) address, the article is able to adapt the presentation of the content to the nearest metropolitan area and zip code. When I accessed the page in Washington, DC, it read, "In 2015, a single-family home there was worth $637,165 on average, about 79 percent more than in 2004. It's a densely populated, mostly black area. The home values are typically higher than most of the homes in the Washington-Arlington-Alexandria, DC-VA- area." The text is straightforward but is adapted to me as someone who at the time was living in the LeDroit Park neighborhood of Washington, DC, making it more contextually relevant.

The Business Case

"For us it's not about saving money—it's about doing stuff we couldn't otherwise do," underscored Ben Welsh about the possibilities for automation in the *LA Times* newsroom. Whether it's speeding up production, increasing breadth, enhancing accuracy, or enabling new types of personalization, there is great potential for applying automated content production in journalism. But as editorial possibilities are explored, the business incentives and value propositions also need to be worked out. Can automated content help with some of the sustainability concerns that face newsrooms with shrinking budgets?

Some organizations are already seeing the business impacts of automated content in terms of competitiveness based on speed or breadth. Law Street Media is a niche publisher of law and policy topics for a millennial audience. It doesn't have a big—or really any—video production staff, but it has been able to use the Wibbitz semi-automated production tool to adapt content for a visuals-seeking audience and thus to expand its reach. Wibbitz, the toolmaker, makes money through revenue sharing. "Instead of having . . . 400 text articles written every day and only having a video on twenty of them, they [publishers] can now have video on 90 percent of them," Zohar Dayan, the founder of Wibbitz told me. Expanding the breadth of video content creates more advertising inventory, and in some cases Wibbitz gets a cut of the revenue that the advertising creates. Value accrues both to the creator of the automation tool and to the publisher.

Automated content can also create business value by reducing or shifting labor costs. Sören Karlsson, the CEO of United Robots, estimated that their soccer recap-writing software has saved one of its clients about $150,000 in a year. Some freelancers were no longer needed to call arenas to find out how each game turned out, for instance. This is more of a shift of labor than anything else since the effort (and cost) needed to collect the data has been subtracted away from each local newsroom and centralized by a new business entity that itself employs people to gather the data. There can be some cost savings by media organizations looking to shift labor onto perhaps more efficient and specialized technology provider companies.

Key business metrics can also be favorably impacted by automated content. The *Washington Post* found that automatically produced articles can drive a substantial number of clicks. The paper published about 500 automatically written articles during the 2016 US elections, which in total generated more than 500,000 page views.[61] In China, Xinhuazhiyun, a joint venture between Alibaba and Xinhua News Agency, created an automated soccer video highlight system and deployed it during the World Cup in 2018. The 37,581 clips produced, including things like goal highlights and coach reactions, generated more than 120 million views in total. Klackspark's automated articles are also generating new traffic for Östgöta Media: the site had about 30,000 unique visitors per month in early 2017, and in an indication of a higher level of engagement, visitors now read more articles per visit on Klackspark. These numbers have made it fairly easy to attract sponsorship for the site from organizations that want to speak to soccer-loving audiences. Klackspark is harnessing the attention and value the automation provides to move toward a subscription model, where access to the site is packaged with access to one of Östgöta

Media's local media properties. It's essentially seen as a value-add to the local news package, along the lines of: "Subscribe to our local paper and get access to this great soccer-news resource as part of the deal." Automated articles can also help drive subscription conversion directly. MittMedia's automatically produced real estate articles have driven hundreds of new subscriptions in the first few months of operation.[62]

Automation can, in some cases, also enhance the visibility of content on search engines such as Google. To the extent that search engine ranking criteria are known, these factors can be baked into how content is automatically produced so that it is ranked more highly by the search engine. This provides more visibility and traffic to the content and, theoretically at least, more advertising revenue as a result. For instance, Google ranks editorial content more highly when a picture is included. Realizing this, the German automated content provider Retresco automatically selects an image or picture to go along with the written football recap articles it generates.

Automated content also creates new opportunities for products. In the future perhaps we will see native content (that is, content sponsored by an organization with a stake in the topic) mass-localized for different markets using automation. But as with any new technical advance, designers should ask if an innovation comes into tension with desired values. Automation for scale appears to assume a "more is better" standard for news content. In the case of financial news at the AP, that has helped liquidity around stocks. But is more content *always* better—for society, or for business? For that matter, is more speed or personalization always better? Practitioners will need to weigh the benefits and trade-offs as they balance business and journalistic commitments.

Barriers to Adoption

Innovation in automated content continues to push the boundary of what can be accomplished by taking advantage of speed, scale, accuracy, and personalization. And while there will be a growing number of use cases where these benefits make sense, either financially or competitively, a range of drawbacks will prevent a fully automated newsroom of the future. The limitations of content automation include a heavy reliance on data, the difficulty of moving beyond the frontier of its initial design, cognitive disadvantages such as a lack of ability to interpret and explain, and bounded writing quality. Some of these limitations, such as the dependency on data, are inherent to algorithmic production processes, whereas other issues may eventually succumb to the forward march of technical progress as artificial intelligence advances.

Data, Data, Data

The availability of data is perhaps the most central limiting factor for automated content production. Whether numerical data, textual or visual media corpora, or knowledge bases, automated content is all about the data that's available to drive the process. Datafication —the process of creating data from observations of the world—becomes a stricture that holds back more widespread use of automation simply because aspects of the world that aren't digitized and represented as data cannot be algorithmically manipulated into content. The quality, breadth, and richness of available data all impact whether the automated content turns out compelling or bland.[63] Data also become a competitive differentiator: exclusive data mean exclusive content.[64] Automated content runs the risk of becoming homogenous and undifferentiated if every news organization simply relies on access to the same data feeds or open data sources. In the content landscape, news organizations may see new competitors (or collaborators) in organizations that already have deep and unique databases and can cheaply transform that data into content. Despite a reluctance among some news organizations,[65] the acquisition of quality numerical data streams and knowledge bases is relatively new territory where news organizations will need to invest to remain competitive.

Investment in data production could involve everything from sensor journalism—the deployment of cheap sensors to gather data—to creating new techniques for digitizing documents acquired during investigations.[66] Public records requests are a method many data journalists use to acquire data for their investigations; however it still remains to be seen whether automated content can be reliably built around this form of data acquisition. *Streams* of data are often the most compelling and valuable for automated content since they facilitate scale and amortization of development costs over time. But engineering a stream of data requires the entire chain from acquisition to editing and quality control to be systematized, and perhaps automated as well. Data quality is essential but is still mostly reliant on iterative human attention and care.[67] News organizations able to innovate processes that can pipeline data acquired via public records requests or other sources will have a competitive advantage in providing unique automated content. The use of more sophisticated structured data and knowledge bases is another promising avenue for advancing the capabilities of automation.[68] The deliberate and editorially oriented design and population of event and knowledge abstractions through structured reporting processes allow for the meticulous datafication of particular events from the world. These data can then be used to drive more sophisticated narrative generation.

The textual outputs of an automated writing system are influenced by the editorial decisions about the data they are fed. There's a certain "algorithmic objectivity" or even "epistemic purity" that has been attributed to automated content—an adherence to a consistent factual rendition that confers a halo of authority.[69] But the apparent authority of automated content belies the messy, complex reality of datafication, which contorts the beautiful complexity of the world into a structured data scheme that invariably excludes nuance and context.[70] The surface realization of content may be autonomous or nearly autonomous, but editorial decisions driven by people or organizations with their own values, concerns, and priorities suffuse the data coursing through the system. The ways data are chosen, evaluated, cleaned, standardized, and validated all entail editorial decision-making that still largely lies outside the realm of automated writing, and in some cases demands closer ethical consideration.[71] For instance, standard linguistic resources that an automated writing system might rely on can embed societal biases (such as race or gender bias) that then refract through the system.[72]

Bias can emerge in automated content in several different ways. The bias of a data source relates to a host of issues that can arise due to the diversity of intents and methods different actors may use in the datafication process. The limitations of datasets must be clearly understood before journalists employ automation. Corporations and governments that create datasets are not creating them for the sake of objective journalism. Why were they created, and how are they intended to be used? Data can be easily pushed past its limits or intended uses, leading to validity issues.

Another issue is coverage bias. If automation has a strong dependency on the availability of data, then there may be a tendency to automatically cover topics or domains only if data are available. And even if data are generally available, a missing row or gap could prevent coverage of a specific event. We already see this type of bias in terms of the initial use cases for automation: weather, sports, and finance all being data-rich domains. Other topics may not receive automated coverage if data are not available, leading to coverage bias. "Just because there are a lot of data in some domains, it doesn't mean that that is actually something that is interesting or important to the society. We need to watch out so that you don't let the data control what you would cover," explained Karlsson from United Robots. Data quality also needs to be considered, since data journalists have been known to prefer datasets that are easily readable and error-free.[73] As a result automation editors may want to consciously consider how data availability and quality influence coverage using automation.

The data that feed automated content production are also sub-ject to little-discussed security concerns that could affect quality. It's not unreasonable to imagine bad actors manipulating or hacking data streams to inject malicious data that would result in misleading content being generated. As a simple example, if a hacker were able to make the data delivered to the AP for the earnings per share of a company appear to beat estimates instead of missing them, this could have an impact on investors' trading decisions and allow the hacker to profit. The AP does have checks in place to catch wild anomalies in the data—such as a stock dropping by 90 percent—as well as means to alert an editor, but more subtle and undetected manipulations could still be possible. Additional research is needed to understand the security vulner-abilities of automated content systems.

Data are the primary and in many cases the only information source for automated content. As a result, datafication puts impor-tant limits on the range of content that can be feasibly auto-mated. Data *must* be available to produce automated content, but sometimes information is locked away in nondigitized documents, difficult-to-index digitized documents such as handwritten forms,[74] or even more problematically, in human heads. If a beat, story, or topic relies on information tied up in human brains (that is, not recorded in some digital or digitizable medium), then in-terviews are needed to draw out that information. The current generation of automated journalism is most applicable when the story rests on information either directly in the data, or derivable from the data, but not outside of that data. Unless the input data captures all the nuances of a situation, which is highly unlikely, there will necessarily be context loss in the automated content. New ways to overcome context loss and lack of nuance inherent to datafication are needed in order to expand the range of utility for automated content.

In cases where necessary information is coming directly from people, and when it may be "sensitive, complex, uncertain, and susceptible to misunderstanding, requiring intimacy, trust, assessment of commitment, and detection of lies,"[75] the interjection of reporters—people tasked with acquiring that information—will be essential. Handling sensitive leaks and meetings in dark alleys with shady sources will be the purview of human journalists for some time to come. Interviewing is relational. Even just getting access may depend on building a rapport with a particular source over time. Moreover, an interview may require not just blindly recording responses but instead demand adversarial push-back on falsehoods, follow-ups to clarify facts, or reframing unanswered questions to press for responses. For all of these reasons, automation may be deeply challenged in terms of its capacity to engage in meaningful journalistic interviews.[76]

But there are some hints for how automated content could be integrated with human question asking, such as when the AP has reporters do follow-up interviews to get a quote to augment some automated earnings stories. This pattern of collaboration could even be systematized by inserting gaps in templates where information acquired from human collaborators would be expected. For instance, a template might include an "insert quote from soccer coach here" flag and send a task request to a reporter to acquire a quote before publishing a story. In such mixed initiative interfaces an algorithm might prompt the reporter for certain inputs it deems necessary.[77] In one experiment potential sources were targeted on Twitter and asked a question about the waiting time in an airport queue (42 percent of users even responded).[78] But the gap between asking simple questions like this and the more substantive questions required of human reporting is vast. Meaningful research awaits to be done on developing automation that can ask meaningful questions and receive meaningful responses. Automation must learn to datify the world.

The Frontier of Design and Capability

Automated content production systems are designed and engineered to fit the use cases for which they're deployed. Rule-based automation is particularly brittle, often functioning reliably only within the boundaries of where its designers had thought through the problem enough to write down rules and program the logic. In certain domains such as sports, finance, weather, elections, or even local coverage of scheduled meetings, there is a fair bit of routine in journalism. Such events are often scheduled in advance and unfold according to a set of expectations that are not particularly surprising. Sports have their own well-defined rules and boundaries. It is in routine events like these where an automated algorithm, itself a highly structured routine, will be most useful. But, almost by definition, routine events in which something nonroutine happens could be extremely newsworthy—like say, stadium rafters collapsing on a soccer match. Unlike automated systems, human journalists are adept at adapting and improvising in cases like these.[79]

Automation fundamentally lacks the flexibility to operate beyond the frontier of its own design. Automated systems don't know what they don't know. They lack a meta-thinking ability to see holes or gaps in their data or knowledge. This makes it difficult to cope with novelty in the world—a severe weakness for the domain of news information given that novelty is quite often newsworthy. When the Norwegian News Agency implemented its soccer writing algorithm, there was a lot of handwringing about what to do in outlier situations. At the end of the day the decision was to simply not create an automated story for events that had some kind of exceptional, out-of-bounds aspect to them. But that kind of recognition itself requires human meta-thinking; human oversight must be built into the system.

The fragility of automated content production algorithms also leads to reliability issues. Yes, once it's set up, an algorithm will run over and over again in the same way. It is reliable in the sense that it is consistent. But if the world changes even just a little bit, such as a data source changing its format, this could lead to an error. Reliability in the sense of being dependable is an issue for adoption of automated systems because it impacts trust.[80] This introduces limits on how far news organizations are willing to push automation: "The more sophisticated you try to get with it, the more you increase the chance of error," said Lisa Gibbs from the AP.[81] In high-risk, high-reward use cases such as finance, which are built around a need for speed, organizations such as Reuters have double and triple redundancy on their automation, including in some cases a human fallback.

The resilience of people allows them to accommodate error conditions and make corrections on the fly. Automated systems, by contrast, continue blindly powering forward until an engineer hits the kill switch, debugs the machine to fix the error, and then restarts the process. As a result, automated content needs editors who can monitor and check the reliability of the process on an ongoing basis. Oftentimes the errors that crop up with automation are data-related, though sometimes they can also be introduced by algorithms that aren't quite up to the task.[82] Ben Welsh at the *LA Times* described an error that their earthquake reporting system made. It published a report based on USGS data, but then ten minutes later the USGS sent a correction saying it was a ghost reading caused by aftershocks in Japan. The *LA Times* updated the post and then wrote a second story about ghost earthquakes that are sometimes incorrectly reflected in the USGS data. Errors of this ilk keep cropping up, though: in June, 2017 the Quake Bot relayed another bogus report from faulty USGS data, this time because a date-time bug at the USGS sent out a faulty alert.[83] These instances point out the weakness of relying on a single, untriangulated stream of data, albeit one that is often reliable. Similar data-driven errors have also arisen at the AP, including a prominent error made in July 2015, when one of its earnings reports erroneously indicated that Netflix's share price was down, when instead it was up. The reason for the error was traced to the fact that the company had undergone a 7–1 stock split, but the algorithm didn't understand what a stock split was.[84] Thankfully, outlets such as the *LA Times* and AP have human oversight and corrections policies that help to mitigate or remediate such algorithmic errors.

Errors in data aside, algorithms have gotten reasonably profi-
cient at automated content creation within the bounds of their
design. But they also still have difficulty with more advanced cognitive tasks. Beyond simply describing *what* happened, algorithms struggle with explaining *why* things happened. They have
difficulty interpreting information in new ways because they lack
context and common sense. In the nomenclature of the classic six
Ws of journalism—who, what, where, when, why, and how—
automation is practicable with *who, what, where,* and *when,*
particularly when given the right data and knowledge bases, but
it still struggles with the *why* and *how,* which demand higher-level
interpretation and causal reasoning abilities.

Generating explanations for why something is happening in
society is daunting, even for people. While data-driven methods
do exist for causal inference, it remains to be seen whether they
rise to the level of reliability publishers would require in order to
automatically publish such inferences. It's more likely that any explanation produced by an automated system would be further
vetted or augmented by people. Explaining a complex social phe-
nomena may demand data, context, or social understanding that
is simply inaccessible to an automated content production system.
One of the critiques of mass localization has been that if statistics
aren't contextualized by reporters with local knowledge, articles
can miss the bigger social reality.[85] Entire strands of journalism,
for instance those pertaining to cultural interpretation, may
also be difficult for automation to address.[86] The lack of com-
monsense reasoning prevents systems from making inferences
that would be easy to make for a human reporter, which further
curtails their usage outside of the narrow domains where they've
been engineered with the requisite knowledge.

One specific type of knowledge and reasoning that automated
content still lacks is the legal kind. As a result, algorithms have
the potential to violate media laws without realizing it. Consider
for a moment the possibility of algorithmic defamation, defined
as "a false statement of fact that exposes a person to hatred,

ridicule or contempt, lowers him in the esteem of his peers, causes him to be shunned, or injures him in his business or trade."[87] In order for a statement to be considered defamation in the United States, it must be false but be perceived as fact and must harm the reputation of an individual or entity.[88] The United States has some of the most permissive free speech laws in the world, and for a defamation suit to hold up in court against a public figure, the statement must have been made with "knowledge of its falsity or reckless disregard for its truth or falsity"—the "actual malice" standard.[89] Presumably this could be proven if a programmer or news organization deliberately acted with malice to create an automated content algorithm that would spew defamatory statements. But there's a lower standard for defamatory speech against private individuals. If a news organization publishes an automatically produced libelous statement against a private individual, it could be liable if it is shown that the organization was negligent, which might include failing to properly clean data or fact check automated outputs.[90] The potential for algorithmic missteps that lead to legal liability is yet another reason to have human editors in the loop, or at the very least to engineer systems away from being able to make public statements that could hurt the reputation of private individuals.

Writing Quality

Despite being able to output perfectly readable and understandable texts, the quality of automated writing still has a way to go before it can reflect human-like standards of nuance and variability, not to mention complex uses of language such as metaphor and humor.[91] Variability is a key concern, especially for content domains such as sports, where it's likely for a single user to consume more than one piece of content at a time. Repetition could lead to boredom. "You really need to be able to express the game outcome in many different ways. Otherwise you will see that this is automated text and you will find that this is repeating itself," explained Karlsson from United Robots. In domains such as finance there may be advantages to keeping the language straightforward and more robot-like—verbal parsimony and repetition can straightforwardly communicate essential facts to users—whereas in domains such as sports users may want more entertaining, emotional, or lively text.

Text quality of course varies greatly with the method used to automate the writing. Template-based methods have the highest quality because they encode the fluency of the human writer of the template. Yet templates also reduce text variability, increasing repetition and the potential to bore readers. Studies have begun to examine the perception of automatically written texts and found that readers can't always differentiate automatic from human-written texts but that there can be substantive differences in readability, credibility, and perception of quality.[92] An early study found that human-written articles were more "pleasant to read" than their automated counterparts.[93] A more recent study of more than 1,100 people in Germany found that computer-written articles were scored as less readable, but more credible than their human-written counterparts.[94] The difference in readability was substantial: the mean rating for the human-written articles was 34 percent higher than for computer-written articles. But the absolute differences for credibility were quite small, only about 7 percent. Another study of 300 European news readers found that message credibility of sports (but not finance) articles was about 6 percent higher for automated content.[95] In Finland, a study of the Valtteri system compared automatically generated municipal election articles to journalist-written articles and found that the automated articles were perceived to be of lower credibility, likability, quality, and relevance.[96] Feedback from the 152 study participants suggested that the automated articles were boring, repetitive, and monotonous, as well as that there were grammatical mistakes and issues with the writing style. Unlike previous studies which evaluated texts generated using templated sentences, Valtteri used phrase-level templates, phrase aggregation, referring expression generation, and automated document planning based on the detection and ranking of newsworthiness of facts to include in the story. In other words, it's a more complex NLG engine. But this complexity appears to introduce the potential for grammatical errors that may undermine the credibility of texts. Moreover, the phrase-level templates used didn't provide enough variability to make the texts interesting to users.

We can contrast template-driven automated content of perhaps passable (if not entirely compelling) quality to even lower-quality statistical NLG approaches. Let's look at an abstractive summarization system trained on *New York Times* articles using a machine-learning technique.[97] Researchers asked human readers to rate the readability of the summaries produced in an evaluation of the system. Here is one example of the output of the model that produced summaries with the highest readability of those tested, run on an input article about a Formula One car race:

> Button was denied his 100th race for McLaren. The ERS prevented him from making it to the start-line. Button was his team mate in the 11 races in Bahrain. He quizzed after Nico Rosberg accused Lewis Hamilton of pulling off such a manoeuvre in China.

Though somewhat recognizable as topical text, the summary has awkward verbs, such as "quizzed," which do not fit the context, it doesn't explain acronyms, and it has fragments of nonsensical text.

The fluency of textual output produced by simple templates (see Figure 3.1), as well as being more straightforward to understand in terms of concrete rules, helps explain its adoption by news agencies in lieu of statistical methods.[98] Publishing garbled text consisting of ungrammatical nonsense would cast a long shadow on the credibility of a news outlet. If more advanced machine-learning approaches are to be integrated into content production, additional technical advances are needed.

Automated Content Is People!

In 2016 the White House predicted that as the result of advances in artificial intelligence, "Many occupations are likely to change as some of their associated tasks become automatable."[99] So what does automation mean for human tasks in news production? Even in scenarios where content is produced entirely autonomously with no human in the loop,[100] there is still a lot of human influence refracted through the system. Automation is designed, maintained, and supervised by people. If people are inserted at key points in the production process, they can oftentimes compensate for the shortcomings of automation described in the last section. And so determining how best to infuse or blend human intelligence into the hybrid process is a key question. "The value of these automated systems is the degree to which you can imbue them with editorial acumen," explained Jeremy Gilbert at the *Washington Post*. Here I consider how that editorial acumen is expressed via the design, development, and operation of automated systems, as well as what this means for how human roles may change.

Design and Development

The design and development process for automated content production systems is rife with opportunities for baking in editorial decision-making according to the editorial values and domain knowledge of whoever is involved in that design process, including reporters, editors, computational linguists, data scientists, software engineers, product managers, and perhaps even end users. Values become embedded into systems through everything from how constructs are defined and operationalized to how knowledge bases and data are structured, collected, or acquired, how content is annotated, how templates or fragments of text are written and translated for various output languages, and how general knowledge about the genre or domain comes to be encoded so that it can be effectively utilized by an algorithm.

One of the key editorial decisions that automated content systems must make is how they define what information is included or excluded. Whether that depends on some notion of "newness," "importance," "relevance," "significance," or "unexpectedness," data scientists will need to carefully define and measure that construct in order to use it in the algorithm. Decisions about these types of editorial criteria will have implications for how people perceive the content. "Some critics of the Quake Bot think it writes too many stories about smaller earthquakes," Ben Welsh explained. This was the result of a decision by the city editor, who simply declared that the bot should cover everything that's a magnitude 3.0 and higher earthquake in the Los Angeles area. These types of human decisions get enshrined in code and repeated over and over by the automation, so it's important to think them through carefully in the design process.[101] Otherwise different or even conflicting notions of newsworthiness may become unconsciously built into how algorithms come to "think" about such inclusion and exclusion decisions. It's often necessary for people involved in the design of these systems to be able to make their implicit judgments explicit, and with clear rationale.

People also heavily influence automated content production in terms of the creation and provision of data. For unstructured data or for systems relying on machine learning, human annotation of data is often an important step. Structured annotations are a key enabler of algorithmic production. For instance, automated video creation systems need a corpus of photos that is reliably annotated so that when a person is referred to in the script, a photo of the correct person can be shown. In early systems for producing automated video such annotations were supplied by people using controlled vocabularies of concepts.[102] Newer systems, such as those of Wochit and Wibbitz, rely on vast corpora of content that have been tagged by professional photo agencies. In cases where yet more classification algorithms are used to automatically tag a photo or video with concepts, those algorithms have to be trained on data that was originally judged by people as containing those concepts. Automated systems are built atop layers and layers of human judgment reflected in concept annotations.

Domain-specific and general knowledge reflecting an understanding of the genre, narrative style, choice of words, or expectations for tone also need to be encoded for automated systems.

For specific content areas, such as politics, sports, or finance, experts need to abstract and encode their domain knowledge and editorial thinking for use by the machine. For instance, semantic enrichment of valence about a particular domain might allow an automated system to write that a trend for a particular data series "improved" instead of just "increased." The meaning of words may also depend on constantly evolving knowledge of a domain: for example, in a story about election polls, the meaning of terms that are not well defined, such as "lead," "trend," or "momentum," could depend on context.[103] Retresco keeps former editors on staff so that different genres of text can be matched in terms of choices in grammar and word choice. Tom Meagher at the Marshall Project explained how the database they designed to support the automation in their "Next to Die" project was influenced by partners who had spent dozens of years covering capital punishment in their own states and as a result knew what factors to quantify for the automation. Wibbitz has an in-house editorial team of video editors and ex-journalists who work with research and development groups to incorporate their knowledge into the technology. "That's one of the most important parts of the company," according to its founder, Zohar Dayan. A key enabler of the next generation of automated content systems will be better user interfaces that will allow experts to impart their journalistic knowledge and domain expertise to the system.

Collaboration in Operation

Once an automated content production system has been designed and developed, it moves into an operational phase. In this stage as well, people are in constant contact and collaboration with the automation as they update it, augment it, edit it, validate it, and otherwise maintain and supervise its overall functioning. There are some tasks humans can't do, there are other tasks that automation can't do, and so a collaboration is the most obvious path forward. This raises important questions about the nature of that human-computer interaction and collaboration, such as how to ensure common ground and understanding between a human user and the automated system, how to monitor the automation to ensure its reliability or to override it, how contributions by people and computers can be seamlessly interleaved, and when and how trust is developed when systems are fairly reliable but not 100 percent reliable.[104] As people interact with these systems, the nature of their skills, tasks, roles, and jobs will necessarily evolve, most likely to privilege abstract thinking, creativity, and problem-solving.[105]

Given the preponderance of template-driven approaches to automated content, writing is one of the areas where people will need to evolve their craft. Template writers need to approach a story with an understanding of what the available data *could* say—in essence to imagine how the data could give rise to different angles and stories and delineate the logic that would drive those variations. Related is the ability to transform the available data and organize it more suitably or advantageously to the way it will be used. Gary Rogers of Urbs London, who creates templates to tell stories using open data in the United Kingdom, explained it this way: "When you're writing a template for a story, you're not writing the story—you're writing the potential for every eventuality of the story." The combinatorics of the data need to be understood in relation to what would be interesting to convey in a story, something that is closely related to the computational thinking concept of parameterization described in Chapter 1. People will also need to be on hand to adapt or reparameterize story templates in view of data contingencies or shifts in data availability for different contexts, such as a national soccer match with lots of rich data and a local soccer match with a relative paucity of data. Available interfaces for template writing don't yet support writers in seeing the multitude of possibilities in a given dataset, or in parameterizing a story in terms of the available data.

But user interfaces are, in general, evolving to better support the template-writing task. Automated Insights, whose technology drives the AP earnings reports, markets a tool called "Wordsmith," while Arria, which is used by Urbs Media, has a tool called "Arria Studio." These are essentially user-interface innovations wrapped around an automated content production algorithm. You could think of it as an alien word processor that lets the author write fragments of text controlled by data-driven if-then-else rules (see Figure 3.4). Automating the document planning and microplanning stages of NLG is complex and demands a fair amount of both engineering and domain knowledge. These interfaces offload the most complex of the document planning and microplanning decisions to a human writer who authors a meta-document of rules and text fragments. Updating and main-

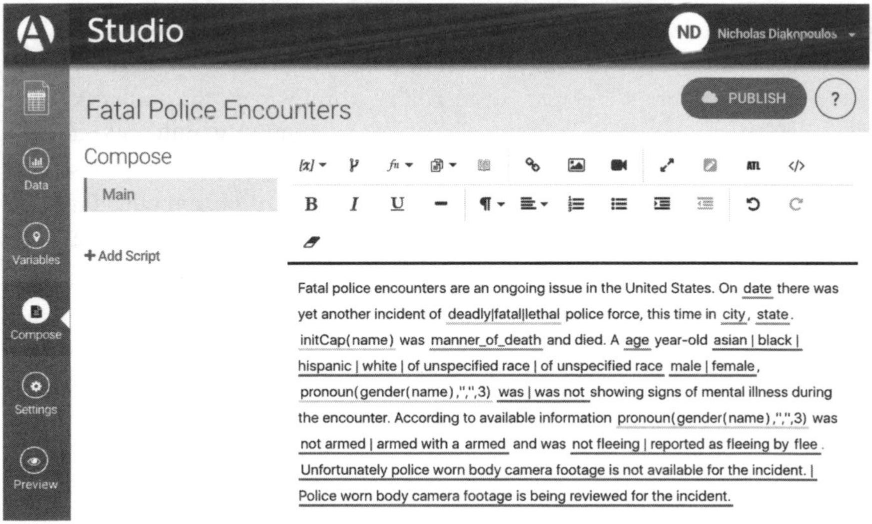

Figure 3.4. The Arria Studio user interface showing a story drafted using data from the *Washington Post* fatal police shootings database. Note the top row of buttons in the toolbar, used for inserting variables, conditional statements, synonyms, or other computational functions to transform the text. An alternative view provides direct access to the templating language. At the left are tabs that allow the user to explore the data, to choose among variables for the purposes of writing, and to preview the template's output with different rows of test data. *Source:* Arria Studio (https://app.studio.arria.com/).

taining a portfolio of templates this way, however, requires a fair bit of new editorial work.

If there's any area where there will be steady growth in employment, it's in the various shades of ongoing maintenance work that automated content systems require. People need to be involved in remediating errors that crop up in automated outputs, for instance. This may very well involve some exciting and creative detective work in debugging the system. But then there is the more prosaic maintenance: making sure the data streams are updated when the soccer leagues announce changes to teams, editing databases or spreadsheets to reflect new corporate details, keeping track of new or updated open data sources, or tweaking any of the myriad rule-sets for structure, genre, or style that have been baked into the design of the system. Lisa Gibbs at the AP told me that their introduction of automated stories has led to new tasks for her colleagues: "One of the responsibilities of an editor on our breaking news desk now is essentially automation maintenance," which involves tracking when companies move headquarters, split their stock, and so on. She estimates this takes about two hours per month of staff time, so it's still a small slice of effort, but you could imagine that growing as more and more automation comes online. When the LA Times' Quake Bot missed a noticeable earthquake out in the middle of the Pacific Ocean, the geographic bounding box of the bot had to be adjusted so that its filter stretched farther out into the ocean. Updates like this will be needed as automated content is put through its paces and exposed to some of the corner or edge cases that designers maybe didn't capture in their initial rules. From a business perspective, automated content probably won't be competitive if it's static for too long. People will need to be involved in continuously assessing and reassessing how it could be improved.

Supervision and management of automated systems are also increasingly occupying humans in the newsroom. As systems are developed, automation editors are needed to assess the quality of the content until it is good enough to publish, ideally foreseeing and rectifying potential errors in the design process. Regarding the development of soccer article-writing software, Helen Vogt from the Norwegian News Agency said, "I think we had at least 70 or 80 versions before we were ready to go live. And they [the sports editors] had a lot of fun testing it and tweaking it." In the production of its Opportunity Gap project, ProPublica's Scott Klein noted that editing 52,000 automatically written stories became a new challenge: "Editing one narrative does not mean you've edited them all."[106] Sensible edits in one case might not entirely fit in another. Automated checks can contribute to quality assurance, but the provision of high-quality text still requires that representative samples of outputs be manually assessed.[107] At the RADAR project about one in ten stories is still manually checked to ensure that the raw data and story flow are accurately reflected in outputs. Much as methods for "distant reading" have helped digital humanities scholars understand corpora of texts via computational methods and visualizations,[108] building tools to support the notion of "distant editing" could allow editors to work on a much larger scale of texts.

There's a distinct quality control or editing function that people must contribute during development of automation. People must also be available to make and post corrections in case the automation doesn't behave as expected once it's put into operation. When the *Washington Post* ran its automated elections articles for the 2016 US elections, people were tasked with monitoring some of the stories using tools like virtual private networks (VPNs) to simulate loading the stories from different locations in order to see if the articles were adapting as expected. Tool makers have noted that a barrier to the adoption of personalized content is the effort needed to edit and check consistency of the many potential outputs.[109] As newsrooms expand their use of automation, people will need to keep an eye on the big picture—to know when to deploy, decommission, or redevelop a system over time.

Shifting Roles

The collaborations that emerge between journalists and automated content systems may lead to deskilling (loss of skills in the
workforce), upskilling (an increase in skills to meet new demands
from sophisticated tools), reskilling (retraining), or otherwise shift
the role of human actors as they adjust to a new algorithmic presence.[110] Maintenance work related to updating datasets and
knowledge bases, or annotating media, may not ultimately be that
sexy, cognitively demanding, or high skill. This could have the effect of creating more entry-level jobs for which there would be
more labor supply and lower wages. At the same time, automation can offload and substitute some of the tedium of, say, determining data-driven facts for a story. This may create more time
for high-skilled journalists to do what they're trained for, namely
reporting, finding and speaking to new sources, and writing in
creative or compelling ways.[111] The need for high-skilled reporters
is reinforced by the shortcomings of the current state-of-the-art
technology, which cannot get at information where there are no
data or answer questions such as why and how an event fits into
the social fabric of society. The design, development, configuration,
and supervision of automation may entail the need for a different
kind of high-skilled individual as well—one who has mastered
computational thinking, is highly creative, and understands the
limits of the technology.

The reskilling of the existing journalistic workforce will involve
learning tasks such as how to write templates to feed the automation. It will also include some light coding or at least familiarity
with coding. "You have to be able to say here's a question a reporter would ask, or a framing of a story, or an angle and how do
I encode that in computer code, or how could computer code ask
and answer that question on its own, and return an answer that
can then be republished," Welsh told me. Writing templates demands domain knowledge and a fluency in writing for that domain, as well as an essential understanding of the possibilities of

what the technology affords. At the *Washington Post*, Jeremy Gilbert observed that more experienced editors are often better at writing the templates because they already have experience helping to shape the writing of reporters and so they "have a better sense of structurally what is or should be." A structured journalism pilot project asked ten reporters to populate event and knowledge data structures, and found that the key skill that enabled some of those reporters to adapt quickly was a "general comfort with abstraction."[112] But this is skill enhancement, not replacement; reporting skills are just as important as ever. On the "Next to Die" project at the Marshall Project Tom Meagher explained that for structured journalism "the core task is keeping the database up to date and adding every new change to a case," but that "in some ways the reporting is almost exactly the same." In other words, reporting skills are still necessary, but the output of those reporting skills is to a structured database that then feeds the automated output.

These shifts are already to some extent reflected in new roles, both at the deskilled and the upskilled ends of the spectrum. Wibbitz claims that the results of its automatic process are a "rough cut" that's about 80 percent of the way there. People manage the last 20 percent, which involves fine tuning the story, swapping images based on relevance, or adjusting the transitions or caption timing. The people who do this don't have to be highly skilled video editors—one media organization I spoke to referred to the person tasked with editing the videos all day as "junior staff," an intern. On the other hand, the sports reporter who worked on the design of the first soccer story-writing software at the Norwegian News Agency decided to take on a new role as "news developer," and he now looks at tools, workflows, and opportunities where automation can provide value to the organization. Reuters has an automation bureau chief who is similarly tasked with both thinking through how to manage the existing automation in use and with envisioning new possibilities. And at the AP, a new position was created in 2014 for an automation editor who engages in much of the supervision, management, and strategy around automation use by the agency. These roles need editorial thinking as much as they need a capacity to understand data and the capabilities of state-of-the-art content automation technology. In other words they could be appropriate for a reskilled journalist or a reskilled data scientist. The implications of labor shifts will be borne out over time. Future research will need to observe how automated content production affects the composition of deskilling, reskilling, and upskilling and how that in turn impacts issues such as worker autonomy and skills education.[113]

Whither Automated Content?

Automated content production is still in a nascent state. It's beginning to gain traction as different organizations recognize the potential for speed and scale, but personalization is still largely on the horizon. There remains untapped communicative potential for combining text, video, and visualization in compelling ways. As limitations on data provision and automation capabilities give way to advances in engineering, what should we expect for automated content moving forward? Where should organizations look for opportunity as the technology advances?

Genre Expansion

One of the criticisms of automated journalism is that it's less "automated journalism" than "automated description."[114] A typology of journalistic forms is useful for seeing where else automation could expand. One such typology draws on rhetorical theory and offers five types of journalistic output: description, narration, exposition, argumentation, and criticism.[115] Description is essential in all of these modes and is well-suited to automation, given that the state of the world can be rendered factually based on collected data. For aspects of description that need to be more phenomenological, human collaborators can step in to add "flavor" such as quotes or other human-interest observations. Narration builds on description but offers more structure in presenting an event, perhaps even making it come across as more of a story by establishing connections between facts, events, and characters. This is what companies such as Narrative Science strive for: to be smart about document planning so that description starts to look more like narrative. The current state of the art in content automation gives us description and narrative.

Exposition starts to be more challenging. Exposition seeks to explain, interpret, predict, or advise and is familiar from formats such as op-ed columns or news analyses. This type of composition is harder for automation to render. Notable research prototypes of heavily engineered systems have, however, created expository essays or documentaries.[116] As explanatory AI becomes more sophisticated and knowledge structures are engineered to incorporate causality, we may see production-level automated content integrating aspects of explanation. Still, some aspects of exposition, such as commentary flavored by individual opinion, will remain outside the purview of automation, or will extrude human commentary that is parameterized and amplified through the machinery of the system. User-interfaces could allow for an opinionated configuration of the content production pipeline. Personal interpretations of the definition of newsworthiness, for instance, as well as the word choices, templates, and tone used could then infuse what would be a more overtly subjective exposition.

Argumentation goes beyond exposition by adding the purpose of persuasion, of trying to sway a reader's attitudes and ultimately behaviors. Provided that the argument is coming from a human author and could be encoded in a template through human-driven document planning and that there is data that supports the argument, there are no real barriers to producing automated content that reflects that argument. Automated argumentation is an area that is ready to colonize, though perhaps less so by traditional journalists than by other strategic communicators.

A strong human collaborator enables automation to also participate in the composition of criticism. Criticism relies on the exercise of personal judgment and taste in appraising some newsworthy object or event. This is precisely what sophisticated sports commentators do when they critique the performance of a team or athlete. One example in this direction is a project from *Der Spiegel* that automatically produces tactical data visualizations, or maps of how a particular soccer team has performed.[117] But the maps are practically unpublishable on their own. A squad of sports reporters interpret the maps and add their own knowledge and critique of the game as they view the automatically produced visualization through their own critical lens. The automated visualization becomes a helpful tool for grounding a particular form of criticism.

Topical Opportunities

There is certainly room for automation to explore opportunities in exposition, argumentation, and criticism, as well as to deepen and expand descriptive and narrative capabilities. But there are also opportunities to apply existing techniques to new topics. We've already seen automation gaining traction in areas such as sports, finance, weather, and elections where data are available. Where else might there be demand for automated content if only data were available? And where is there enough of a potential for scale in terms of either raw scale of interest in publication of an event by different publishers or for scale over time because an event is routine or repetitive?

To examine these questions I gathered data from Event Registry, a content aggregator that as of mid-2017 had slurped up more than 180 million news articles from more than 30,000 news publishers worldwide. You might have guessed that Event Registry is about *events*. The database clusters news articles that are about the same event, not unlike how Google News groups articles. Event Registry then enriches these events by automatically tagging them with categories—high-level groupings such as "Health" or "Science" but also much more fine-grained ones such as "Climate Change." I collected all of the events from the Event Registry database for June 2017—more than 20,000—that referred to events in the United States and had at least some content in English. From these I tabulated the dominant categories of content based on number of events to see which categories show promise for scale over time. I also looked at the average number of articles per event to see which categories might benefit from scaling coverage over a range of different audiences.

Table 3.1 lists the top categories of content according to the number of events observed. Categories such as "Law Enforcement," "Crime and Justice," "Murder," "Sex Offenses," and "Fire and Security" all clocked hundreds to thousands of events over the course of a month, with the average number of articles per event being in the range of fifteen to twenty. The dominance of these categories is perhaps unsurprising given the old journalism adage, "If it bleeds, it leads." It is also no surprise that categories relating to sports hit a sweet spot across the board—a great variety of sports-related topics received both routine and fairly widespread coverage. These include American favorites such as "Baseball," "Professional Basketball," and "Ice Hockey" as well as new classics such as "Competition Shooting" and "Auto Racing." "Martial Arts" was another standout: there were about forty-six articles on average for each of the events, suggesting an opportunity for breadth. One surprise in the data was the apparent extent of media produced about video game events, which includes e-sports, video game tournaments, and fantasy sports. However, upon closer inspection, it appears Event Registry miscategorized some regular sporting events as "Video Game" events making it difficult to say how prevalent coverage of video game events really was.

Besides crime, sports, and potentially games there are several other categories of content that could take advantage of the potential for scale. Service-oriented topics related to transportation such as "Aviation" are promising, with 118 events and about 21 articles per event, as is "Health" with 178 events and 16 articles per event. Policy-oriented topics also have a potential for scale: "Immigration" had 109 events with an average of 19 articles per

Table 3.1.   Categories of news in Event Registry with more than 100 distinct events in June 2017.*

Category	Event Count	Mean Article Count	Median Article Count
Society/Law/Law Enforcement	1,440	17	8
Reference/Education/Colleges & Universities	767	15	8
Business/Business_Services/Fire & Security	657	14	8
Games/Video_Games/Recreation	564	21	10
Games/Video_Games/Browser_Based	495	30	11
Society/Religion & Spirituality/Christianity	447	15	8
Society/Issues/Crime & Justice	389	18	8
Sports/Football/American	381	15	10
Society/Law/Services	355	26	9
Society/Law/Legal Information	235	30	9
Business/Industrial Goods & Services/Industrial Supply	221	13	7
Sports/Basketball/Professional	194	31	11
Recreation/Guns/Competition Shooting	190	31	8
Health/Public Health & Safety/Emergency Services	188	12	8
Society/Issues/Health	178	16	8
Shopping/Sports/Baseball	178	25	9
Home/Family/Parenting	176	14	10
Sports/Hockey/Ice Hockey	174	16	10
Arts/Performing Arts/Theater	160	24	8

(continued)

Table 3.1.   (continued)

Category	Event Count	Mean Article Count	Median Article Count
Science/Biology/Flora & Fauna	155	18	8
Sports/Baseball/Youth	154	15	8
Society/Issues/Business	152	41	10
Society/Crime/Murder	148	17	8
Games/Video_Games/Downloads	140	25	10
Society/Issues/Transportation	139	15	7
Computers/Software/Accounting	129	20	9
Society/Crime/Sex Offenses	128	46	7
Society/People/Generations & Age Groups	120	14	7.5
Society/Issues/Warfare & Conflict	120	20	10
Business/Transportation & Logistics/Aviation	118	21	8
Computers/Internet/On the Web	117	25	11
Science/Technology/Energy	114	13	8
Sports/Motorsports/Auto Racing	114	19	8
Reference/Education/K through 12	113	10	8
Society/Politics/Campaigns & Elections	110	21	8
Society/Issues/Immigration	109	19	10
Arts/Television/Programs	108	16	8
Business/Energy/Utilities	108	18	8
Society/Issues/Environment	103	19	9
Recreation/Pets/Dogs	103	21	9

* Each category is shown with the mean and median number of English articles published for each event.

event, "Environment" had 103 events also with 19 articles on average, "Economic" issues had 79 events with an average of 24 articles, and "Campaigns & Elections" had 110 events with 21 articles on average. There is a range of openly available data related to economic issues, as well as for immigration and the environment, suggesting that these topics could perhaps be covered using automated content techniques. In general, however, cataloging the available data resources for each of these topics would be necessary to identify where the best opportunities lie.

Of course, there are limitations to Event Registry data in terms of coverage and the extent of representation of media. Also, the numbers noted above deal only with the supply side of content, and the strategic deployment of automated content should also consider reader demand. But these data do provide hints about what categories or topics might be promising for automation. It's not an entirely unreasonable assumption that the coverage of these topics is in response to demand that's been expressed in some way by media consumers. The numbers suggest that there may still be opportunities for finding underexplored niches where data availability, technical capability, editorial interest, and some form of need for scale—either over time or for breadth— all intersect.

Automated content production offers a host of new opportunities to increase the speed, scale, accuracy, and personalization of news information, some of which are already creating revenue and competitive advantages for news organizations. At the same time, human roles and tasks are evolving to accommodate the design, maintenance, and supervision of automated content systems. Far from a panacea for news production, there are a host of limitations that go along with content automation. A dependency on data, as well as bounds on flexibility, interpretive ability, and writing quality place real constraints on how widely automated news production can spread. Still, some domains of content may yet be colonized by automated news content, as journalists find where end-user demand intersects with technical capabilities and constraints. Another milieu where these intersections are increasingly being explored is social media, where automated content takes on a social face in the form of newsbots.

4

NEWSDOTS: AGENTS OF INFORMATION

In just one month in 2017 an unpretentious little bot going by the handle "AnecbotalNYT" methodically pumped out 1,191 tweets addressed at news consumers on Twitter. It's perhaps surprising to see people genuinely engage the bot—a software agent that presents itself as nothing more—replying to or agreeing with it, elaborating on the views it curates, responding emotionally, rebutting or explicitly disagreeing with it, even linking to contradictory videos or articles. Eighty-eight percent of the replies were from the user the bot had initiated contact with, but 12 percent were actually replies from other Twitter users. By catalyzing engagement both with the targeted user and with others who could then chime in, the bot opened the door for human users to interact more with each other.

I designed AnecbotalNYT as an experiment to help raise awareness for interesting personal experiences or anecdotes written as comments to *New York Times* articles. It works by first listening for tweets that have a link to a *New York Times* article. Then it harvests all the article's comments, scoring each text based on metrics such as length, readability, and whether it describes a personal experience.[1] The comments are ranked by an overall weighted score, and the bot selects a comment likely to contain a personal story or anecdote. The selected comment is then tweeted back at the person who had originally shared the article link.[2] If the person was interested enough to share the link on Twitter, maybe they'd also be interested in someone's personal experience reflecting on the story.

The goal of AnecbotalNYT was to bridge the *New York Times* commenting community back into the network of people sharing links to *New York Times* articles on Twitter. People who might not otherwise pay attention to *New York Times* comments thus became a new potential audience to engage. And engage it did. One tweet the bot sent received 124 retweets, 291 likes, and 5,374 people clicking on the comment to read it in full (see Figure 4.1).[3] That article was about Cassandra Butts, an Obama-era appointee who died waiting for confirmation from a Republican Senate.

Replying to @Maribo17

HT @Maribo17 for sharing this NYT article: nytimes.com/2016/06/07/opi ... Here's an anecdote from the comments:

> "The Republican Senate is the single most unpatriotic and dysfunctional body politic I have seen in my lifetime. Cruz, Cotton, McConnell disgrace our country day in, day out. The oath a Senator takes does not include 'inflicting special pain on the president'. It does not include stymieing foreign relations or our justice system. It does not include thwarting good people from serving our country. The trajectory that Republican legislators are taking our country will run it into the ground. "
>
> — Suzanne Moniz, Providence

9:07 PM - 22 Jan 2017

124 Retweets 291 Likes

💬 3   ↻ 124   ♡ 291

Figure 4.1. An example tweet showing the AnecbotalNYT bot responding to a user sharing an article.

AnecbotalNYT's curated comment for the story struck a chord
with liberals, capturing a common sentiment and sharply critical
attitude toward a US Senate viewed as playing political games at
the expense of individuals like Cassandra. That's just one example
of the kind of engagement the bot can generate. Over the course
of April 2017 Twitter users engaged with 57 percent of the 1,191
tweets the bot sent, including some combination of retweets, likes,
and replies. That month the bot drove engagement activity of 150
retweets, 52 replies, 247 likes, and 210 link clicks. Every extra
person clicking a link generates additional traffic back to the *New
York Times* site, possibly adding to advertising revenue. And this
is just a fraction of the engagement the bot *could* generate if it
weren't hamstrung by Twitter's Application Programming Interface (API) limitations.

Bots often appear as productive social agents that populate
chat apps and social network platforms such as Twitter, Facebook, and Reddit. They can contribute to news and information
dissemination during news events, catalyze new interactions, as
is the case with AnecbotalNYT, and even scaffold the network
by stimulating human interactions that might not otherwise
occur. They are seeds that when strategically planted can estab-
lish community bridges or increase exposure to more diverse
perspectives.[4] This is not to discount the potential dark side of
bots though. Bad actors can just as easily aim automated social
agents at creating spam, disingenuous political nudges, false followers and audiences, or influence campaigns.[5] Either way, bots
are proliferating. A Pew study indicated that two-thirds of links
tweeted about popular news and current events are from sus-
pected bots.[6] Another research study put the count of bots on
Twitter at anywhere between 9 and 15 percent of accounts—
that's as many as 48 million potential bots.[7] The presence of bots
on popular social media networks makes them a substantive
part of the public face of news and information automation.

Bots have been defined in a host of different ways, including
as "automated social actors," "software agents that interact on

social networking services," "automatic or semi-automatic computer programs that mimic humans and/or human behavior," and
"software processes that are programmed to appear to be human-
generated within the context of social networking sites."[8] The
term "bot" can refer to a range of activity that spans different
degrees of sociality and of sociality in different contexts.[9] For example, a specific form of bot, the chatbot, refers to a computer
algorithm that engages humans in dialog using natural language
and provides for a more conversational experience than would
otherwise occur.[10] Chatbots tend toward higher levels of social
interaction. On the other hand, some bots may be no more social
than posing as a visitor to a website in order to, say, interact with
content or scrape information from the site.[11]

The emphasis in this chapter is on bots that are at the higher
end of the sociality spectrum and are public facing, in contrast to
those that lack any visible social presence or are used internally
to a news organization. For the purposes of this chapter, the most
apt synthesis of definitions for a social bot is "a computer algorithm that automatically produces content and interacts with
humans on social media."[12] Newsbots are social bots that have a
particular focus on news and information content. They are the
social face of news automation, tightly integrating analytic automation with content automation in an interaction loop with users.
This social presence offers both an interface to automation and
a new medium of expression all its own.

As user interfaces, newsbots enable people to access information, ask questions, or delegate tasks via natural language
conversation. Such bots can provide weather, traffic, or other information services via a conversational interaction. As an interaction paradigm, conversation offers potential benefits for browsing
information, for navigating directly rather than steering through
cumbersome menus, or for referring to things that aren't visible
in the interface.[13] In order to keep ongoing interactions fluid in
conversational user interfaces, bots must exhibit a high degree of
autonomy both in their analytic capabilities (such as inferring, ac-

cessing, or analyzing knowledge) and their content production capabilities (such as creating appropriate and meaningful prompts or responses). Bots operate along a spectrum of interactivity, ranging from bots that feed off of public prompts such as a *New York Times* link, as is the case with AnecdotalNYT, to those rooted in understanding and responding to textual (or voice) input. Some bots may themselves take the initiative to start a conversation, prompting users with an information solicitation.

Bots that tend toward the conversational must be able to understand the goals and intents of their interlocutors based on the often imprecise, varied, and ambiguous utterances of human beings. Because of this ambiguity, bots must also be designed to fail gracefully, to recover from misunderstandings, and to get a conversation back on track. They may need mechanisms for developing common ground with users, for instance by ensuring both the user and the bot are referring to the same concept. Bots may need to communicate feedback about whether and how they understood a user.[14] To make conversation less mechanical, more cohesive, and extend over multiple turns, they also need a memory to recall what was said previously. Grounding, memory, turn-taking, graceful failure, and conversation repair behaviors are still active areas of research, making natural language understanding (NLU) an important area of technical development for advancing conversational user interfaces.[15]

The limitations of autonomy are again often overcome through a human-computer hybrid system, wherein humans are responsible for complex communication, expert thinking, and nuanced contextual judgments. But in the case of bots, the perceptive, analytic, and output phases of production must be completely autonomous, otherwise the interface would not meet basic requirements for responsiveness. In practice this means that the human influence over bots gets compressed into and expressed via the design of the bot, as well as in its ongoing maintenance. Authoring and designing narrowly scoped bots allows for humans to prebake analytic interpretations, judgments, knowledge bases, task-models, and responses so the bot can act autonomously when interacting with end users in the moment. Designers must try to anticipate how a bot will be used so that it is able to recognize and robustly respond to an appropriate array of user intents, while coping with situations in which users push it past its boundaries of operation and understanding. Of course, it's impossible to anticipate everything. News organizations deploying bots, such as the *Washington Post,* have underscored the importance of user testing to understand the varied ways different people might try to ask the same thing.[16] Research efforts have begun to examine a wider range of automated questioning and answering by bots by injecting typos or substituting synonyms into simulated user questions to see how well the bot copes.[17]

Bots shouldn't be thought of only as task-oriented interfaces though. In fact, for many tasks a graphical user interface may be more efficient or otherwise preferable for a variety of reasons, including lower human memory demands, ease of pointing and clicking, and immediate and persistent visual feedback.[18] Alternatively, bots that are not task oriented can be seen as a form of content that offers an altogether new model for interactive media experiences. They can entertain, help pass the time, react and respond to questions, offer conversation-sized chunks of content and information, and provide an ostensibly social interplay that moves beyond the typical task orientation of human-computer interfaces. For instance, the *Guardian*'s Sous-Chef Facebook bot inspires users with recipes, while *British Vogue*'s Fashion Week bot delivers personalized information about a user's favorite clothing brands.[19] While some publishers may see bots as a convenient mechanism for distributing and statically dumping their content on social media, and others will want to build out task-oriented bots as interfaces to data, the opportunities to explore this nascent new medium in terms of engagement, interactivity, and communication are much broader.[20]

How will social bots come to interact with people and with society in the context of news? Newsbots have already proven useful in a number of journalistic scenarios, from identifying and sharing newsworthy events to spreading information during crises and providing new mechanisms for social critique or accountability. At the same time there is immense potential for the misuse of social bots by bad actors for the purposes of shaping user perceptions, polluting content, gaming social metrics, infiltrating social networks, astroturfing disingenuous comments, misdirecting attention, and so on. This chapter sets out to explore the possibility space for the use of newsbots and considers a range of journalistic functions, design challenges, and liabilities that they pose.

Journalistic Uses for Bots

In December 2014, communication studies scholar Tanya Lokot and I analyzed a sample of 238 newsbots from Twitter, qualitatively examining the behavior and "self"-presentation of the bots we found.[21] We observed newsbots enabling a range of information tasks from curating and aggregating sources to analyzing and processing data and bridging different platforms in order to raise awareness and amplify dissemination to diverse audiences (one of the inspirations for AnecbotalNYT). In the next sections, I extend and expand on the journalistic potential of bots that we identified in that initial work. Bots are in a nascent stage of mainstream adoption by the media, which are developing experimental prototypes to prod whether audiences have any real appetite for them. The level of artificial intelligence in the natural language understanding that typical bots deploy is often still quite low—any illusion of intelligence is due to careful design work. As detailed next, early endeavors have explored not only how bots can help to disseminate information in a casual and even entertaining way, but also how they can gather information and monitor the world, contribute to accountability, and offer a new avenue for social commentary and critique.

Bots with Informational Benefits

Content Dissemination

Perhaps the most straightforward implementation of bots within the domain of journalism is as a channel for disseminating informational content. Users can perceive social bots as credible sources of information, making them potentially useful vectors for trusted content from news organizations.[22] About three-quarters of the bots analyzed in our initial Twitter study were information disseminators. Likewise on Facebook, some of the first bots to emerge in early 2016 were essentially syndicated feeds, spreading links back to online content.[23] At the BBC, for example, where their News Lab is exploring a range of bot applications, repurposing content was the initial motivation for use of bots. The BBC already produces heaps of content, and bots are a convenient new mechanism for spreading that content through social media.[24] This approach has the added benefit of not upending existing content production workflows.

Bots can complement traditional data journalism to help extend the reach of those stories into social media in new ways. For instance, the *Quartz* article "The Injuries Most Likely to Land You in an Emergency Room in America,"[25] pairs a series of data visualizations online with a bot (@usinjuries) that Tweets out examples from the database of emergency room visits used for the story. Some examples include: "16-YR-OLD MALE HURT KNEE PLAYING BASKETBALL DX CONTUSION" and "29-YR-OLD F GETTING A SWEET POTATO OUT OF THE OVEN AND SUSTAINED A THERMAL BURN TO LOWER ARM." The bot has more than 8,000 followers. Also in the genre of bots that connect databases to social media is the @censusAmericans bot from FiveThirtyEight. This bot puts a face on US census data, otherwise often only presented in abstract aggregates, by using slices of the data to build mini biographies about individuals, such as "I work less than 40 hrs a week. I went to college for less than a year. I'm on active duty for training in the Reserves/National

Guard."[26] Bots such as @usinjuries and @censusAmericans show a promising direction for news automation because they corral facts locked up in databases into a stream of engaging and informative nuggets of content.

Beyond the dispersal of content and information, the medium is evolving quickly. The conversational affordances of bots also offer new possibilities for interactively informing users about the news. Take for example Politibot, a bot originally launched on the Telegram chat app to help inform voters about the Spanish elections in 2016.[27] While the bot delivered digests of politics-related content several times per day, including original charts, as well as links back to curated articles, it could also solicit basic demographic information from users, which was then used to help users understand where they fit with respect to peers. The affordances of chat interfaces as "one-on-one" experiences offer possibilities to personalize and individually adapt the information delivered to each of the bot's interlocutors.

Politics appears to be one domain where news organizations are actively deploying chatbots. In early 2017, for example, the *Texas Tribune* launched a Facebook Messenger bot named "Paige," designed to make it easier for users to follow Texas politics.[28] In addition to providing Monday and Friday briefings, the bot also serves as a sort of quiz game, allowing users to exercise their knowledge of Texas government. At the *Fort Collins Coloradoan*, the Elexi bot was produced for the 2016 elections as a way to provide information about local candidates and races in a more conversational way.[29] Users could ask questions such as "Who is running for Senate in Colorado?" and the bot might respond with a story written and curated for the purposes of comparing and contrasting the two candidates. Users could ask questions about where to vote or if they were registered and receive links to pages that would help answer those questions. Where data or curated content is available, bots can become services, answering questions and surfacing buried information to meet the explicitly articulated information needs of users.

Presenting information via chat interfaces also offers new possibilities for framing that information using the persona of the bot, which can enliven and provide levity to the interaction and make complex material more accessible. It's here where we truly see the medium start to differentiate itself as something more than a straightforward disseminator of information. One of the more offbeat examples of this approach is a project from the German broadcasting corporation Westdeutscher Rundfunk called "Superkühe" (German for "super cows").[30] The project followed three cows (Uschi, Emma, and Connie) from three different farms over the course of thirty days in 2017, exposing and contrasting differences in the agricultural production of milk on an organic farm, a family farm, and a factory farm. Daily reports included images, videos, and written content produced by reporters who were following each cow as it gave birth to a new calf and entered into milk production. Sensors placed around (and inside) the cows tracked milk production, health, eating behavior, and activity level.

All of the structured data and content about the cows then fed into a chatbot on Facebook Messenger, which allowed users to interact and chat with a simulation of any of the three cows. By personifying the experiences of each cow and using the chat interface to frame a more intimate encounter, the bot creates an opportunity to empathize with the animal's experience and learn about animal conditions and treatment relating to different agricultural approaches in a casual and even entertaining format. Instead of reporting *about* an entity such as a cow, the use of bots creates an opportunity to interact directly *with* a simulation of that cow, leading to a shift in perspective from third- to second-person. Consider the possibilities for news storytelling: instead of reading a quote from a source a reporter had interviewed, readers themselves could chat with that source via a bot that simulated responses based on the information the reporter had collected.[31] One advantage might be to draw users in closer to the story and the "characters" of the news.

Information Gathering

Besides their role as information conveyors, bots can also contribute to information gathering with varying amounts of success. For instance, ProPublica launched a bot in late 2017 with the goal of collecting examples of hate speech on Facebook.[32] Ordinarily journalists might try to crowdsource this information using a survey or form, and ProPublica certainly did this, but to make information collection even easier, it also presented the survey in the guise of a bot that users can chat with on Facebook Messenger. The bot asks informational questions about a user's experience with hate speech on the platform, soliciting screenshots or wordings of posts that were deleted and then parsing responses into structured data for further analysis by reporters. The news organization received more than one hundred responses via the bot on its first day of operation.[33] These tips fed a larger corpus of examples that enabled additional reporting on errors in the enforcement of hate speech rules on the site.[34]

Another bot that was successful in soliciting responses from users was the Feels Facebook bot operated during the 2016 elections by the *Washington Post*.[35] The bot would ask users on a daily basis questions such as "How is the election making you feel today?" and they could respond along a scale of emojis and write a sentence or two of context to explain how they felt. The next morning the bot would send a report (curated by reporters) that showed aggregate reactions and highlighted quotes from users. About a third of users participated every single day in the simple poll and response. These types of information-gathering scenarios are helped by the affordances of the chat apps that are hosting these bots. In particular, they offer private channels for one-on-one solicitation, which allow sources to share information discreetly without publishing openly to everyone. Still, questions remain about what types of information people feel comfortable reporting to a bot, how trust may form, and whether there may be privacy sensitivities, particularly in regimes where social platforms are monitored by the government.[36]

Not all information-gathering bots are successful. Buzzfeed's Buzz Bot was an attempt to engage with and gather information from attendees of the Republican Party and the Democratic Party conventions in the summer of 2016.[37] After users signed up with the bot on Facebook and disclosed if they were physically present at the conventions, the bot could target questions to them about events unfolding at the conventions. Users contributed media in response to the bot's solicitations, but they were often too slow to compete with the swarm of professional reporters at the events. As Amanda Hickman from BuzzFeed explained, "We did develop some sources through the bot but ultimately BuzzFeed reporters were much better and faster at getting information on the ground in almost every instance. . . . By the time anybody who was a bot user got back to us, and sometimes they did, the reporters had already figured out what was going on and documented it and published it." The bot did have another type of value though: looking at what users asked the bot provided a signal back to the newsroom about how reporters might cover the event in such a way as to answer common questions. While bots may have some potential for helping to gather information about critical incidents and emotional reactions, their utility for breaking news scenarios or in situations where they are in direct competition with reporters at preplanned events may be more limited. Bots still need to find the niche of stories where they are most productively employed for information gathering.

Monitoring

In some cases bots not only gather information but also process that information to operate as public-facing monitoring and alerting tools. Given the importance of Twitter to the Trump presidency, Twitter bots are routinely oriented toward monitoring Trump-related activity on the platform. For instance, the @TrumpsAlert bot tracks and tweets about the following and unfollowing actions of Trump and his family and inner circle in order to bring additional attention to relationships at the White House. The @BOTUS bot produced by National Public Radio (NPR) had the goal of automatically making stock trades based on monitoring the sentiment of Trump's tweets when he mentioned publicly traded companies. Another Twitter bot, @big_cases, from *USA Today* monitors major cases in US district courts, including those relating to Trump executive orders. *Quartz* built a bot called @actual_ransom that monitored the Bitcoin wallets of hackers who had blackmailed people into sending a ransom in order to unlock their computers.[38] The bot, which broke news on Twitter, was the first to report that the hackers had started withdrawing money from the bitcoin wallets. Although none of these monitoring bots is interactive, all do demonstrate the potential of bots to complete the autonomous gathering, analysis, and dissemination circuit in narrowly defined domains.

Bots can also be connected up to streams of data produced by sensors to provide additional monitoring capabilities over time, including of environmental conditions such as air quality.[39] A notable example of a monitoring bot is @GVA_Watcher, which posts to various social media channels when air traffic sensors run by amateur plane-spotters around Geneva's airport in Switzerland recognize a signal from a plane registered to an authoritarian regime. The bot is intended to draw attention to the travel patterns of authoritarian leaders who may be entering Switzerland for nondiplomatic reasons, such as money laundering.[40] The goal of this type of monitoring starts to veer in the direction of accountability, which I discuss in more detail next.

Accountability Machines

Accountability journalism seeks to bring to light behavior by individuals or institutions that violates norms or laws. This might, for instance, include investigating a public official about an abuse of power or a corporation deceiving the public about environmental impacts. The news media functions as an accountability organ by creating awareness and inducing public pressure that then demands a response from the actor to explain and be held responsible for that behavior. The impacts of accountability investigations range from an individual being fired or indicted to an audit or review of policies and even to a new law being enacted. Awareness of the actor's behavior by the public may spur debate and induce a shift in behavior to avoid ongoing negative public exposure. The ability of bots to monitor aspects of public life and behavior invites examination of how they may contribute to the accountability function of journalism. Can bots help hold public actors accountable for their behavior by drawing more attention to those behaviors on social media platforms?

The attention bots bring to an issue can, at the very least, serve as a constructive starting point for discussion. Take the @NYTAnon bot on Twitter, for example. John Emerson designed the bot for the express purpose of accountability. "It was to kind of put pressure on the *Times* to be a little stricter about when its sources are or are not anonymous," he told me. The practice of using anonymous sources by news media is a fraught one, because while it may be justified in some cases in order to protect sources, it also undermines the reader's ability to evaluate the trustworthiness of the information source on their own. The key is to not overuse anonymous sources or be lax in offering anonymity just because a source is feeling timid. The bot actively monitors all articles published by the *New York Times* for the use of language relating to the reliance on unnamed or anonymous sources. If an article uses any of 170 different phrases such as "sources say," "military officials said," or "requested anonymity," the bot will excerpt that piece of the article and tweet it out as an image to draw attention to the context in which the *New York Times* is using an anonymous source. The initial reaction to the bot included some independent blog posts as well as a post by then—*New York Times* public editor Margaret Sullivan suggesting that at the very least she and perhaps others in the newsroom were aware the bot was monitoring their use of anonymous sources.[41] Still, despite the NYT's awareness of the bot's exposure of its practices, Emerson lamented that he still didn't know "if it's changed policy or made reporters think twice about anything."

To try to answer this question I collected some data on the pro portion of *New York Times* news articles that had used any of the 170 terms the bot was tracking over time, both before and after the bot was launched.[42] Did reporters use fewer phrases with respect to anonymous sourcing after the bot started monitoring? The results indicated that there was slight shift downward in the use of anonymous sources, perhaps as much as 15 percent, in the three months after the bot launched, but that the use of anonymous sources then increased again. There was no clear or definitive signal. I talked to Phil Corbett, the associate managing editor for standards at the *New York Times* about the pattern. According to Corbett they didn't "detect any major shift" in their use of anonymous sources during that period, but he wasn't able to firmly refute the possibility of a change either. "I will say that I don't think much attention was paid to the Anon bot, so that seems to me unlikely to have had much effect. On the other hand, Margaret and some of the other public editors did periodically focus attention on this issue, so that could have had some impact," Corbett added. The more likely route to accountability here was perhaps not the bot directly, but rather the public editor drawing attention to the issue, which in at least one instance was spurred by the bot when she blogged about it. Bots may not be able to provide enough publicity or public pressure all by themselves. But to be more effective they could be designed to attract attention and cause other media to amplify the issue the bot exposes.

Let's consider another study of the deployment of a bot for accountability purposes, the @GCCAEdits Twitter bot launched in Canada in 2014.[43] This bot was a specific instance of a class of bots that monitors anonymous edits of Wikipedia pages from internet protocol (IP) address ranges that are associated with particular institutions. So, for instance, the @GCCAEdits version of the bot traced edits to Wikipedia pages about the Parliament of

Canada, the Senate of Canada, and various governmental agencies to IP addresses indicating the editor was using a computer address assigned to one of those entities. In principle, such a bot presents a way to track if there are conflicts of interest in attempts to anonymously edit pages in ways that may hide or alter the framing of official information.

The initial coverage of the bot by other media reinforced a narrative about government waste or manipulation in relation to anonymous Wikipedia editing behavior: Why should officials be editing Wikipedia to begin with, and could anonymous government officials be shaping Wikipedia content in politically expedient ways? This framing was in spite of the fact that only 10 percent of edits were substantive in altering more than a sentence on a page. Most editing activity, even when done anonymously, was quite innocuous. After the initial media storm over the existence of the bot, the volume of tweeting from the bot decreased. In other words, after the media raised awareness in the government that the bot was monitoring its editing activity, the pace of its edits diminished. The researchers interviewed a government minister who confirmed he had warned staffers to beware of the bot's surveillance. In response, people may have shifted their behavior to evade detection by the bot, such as by logging in so they weren't editing anonymously. Or, they may have simply reduced their editing of Wikipedia altogether.

This case makes clear that bots can affect human behavior, but it also raises interesting challenges for the deployment of such bots for accountability purposes. While there may have been cases of inappropriate anonymous editing of Wikipedia by government officials, a failure of the bot was that the behavior captured and monitored was overly broad and included what was mostly banal editing. Ideally a bot must precisely operationalize the negative behavior it seeks to publicize. But designing a bot to detect an edit that shows an actual conflict of interest may be quite difficult, or perhaps even entirely infeasible. As is, when a bot is not specific enough about the behavior it calls out, it might end up dampening other innocuous, or even productive behaviors. More-over, due to the inflexibility of bots in the behaviors they mon-itor, it is potentially quite easy for people to alter their trail to avoid detection. Journalists will need to stay involved, reorienting bot attention over time in order to track actors attempting to evade attention. Accountability bots will need to be designed to work together closely with people in order to achieve lasting ac-countability goals.

The Opinionator

Artificial intelligence is far from having its own opinions. But bots do enable new ways for people to indirectly opine by allowing designers to embed their opinion, critique, and commentary into the interactions and messages the bot enacts. Through careful and deliberate design, bots can be used to convey particular points of view. Although such use is still being explored, the expressivity of bots as opinion performers appears to hinge on a few affor-dances of the medium. For instance, bots can function continu-ally and exhaustively, which means that a bot can hammer on a topic by accumulating a particular perspective over time. This enables critiques that are in some sense comprehensive and unre-lenting. Bots also thrive in the expression of absurdism and com-ical juxtaposition.[44] Like The Three Stooges they present as bumbling dummies that don't understand the accidental irony or import of what they say and do. Their lack of self-awareness be-comes an expressive tool for the human opinion-maker seeking to point out a parallel to human stupidity or lack of awareness.

The FISA bot (@FISAbot) is an example of a commentary bot on Twitter that hinges on both the cumulative and absurdist af-fordances of bots as medium. In the United States the Foreign Intelligence Surveillance Court (FISC, but also called the FISA Court as it was authorized under the Foreign Intelligence Surveil-lance Act) oversees requests for surveillance warrants. In 2013 it was reported that in its thirty-three-year history the court had denied only twelve of the more than 35,000 requests it had received, essentially acting as a rubber stamp on requests from the intelligence community.[45] In 2016 the FISA bot was launched to satirize the ease with which surveillance requests were approved by the court. Twitter users could tweet at the bot to request warrants and the bot would automatically tweet back saying, "I authorize this request" according to the statistical distribution of the rate of approvals of the actual court—so, basically always. As John Emerson, the creator, explained to me, "It's obviously a commentary on the kind of rubber stamp rate aspect of it." The mechanical responses of the bot were a mirror for how the court was acting, allowing it to effectively drive home the critical point the bot's designer was trying to make. Some people really enjoyed the joke and treated it as a form of entertainment, asking the bot things like whether they could have a search warrant for the White House, with the bot of course responding, "I authorize this request." Other people thought the bot got annoying, and it was "retired" after about 5,000 tweets.

Another example of an absurdist commentary bot on Twitter is the Pundibot.[46] The point was to show that a bot could make predictive statements about the 2016 election that were just as vacuous as those being made by pundits on cable news. PundiBot can "imitate cable-news pundits or sports commentators filling airtime with useless predictions," explained the creator, Jeremy Merrill, in his write-up of the project. The bot operates by randomly selecting a dataset containing time series information, which it then uses to generate and share a true but meaningless correlation such as "Whenever personal consumption expenditures declined year over year, after 1930, the Democrats have never lost the House." It can add little twists about odd and even years and with exceptions that make the bot's tweets seem even more absurd (though not inaccurate!). One tweet read, "Since 1990, the G.O.P. has not lost the House in any year when Super Bowl attendance's digits add up to an odd number, except 1992." Clearly a silly thing to say, but maybe not all that far off from the flavor of predictions TV commentators sometimes offer about political events.

Quartz fittingly used a Twitter bot to comment on the often contradictory nature of President Trump's tweets in terms of past policy positions he's expressed.[47] The @TrumpOfYore bot juxtaposes recent tweets by Trump against tweets that he's made in the past on similar topics or issues. The end goal is to surface comical juxtapositions or ironic contrasts that show how Trump is contradicting himself by flip-flopping on issues. Sometimes it works, sometimes it doesn't. That's because the bot doesn't really understand the text of the tweets it's juxtaposing. It's using a text similarity algorithm to try to find related tweets, but doesn't grasp the meaning of the words. And so while the bot can occasionally get lucky and tweet a zinger, it can also come across as entirely nonsensical.

Bots that express opinion on politics or other sensitive issues can expose a fraught relationship with the social platforms that bound their existence. Whether it's Twitter, Facebook, Amazon, or some other private system, such platforms may choose to impose and enforce their own rules and terms on bots that use the service. Twitter goes so far as to spell out what the rules of the road are for bots in an "Automation Rules" help page.[48] While the rules encourage creators to "try new things that help people," Twitter also makes explicit that bots definitely shouldn't try to circumvent rate limits or "spam or bother users, or otherwise send them unsolicited messages." The problem is that a bother to one person might be helpful to another, and so there's an immediate element of subjectivity in weighing and judging a bot's impacts on diverse stakeholders. "The way that they identify spam often ends up flagging bots so you can't push out the same message to a bunch of different people. . . . They'll flag you as spam," explained Emily Withrow, an editor at the Quartz Bot Studio. Platforms routinely scrub out accounts they've identified as spam, but if applied too broadly, such activities could easily sweep out legitimate political speech being exercised by bots on behalf of their creators.

In some cases the rules of the platform may hinder free speech and come into tension with journalistic norms, such as a focus on the public interest. For instance, topics such as sex education may warrant public attention but could trigger algorithmic censors that create friction in publishing on those topics.[49] Moreover, individuals who disagree with the output or intent of a bot could flag it as "offensive" or "spam" and trigger the platform to block the bot. Emerson, who created the FISA bot, retired it at the request of Twitter. "Some people got the jokes and [other] people really didn't or were kind of pissed off about it. Eventually, Twitter asked me to stop because . . . it was kind of against the terms of service. And so I stopped it," he remarked. In the case of Politwoops, which tracks when politicians delete a Tweet, the bot was shut down when Twitter decided it violated the company's API Terms of Service agreement.[50] About six months later Twitter changed its mind and reinstated the bot's access to the API, allowing it to begin publishing again.[51] Fickle platforms create an additional layer of uncertainty about the viability of bots for certain types of journalistic acts. The core issue is really about the degree of freedom of speech afforded to bots on the platforms where they exist. Who will decide what rights newsbots have in comparison to human journalists, though either may be exercising important critique of those in power?

Designing Newsbots

Bots can function in a variety of ways: they can disseminate, gatherer, and monitor information, and they can contribute to accountability or function as mechanisms for expressing critique and commentary in new ways. It's important to underscore that these bots are not acting in any sort of artificially intelligent way, but are rather extensions of the intents and purposes of their human designers. They are able to act autonomously in interactions with end users because designers have taken the care to define and engineer the bounds of operation for them. Designers make many consequential decisions about bot behavior, including how that behavior is framed by the persona or personality that the bot projects, as well as the ways in which the bot conveys itself through authored dialogue patterns. Taken carefully, such decisions may reflect the ideology and value propositions of journalism.

Anthropomorphism in user interfaces has been a topic of debate for some time.[52] How closely should bots try to mimic human behavior and personality? Should a bot make a run at acting friendly, aloof, hostile, skeptical, arrogant, considerate, gregarious, or any of a number of other character traits? Early research on embodied conversational agents articulated the challenges of designing agents that reflect natural human conversational interaction and intonation, as well as corporeal components such as posture and gesture.[53] Agents with a persona can get in the way, as evidenced by the failure of early attempts such as Microsoft Word's Clippy assistant to gain traction with users. For task-oriented scenarios a bot with personality may needlessly slow down an interaction, thus hindering efficiency. But this view alone is too narrow for newsbots, which are also a form of media that users can engage with in non-task-oriented terms. The presence of a persona can itself be a cue to treat the bot in a less task-oriented way.

Conveying personality in a bot is a double-edged sword. While an approachable personality makes it easier to initiate engagement with users, it also creates a mental model of the bot that can mislead users and create unrealistic expectations. In a 2016 study of fourteen users of general purpose conversational assistants, such as Siri, researchers found that user expectations were "dramatically out of step with the operation of the systems, particularly in terms of known machine intelligence, system capability and goals."[54] Although the playful and humorous responses of the bots were useful for drawing in and engaging users, these interactions reinforced anthropomorphic qualities and exacerbated the mismatch between the perception of intelligence and the agents' actual level of intelligence. The more designers tune a bot to exhibit social interactional intelligence, including behaviors such as initiation, interruption, feedback, turn-taking, and conversational repair, the more users may then infer a greater degree of intelligence than is warranted. The design of bots with personality is difficult; a dose of character must be paired with straightforward feedback that articulates the boundaries of capabilities, or an avenue to get to a real person if there's a complete breakdown in communication.

Content creators will need to learn and adapt new writing and authoring skills to effectively shape the experiences that users have with bots. At the BBC, one pilot project tasked a personal finance writer who was already writing a Q/A type of article to write up the information a second time in a more chatty, conversational style for the bot. Writing for bots is even becoming a new career opportunity for artists, poets, and script writers, who can use their creative skills to craft an entertaining experience.[55] This is because linguistic expression, including choices in words and tone, can convey important differences in personality.[56] A bot that greets a user with "Hi, how may I help you?" might get a different response than one that begins "What is it you need *now,* Kevin?" Like any other form of media, the output of bots will need to take into account its intended audience. In order to fit the genre of chatbots, dialogues need to feel casual, as though they could exist alongside other personal chats a user is having. Use of complex vocabulary and grammatical constructs might be appropriate for some audiences but not others. In some cases users may even mirror and match a bot's vocabulary diversity and message length, indicating they are adapting to the standard set by the bot (much as people adapt conversation to suit children or foreign speakers).[57] Outward appearances, including the identity of the bot, such as the name, sex (or lack thereof), and race the bot assumes, can also be consequential to how people react to it.[58] This raises new questions about the identity diversity of a stable of bots that an organization is running. Creators also find new ways to signal personality via the capabilities of the social platforms where they live. Politibot, for instance, is friends with only one person on Twitter—Teddy Roosevelt. What does that say about the bot's (or its creators') politics?

Designing bots is also about accounting for the peculiarities of how people might treat them. Typical users will pursue inquisitive limit-testing behavior to better understand the bounds of operation of a bot.[59] People like to try to stump bots, or get them to do something they weren't designed to do. It's not uncommon for people to insult or make sexual advances on bots. Eduardo Suarez, one of the designers of Politibot, explained that part of the authoring effort involved brainstorming a long list of potential insults and then mapping out how the bot would respond to each. How the bot reacts to these types of interactions can send an implicit signal about whether certain norm-breaking behaviors are ok. In other words, if a bot is verbally assaulted, but doesn't convey the inappropriateness of that in a response, does this train users to treat other individuals who fit the persona projected by the bot in similar ways?

Bots not only rely on people during their design phase, they often also require maintenance efforts at regular intervals while they are in operation. While they may act autonomously in moment-to-moment interactions with users, they are better understood as hybrid entities that are backed by people that edit, manage, update, and eventually decommission the bot. This hybridization requires consideration of the workflow of journalists and how new tasks associated with the bot fit into the rhythms of the newsroom.

The Elexi bot, created by the *Coloradoan* for the 2016 US elections, required a producer to spend at least five minutes a day to update and send top stories through the bot. For BuzzFeed's Buzzbot, a team of reporters could set up dialogue trees for the bot on the fly as events were unfolding. The Politibot, which includes curated as well as original content, requires even more human effort, one to two hours per day. "The problem is that the bot is very time consuming and requires that someone compose these daily digests that we send every day," explained Suarez. Andrew Haeg, who helped with the design of the *Texas Tribune*'s Paige bot, estimated that bot maintenance amounts to a couple of hours of human effort every Monday, and then another twenty to thirty minutes per day to keep it going during the rest of the week. "There's the process of getting the content, chunking it out, putting it into a spreadsheet, finding some emojis, finding some images, figuring out what options to give people like 'read more' or 'I'm all done' or 'skip to next story.'" Additional tasks include monitoring questions users may ask the bot and then triaging those to see if they should be passed on to reporters. "You can't just stop everything and say 'All right we're reorganizing ourselves . . . to create this pilot,'" explained Haeg. Since these are all prototype projects, they must be sustained in parallel with other ongoing reporting and writing efforts. Robert McKenzie, the editor at BBC News Lab, is concerned that new workflow tasks may distract from core tasks such as source development and information gathering. As a response the Lab has developed a tool called BotBuilder, which allows journalists to convert already written explainer articles into interactive Q/A content that can be directly plugged into a bot.[60] The broader challenge moving forward is to develop and iron out workflows that effectively combine human practices with the deployment of bot-based experiences and content.

Automated Sociopaths

Bots can be designed for the most benevolent of purposes, to commit genuine acts of journalism in the public interest. But they can just as easily be imbued with more ignoble intentions and values and deployed or hired by governments, corporations, or individuals to reach foul ends. A central concern is a lack of authenticity in which an approachable social persona conceals some unscrupulous goal. Deception as to their nature as bots and to the mal-intent of their designers creates the conditions for the surreptitious manipulation, pollution, and corruption of information. It doesn't take a terribly smart bot to mimic nasty behavior such as spamming, flaming, stalking, shaming, or bullying.[61] Bots can be used as political cogs in a computational propaganda machine that uses automation to shape public opinion. These so-called political bots "mimic real people so as to manipulate public opinion across a diverse range of social media."[62] Typically they surface as part of botnets—networks of bots controlled and coordinated centrally by some entity such as a state actor—to manipulate discourse. Such bots and botnets are in active use, and have been for several years now. Analyses done on the 2016 US election suggest that perhaps 10–15 percent of the accounts participating on a sampling of election-related hashtags on Twitter were automated.[63] During the third presidential debate estimates put the proportion of tweets from automated accounts at 25 percent—fully a quarter of all communications.[64] And the attention of the bots was not uniform: they produced seven times as many tweets for Donald Trump as for Hillary Clinton. What liabilities does such activity create for public discourse?

There are at least four mechanisms through which bots hack public media. Bots can (1) manipulate the credibility of people or issues, (2) amplify and spread propaganda or junk news, (3) dampen or suppress opposition and debate, and (4) intimidate or deny access to people wishing to participate in communication. I'll consider each of these in turn.

Bots influence the credibility and legitimacy of information by manipulating social signals, such as the amount of feedback a message receives. Although their actions are inauthentic—they are coordinated by the agenda of some bot master—the aggregated likes and shares they produce may be perceived as a signal of the genuine activities of independently thinking people. Their deception corrupts the true social signal and reactions of real people. For instance, one pro-Trump bot spewing anti-Clinton conspiracy theories into the Tweet ether had more than 33,000 followers just prior to the election.[65] This creates fake social proof people read as indicating that "this source is important because many other people are listening to it." Bots inflate political figures by following, retweeting, or liking their content, making them appear to have greater support and perhaps more legitimacy than they really do. An estimate published in May 2017 put the number of bots following Donald Trump's twitter account at more than 15 million—about 49 percent of his following at the time and a huge increase from the 8 percent of bot followers his account recorded in April 2016.[66] Trusted actors, such as journalists, can have their credibility undermined if they are exposed as having a large bot following, even if they themselves did not purchase or otherwise induce those bots to follow them.[67] In Mexico, bots are thought to have inflated the perception of support for energy reform ideas in 2013 by selectively retweeting government officials.[68] And in the German parliamentary elections in 2017, the far-right Alternative für Deutschland party received a relatively higher rate of tweets from automated accounts.[69] On some topics of relevance to Russian interests in Eastern Europe, such as military exercises or troop deployments, bots produce as much as 84 percent of the content in Russian.[70] Such approaches fake the appearance of a grassroots movement or consensus of ideas in a strategy known as "astroturfing."[71] The end-goal is to project an image of significant and widespread support that may in turn jumpstart actual political support.

Journalists can use bots to disseminate quality news information, but activists can just as easily harness bots to push a call to action for their desired outcome, while propagandists can amplify and spread rumors, misinformation, and their prevailing perspective.[72] Information junk can overwhelm attention, distract from what may be genuinely important, and steer the conversation by reframing it.[73] An avalanche of junk information matters because people often actually fall for it. One study showed that people retweet false claims posted by bots as often as they retweet them from other people—showing a lack of discernment in choosing what to retweet.[74] So-called twitter bombs target specific users with unsolicited messages in order to get them to pay attention to the agenda of the manipulator.[75] A dozen different bots might pair a message mentioning an influential user with a link to a false piece of information in the hopes that that user will reshare the misleading link because it looks popular.[76] Such targeting strate gies, which involve multiple exposures to an idea from multiple ostensibly independent sources, have been shown to be highly contagious insofar as they increase the probability the targeted user will spread that piece of information.[77] Another study looking at an October 2016 sample of US election–related tweets found that about 11 percent of human accounts had retweeted any of 695 different bots. Bot accounts were distributed throughout the communications network, including in densely connected areas.[78] But while some humans appear to indiscriminately reshare questionable information from bots, they do still engage in replying more to other humans than to bots.[79]

Bots can also be tools of opposition and suppression, functioning to dampen particular ideas or positions and limit their spread by influencing attention patterns. One way this works is by jamming trending topics or hashtags with "noise." This is what happened in Mexico on the #YaMeCanse (Spanish for "I am tired") hashtag that arose after forty-three students went missing on their way to a protest in 2014. Journalists noticed that bots attacked the hashtag with gibberish, tweeting out a few random characters such as commas and semicolons together with the hashtag.[80] Flooding the hashtag with nonsense messages created a smokescreen that made it difficult for people to find genuine and meaningful content about the story on social media. This had the added effect of impeding the development of an online community around the issue. Misdirection is a strategy that diverts attention on a particular hashtag to other unrelated content. For instance, one botnet in Syria was used to direct attention away from the Syrian civil war to other Syria-related topics.[81] Another tack is for bots to create new hashtags and generate a huge volume of activity to push those hashtags into a top-trending list. For only €1,000 BuzzFeed found a Russian hacker who would do this for political hashtags on Twitter during the German elections.[82] This type of activity can elbow out legitimate hashtags and make them less visible, while simultaneously attracting real people that organically spread the disingenuous hashtag.

Bots can also be bullies, targeting individuals through intimidation or harassment or by denying access to a social platform. In late August 2017 two staffers at the Digital Forensics Research Lab, a think-tank tracking global disinformation campaigns, experienced this first hand. The attack created two fake Twitter profiles using genuine photos of the staffers, one of whom is the director of the lab. The fake director's account then tweeted a piece of false information indicating that the second staffer was now dead: "Our beloved friend and colleague Ben Nimmo passed away this morning. Ben, we will never forget you. May God give you eternal rest. RIP!" This was then retweeted more than 21,000 times by bots.[83] Such an attack is meant to shock and deceive, and might even be construed as an oblique death threat.

Intimidation can come in different forms and is not always quite so blatant, though. In Canada, a law professor commented on Twitter about a trending hashtag #GoodRiddanceHarper, to which he received a negative reply. But then that negative reply received more than 1,000 likes and retweets, many from bots.[84] This type of activity discourages future statements and could lead to self-censorship in order to avoid a blast of negative feedback. In the US context, bots are reported to have attacked Texas Senator Ted Cruz by urging users who had received his campaign's robocalls to report him for violating political media regulations, creating a legal threat to the senator.[85] The ways in which bots attack individuals can be quite creative. For instance, by flooding the notifications a target user receives from a platform, bots can create a form of "denial of service" attack, making it difficult to pay attention to real messages. If a bunch of bots all follow an account at the same time, or report the account as spam, this can trigger an account suspension. In this way Twitter's antispam and antibot tools are weaponized to create additional friction for the legitimate use of the service by targeted users.[86]

All of this antisocial bot behavior also has implications for how automation is deployed by journalists and news organizations with positive and productive intentions—so-called "good" bots. If public and civic engagement is to be supported, authenticity of the participating actors is key. Productive bots in their many forms deserve to coexist with real individuals on platforms. But in order to be used ethically bots need to identify themselves.[87] This in turn will make ferreting out truly deceptive bots an easier undertaking. If bots do need to violate laws, social norms, or involve deception, they and their creators should be prepared with ethically sound justifications.[88]

Good bots also need to be designed with resilience in case a bad bot tries to coopt or manipulate it. Bots that feed off of public and easily manipulated signals such as top trending lists, retweet counts, or interactions with other agents need to be designed with consideration to the extent to which they should act on those signals, lest they become unwitting participants in a manipulative bot's agenda. (Incidentally, *people* should stop to think about whether they act on these signals too.) The designers of good bots may weigh whether their bots automatically reshare information that could actually just be misinformation, propaganda, or noise being pumped out by bad actors. This may in turn call for the development of more sophisticated filters on the input signals to good bots. But some attacks that work against people will not be effective against bots. For instance, bots are not susceptible to intimidation or attentional blocking in the same way that individual humans are.

The Bot War

Bot armies that bully, intimidate, harass, pollute, and push political agendas are making it easier and easier to manipulate legitimate flows of information and attention online. This is probably going to get worse. Malicious actors will continue building bots that are better and better at mimicking human behavior so that they can go unnoticed in covert influence campaigns. Synthesized content such as photos of people for profile photos or even entire comments that are indistinguishable from human-authored ones will eventually enable believable social posts and profiles to be automatically synthesized. Ensuring the legitimacy of online public discourse and securing the online media environment for authentic civic engagement will not be easy.

One approach is to develop computational techniques able to identify bots at scale. For instance, early bot detection work was able to uncover political astroturf campaigns on Twitter during the 2010 US elections.[89] Recognizing the threat to open-source intelligence, the Defense Advanced Research Projects Agency (DARPA) has invested heavily in trying to identify bots, including running a competition in 2015 that challenged teams to identify bots that were influencing views on the topic of vaccination on a simulated version of Twitter.[90] The winning teams used features such as inconsistencies in behavior, text analysis, and network analysis to sort the bots from the nonbots and incorporated machine-learning models along with user interfaces so that humans could rapidly review suspicious accounts. In comparison to human accounts bots tend to retweet more often, originate tweets less often, have more recently created accounts, and receive fewer replies, mentions, and retweets.[91] Bot detection is complicated by the fact that many online bots are in fact cyborgs, in that a person is composing messages that an algorithm is then retweeting or replying to.[92] Bot versus not-bot is not always a simple binary distinction. And bot detection algorithms will never be fully error free. Another barrier to detecting bots and their influence is that access to data about bot behavior is needed. Limited data access offered by platforms such as Facebook presents a very real impediment. Moreover, bots may be operating on non-public chat apps, functioning in closed or encrypted groups that are difficult to access and study.[93] Social platforms will surely step up their internal methods for identifying and purging inauthentic bot accounts,[94] but they should also consider opening up their data to civil society so a greater number and diversity of eyes can be trained on the problem.

Journalists will play a much larger role in securing online communications against bots as they gain access to data and develop computational tools and techniques. The same tools that DARPA is developing can and should be used by news organizations hoping to shed light on how bots may be influencing the media. Bots, botnets, and their misinformation campaigns are a new beat that journalists need to cover more diligently and comprehensively.[95] Creative ways for covering the beat are starting to emerge. For instance, *Quartz'* @probabot_ searches for and marks accounts with high "Botometer"[96] scores that are talking about politics. In a Blade-Runner-esque display, the probabot_ locates other accounts that are likely to be bots and calls them out. There are many other possibilities for news coverage based on such a bot score. Scores could be used to quantify the degree of support bots provide to politicians' tweets, to analyze whether a hashtag is trending because a majority of accounts sharing it are bots, or simply to measure how many fake followers various influencers may have.[97] New computational tools in the hands of expert analysts will help interpret the patterns of information flow on social networks and make periodic reports—perhaps even like weather reports—on which way the bot winds are blowing. As this beat develops, it will help to fortify the public to the risks of automation on social platforms.

Newsbots are a burgeoning opportunity for journalists to provide task-oriented information services, as well as to build entirely new experiences around news content. As social agents, bots offer a new channel for journalists to stay in contact and engage with users in the online spaces where they spend time. While that engagement may not be at the scale of driving revenue just yet, bots do offer entirely new ways of exercising journalistic goals, such as sharing or gathering information, practicing accountability, or expressing opinion and critique. Workflows will need to be updated to maintain and operate bots, causing changes to fundamental practices such as writing and editing. As public-interest newsbots come into conflict with those operated by bad actors and an entirely new set of challenges emerges, journalists will have to grapple even more with differentiating good from bad automation, while platforms will have to don the mantle of media organizations in order to function as both enablers and adjudicators of bot free speech.

5

DIGITAL PAPERBOYS: ALGORITHMS
IN NEWS DISTRIBUTION

On November 16, 2017, the US House of Representatives passed sweeping legislation to overhaul the federal tax code. As the Senate advanced its own version of the bill, major changes to tax law were just around the corner. By the morning of the eighteenth Google searches for "tax reform" were trending, indicating a surge of interest as the public earnestly looked for information about the bill and what it might mean for their wallets. As powerful windows into online information, search engines were mediating and shaping the news people saw about the issue. But were those search engines providing accurate information? Were they providing diverse or balanced information? As Congress hammered out details and the public sought to make sense of what it all meant, exactly what kinds of news information did the likes of Google serve up?

We measured this, in fact, by scraping nonpersonalized Google results for "tax reform" every minute for twenty-four hours starting around noon on the eighteenth. What we found was a startling lack of diversity of news sources. During that twenty-four-hour period only twelve unique sources of news surfaced in the "Top Stories" section of Google results, which sits above the main "organic" results and is presented with eye-catching images. The top five of those sources accounted for almost 93 percent of links to articles that appeared. These included brand names

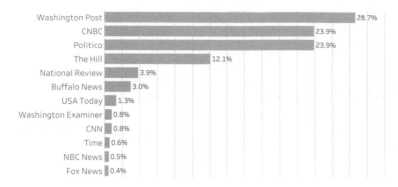

Figure 5.1. Proportion of links from different news sources that appeared in Google "Top Stories" when searching for "tax reform" every minute for a twenty-four-hour period, starting on November 18, 2017, at noon CST.

such as the *Washington Post* and CNBC as well as more focused political outlets such as Politico, the *Hill,* and the *National Review.*[1] The only source you might consider local in the results was buffalonews.com, which accounted for 3 percent of links (see Figure 5.1).[2]

A similar experiment on the issue of "net neutrality" found slightly better diversity metrics. There were fifty-five unique sources with 80 percent of the links coming from the top ten. But a moderate increase in news source diversity brought with it questions about the quality and independence of information presented. In almost 1 percent of the searches, links to RT.com were listed prominently at the top of results. Google was highlighting information from a media outlet funded by the Russian government—state-sponsored media now considered an agent of a foreign state. This is symptomatic of Google's permissive definition of what counts as news. The search engine has been known to highlight unvetted tweets, YouTube videos, and other nonprofessional publishers as "news" as well.[3] A 2016 study of search results for hundreds of congressional candidates found 85 "fake news" sources in the results for Democratic candidates, 139 for Republicans, and 27 for Independents.[4] Ensuring the quality of information at the scale at which Google operates is a challenging proposition indeed.

For people seeking to inform themselves on important civic issues, search engines such as Google play an increasingly important role as algorithmic gatekeepers, steering massive amounts of human attention through their relevance algorithms. A 2014 survey from the Media Insight Project found that 51 percent of US respondents got news in the last week via a search engine.[5] A Reuters Institute survey from 2017 indicated that 25 percent of respondents listed search engines as the *main* way they come across news.[6] Facebook as well as other social media channels are also important arbiters of human attention to news information. A Pew survey in 2017 found that 67 percent of adults in the United States get some form of news via social media, with Facebook having the most widespread usage.[7] By the end of 2017, roughly 45 percent of *external* traffic to news web sites (that is, not internal circulation or direct traffic to a homepage) was being driven by clicks on Google's search results, and another 25 percent was being driven by Facebook.[8] Just these two information intermediaries influence the shape of about 70 percent of attention to news coming from external sources, and just over a third of the overall traffic pie when internal and direct traffic is included.

The dominance of such platforms in the market for attention affords them leverage over media organizations. They can drive particular content formats such as video, or make the tools and data they offer indispensable to publishers seeking to extend or optimize their audience.[9] Shifts in platform algorithms can lead to striking declines in referral traffic. For instance, Facebook's move to prioritize posts from friends and family in its newsfeed algorithm meant that referral traffic from the site declined from 40 percent to 25 percent of external referral traffic over the course of 2017 (see Figure 5.2). Some publishers, such as *Slate,* have seen even more dramatic drops: from May 2017 to May 2018 referrals

External referrals in the Parse.ly network
100% = all external referrers

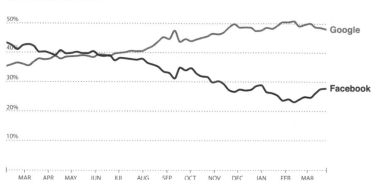

Figure 5.2. The percentage of external referrals coming from Google and Facebook from early 2017 into early 2018 for customers of the Parse.ly news analytics product. *Source:* Data from Parse.ly Network Referral Dashboard (https://www.parse.ly/resources/data-studies/referrer-dashboard/).

from Facebook dropped by 81 percent—that's 15.4 million fewer referrals per month.[10] Moreover, publishers in relatively smaller media markets become guinea pigs for product testing as platforms try out new versions of algorithms that can choke off traffic.[11] Of course, platform algorithms can create unexpected traffic winners too. *USA Today* became the biggest US news publisher on Facebook in February 2017 as the unwitting recipient of fake user engagement stoking the algorithm.[12] While publishers may catch whiffs of these shifts in their data streams before any official announcements, constantly evolving algorithms create an uncertain environment for news distribution. From an economics perspective, platforms dominate ad spending, drawing revenue away from publishers while they bear none of the content production costs.[13] Yet the platforms distance themselves from being seen as media companies, which would provoke a different regulatory regime than if they maintain a rhetoric and public countenance as technology companies.[14]

The algorithms that Google and Facebook employ for filtering and ranking information are core to their value proposition. They reduce the cacophony of information online to something more manageable. As a result, platforms like Google and Facebook have become moderators and arbiters of speech.[15] One dimension of this role is economically motivated: they aim to avoid repulsing offended or harassed users, keep users engaged, and keep advertisers comfortable with how their brands are associated with content; another comes from the moral imperative to mitigate illicit content of the sexually explicit, graphically violent, self-harming, hateful, extremist, racist, or otherwise trolling variety.[16] Platforms play a fundamental janitorial role by making the worst parts of humanity less visible, and they increasingly do so at scale using a combination of both algorithmic and human moderators.[17]

In the process of moderating content, platforms test the boundaries of what speech is legitimated and visible as the topic of public or individual interest. Context-deprived algorithms meant to shield advertisers from sensitive content can end up denying ad revenue to legitimate news publishers if those publishers happen to cross an automatically drawn invisible line.[18] A shift to prioritize posts that generate discussion means that individually informative topics (for instance, those related to sensitive or embarrassing personal health issues), which people may not want to discuss publicly, will be less prioritized by the algorithm. A moral desire to censor sexually explicit language may cause news about sexual health or education to be swept away from view.[19] Because filtering algorithms can easily make mistakes and lack context for their classifications, some legitimate speech will be unavoidably stifled. At-scale moderation on platforms such as YouTube takes a composition of machine learning, user-reported flags, and trained professionals working in concert, but mistakes will be made and disagreements over where to draw the lines for free speech will always fester.

One of the most consequential aspects of platforms' information filtering and ranking algorithms relates to how voters become

engaged and informed about candidates or issues during elections.[20] A Facebook experiment in 2012 showed that boosting
the visibility of hard news within the newsfeed (ranking it at the
top) increased self-reported voter turnout by about 3 percent.[21]
Increased voter turnout and democratic engagement are great for
society, right? Well, yes, except that if the intervention were
deployed differentially to particular demographics or geogra-
phies, it could easily be enough to swing an electoral outcome.
Attention control is a powerful weapon if misused, abused, or
corrupted. For search engines, the ranking of information on the
results page is likewise a powerful factor that drives attention and
interaction with electoral information.[22] Laboratory studies of
mock search engine results have shown that ordering can impact
undecided voters' perceptions of candidates and shift their voting
preferences.[23] The mouths of despots water as they eye the political power of information intermediaries such as Google and
Facebook.

In determining what is highly visible and what is hidden, platform algorithms play a key role in how people develop robust and
diverse viewpoints on societally relevant issues, access the latest
information that may pertain to personal decisions of health,
education, and employment, and inform themselves about important policy issues. Attention-mediating algorithms govern the
visibility of information online, acting not only as algorithmic
gatekeepers but also serving to frame issues and set agendas.
Trending algorithms may reflect back what is popular while
raising awareness among an even broader set of people, in effect
helping to conjure an interested public around an issue.[24] On the
other hand, questions may reasonably be raised when a newsfeed
fails to notify its users of important civil unrest while continuing
to amuse and divert attention to popular events.[25] Individuals in
a democracy must have ways to track when events occur that may
have important ramifications not only for themselves, but for all
of society.[26] The implications of algorithmic shaping of attention
are exacerbated by the fact that many users are not even aware

that their newsfeed is algorithmically mediated, thereby depriving them of the ability to determine their own interests in the marketplace of ideas.[27]

The power of media platforms such as Google and Facebook is broad, and ranges from shaping public opinion during political elections, to enabling or hindering community formation, moderating speech, and dictating the conditions under which news organizations disseminate content. Given their ability to influence attention, interaction, and communication, the choices made in the design of their interfaces and algorithms are anything but neutral.[28] In recognition of their impact on the dissemination of news content, a growing number of scholars have begun to ask how the values driving these organizations differ from the values that have traditionally motivated the news media.[29] Legacy media outlets and their codes of conduct are often deeply motivated by public interest values, whereas the coders creating news apps and platforms that now dominate information distribution may have no inclination whatsoever toward traditional journalistic values and practices, such as truth and verification, loyalty to the public, independence from those whom they cover, and dedication to building community and fostering deliberative conversation. But to what extent do platforms (or news organizations' own content optimizations, for that matter) embody such commitments in their algorithms, code, and broader sociotechnical processes? And if they don't, should they?

This chapter examines the forces and values underpinning the algorithmic distribution of news information, with an eye toward how practices surrounding news distribution are adapting in relation to these forces. On the one hand, news organizations often play to the market logic radiated by the platforms in an effort to stay relevant and attract new audiences.[30] The rules and values projected by platforms via the data they provide and the algorithms they wield set the stage, orienting how news organizations go about growing and optimizing the audience for their content.[31] In the process, new practices are emerging to help maximize those audiences using data and algorithms. On the other hand, some news organizations are starting to take the reins of algorithmic distribution back into their own hands. Using the digital channels they control, such as apps and webpages, they are beginning to actively shape algorithms and workflows for news distribution in ways that reflect more traditionally recognizable editorial values.

Content Optimization

Audience analytics are an essential part of the modern newsroom.[32] Large flat-screen monitors projecting real-time metrics of "most read" or "trending" articles hang from the walls of major newsrooms, saturating the visual periphery with the subliminal signal: "follow the data." News organizations actively monitor audience clicks and other metrics both to gain insights into reader behavior and to plan content production.[33] A variety of tools with names like Chartbeat, Parsely, and NewsWhip provide dashboards, filters, and data visualizations that help newsrooms understand how content performs and where there may be unmet demand from audiences.[34] These tools impact editorial decisions including everything from topic selection, story placement, and monitoring of competitors to rewriting or adapting content to make it more appealing and attention-getting.[35]

Data-mining algorithms are increasingly applied to audience data with an eye toward expanding the monetizable audience by predicting and optimizing the performance of content based on historical patterns. Optimization algorithms help wring extra commercial value out of the content news organizations so laboriously produce. Algorithms can be used in a variety of ways to optimize attention and traffic to content, including methods such as testing of headlines, predicting article shelf-life, selecting and timing postings to various social channels, modeling the impact of platform changes on traffic patterns, developing recommendation and personalization modules to make sites more sticky, and so on. Publishing decisions such as what, where, and when to post content can all be informed so as to maximize some metric with respect to an audience.

Many publishers now experiment with a number of variations of content before they find the one that resonates best with their audience. Headlines written by editors can be optimized through audience testing or directly analyzed according to their text and style to predict which version will perform best on any given social platform.[36] At the *Chicago Tribune,* for example, stories may go through ten headlines before editors find the one that performs optimally in grabbing the audience's attention. Different versions of the headline are shown to different people viewing the webpage to evaluate which one performs best. Referred to as "A/B testing," this technique uses a mathematical calculation to quickly resolve which version of the content is performing better according to some metric, usually the click-through rate though possibly other metrics such as time spent or scroll depth on the article page. "We encourage our newsroom to do as many headlines as possible, as many images as possible, as many blurbs as possible," noted the *Washington Post*'s chief information officer, Shailesh Prakash, adding that the optimization algorithm takes care of finding the combination of content that works best to drive traffic, including for different audience segments such as "women" or "people in Canada."[37] The *Post* is even beginning to knit this optimization technology to automatic content generation so that headline variations can be automatically produced from the article text and evaluated quickly to find the best version.[38]

Algorithmic predictions of expected article performance are also used to inform how editors promote articles across the home page or on different social networks. For instance, the *Washington Post* clusters articles based on their traffic patterns to predict when the traffic for a given article will peak. Editors can then use this information to prioritize article placements that further boost popular content or identify underperforming content that might need A/B testing of new variants.[39] The *New York Times* uses predictive modeling tied to a chat interface to help editors choose which articles to promote on which social channels based on their expected performance.[40] At *Al Jazeera,* an early prototype demonstrated that final article traffic could be accurately predicted based on the data signals that come back during the first few hours after publication.[41] Data-driven modeling can also be used to help cope with the not infrequent changes in platform algorithms. So, for instance, if Google decides it is going to downweight articles that contain interstitial ads, a data science team will model out the predicted loss of a certain amount of traffic as compared to how much money interstitial ads make. The goal is a data-driven decision about how to strategically respond to the platform change. These techniques can also drive better decisions about changes to publisher's own paywalls, enabling them to take into account predictions about expected impacts to revenue. The audience, and what it wants to read, is increasingly modeled and predicted.

News organizations also utilize widgets that encapsulate article recommendation and personalization algorithms in order to make their sites more sticky and increase reader engagement. Based on factors such as an individual's reading history, his or her interest in particular topics, and what similar individuals read, articles more likely to be clicked can be recommended.[42] This can extend the amount of time a user spends on the site. At the *Washington Post,* the article recommendation module increases clicks by about 9 percent over a random baseline.[43] Alejandro Cantarero, the vice president for data at Tronc (before it changed its name back to Tribune Publishing and he joined the *Los Angeles Times*), explained that their personalized article recommendation algorithm, which was running in half of their markets as of the end of 2017, boosts reengagement anywhere from 50 percent to 60 percent in comparison to a baseline nonpersonalized popularity-based recommendation. At Google News the personalized article recommender introduced in 2010 increased the click-through rate by 31 percent, while also driving users to visit the site 14 percent more often in comparison to the nonpersonalized version.[44] There is a fair bit of variance in the efficacy of these systems, some of which may relate to other factors such as page layout, but the trend is clearly to the upside.

Hybrid Practices

Many of the content optimization approaches I've just outlined rely on humans in the loop in some capacity, whether writing headlines, making strategic decisions based on predictions, or setting the parameters for recommendation modules. But that hasn't stopped some from trying push-button content optimization processes that rely more fully on automation and algorithms. Products with names like "Echobox" and "True Anthem" mine the click patterns of piles of articles in order to predict not only *when* to post but also *what* to post to a social channel such as Facebook. Echobox claims that its clients see a 57 percent boost in Facebook traffic and a 100 percent boost in Twitter traffic when they hand the keys over to its algorithm. A primary benefit of such extensive automation is that an algorithm such as Echobox's will adapt as the platform changes its distribution algorithm. Responding to capricious platform algorithms with other adaptive optimization algorithms is appealing since it obviates the need to divine what aspects of content the platform algorithm is keyed into. One algorithm learns how to optimize with respect to the other.

The efficacy of the fully automated approach hinges on the assumption that the optimized model is tuned not only to the content and context, but also to the goals of the publisher. For instance, a model built to optimize aggregate click-through rates will fail if the publisher is trying to build a subscription-oriented business. The *Chicago Tribune* evaluated an automated tool for content optimization on its Facebook page by comparing it to manual curation and found that staff selections had 2.5 times more engagement than the automated posts. The algorithm was missing all of the content-specific tailoring of messaging that a good social media engagement editor is versed in, whether that be excerpting a juicy quote for the post, summarizing a key point, or emphasizing the local interest of the story. The superiority of hybrid curation has also been demonstrated in the domain of push notifications from news apps. SmartNews is one such app that sends four scheduled news alerts every day. The company ran a test comparing a fully manual selection of headlines to a fully automated selection and to a hybrid system that suggested five headlines algorithmically which an editor then chose from. The hybrid system beat both the purely manual selection of headlines and the purely algorithmic selection of headlines across metrics such as open rate and recirculation to other content after looking at the alert.

It seems more likely, at least in the short term, that a human-machine hybrid will have an edge for content optimization tasks. This is because of the complex communication skills often needed to understand how to match or adapt a particular news story happening at a particular moment and perhaps with particular cultural resonances to a perceived audience need or demand. Moreover, an algorithm may be lacking key context that informs which metric is the relevant one to track for a particular piece of content. At BuzzFeed the approach has predominantly been to empower curators to work more efficiently, while debunking myths of the practice using evidence drawn from vast stores of historical performance data. The machine-learned predictions about optimal placements of content, such as where to post on Facebook and how to route a posting from one page to another, are offered as suggestions to editors. "What we're doing with that is showing it to curators . . . giving them this prediction and saying, 'What do you think?,'" explained Gilad Lotan, the vice president for data at BuzzFeed. Alejandro Cantarero concurred with the approach: "A lot of what we try to do is build things where the output is being presented to people in the newsroom as like 'Hey here's more data to help you make an informed decision. But we're not telling you what to do. The decision is still in your hands but we're just trying to give you more tools that make a more informed decision.'"

If hybrid content optimization is the default, an important challenge then becomes how to integrate the output of content optimization algorithms, or even just audience feedback metrics, into other editorial workflow routines. For instance, the *New York Times* and the *Guardian* have built internal dashboards that pull together much of the analytics data they collect so that reporters and editors can see the data in context.[45] BuzzFeed uses "triggers" that push alerts about content into Slack channels that are more attention-getting than a passively monitored dashboard.[46] At the *Washington Post*, the "Virality Oracle"—their article popularity predictor—spits messages into Slack such as "This article may be popular soon! 4311 visits 5 mins since its first visit and > 100k visits @24 hours forecast." Metrics, historical benchmarks, and forecasts are used in alerts that algorithmically orient and direct editorial attention to publication and promotion decisions.

Toward Principled Metrics

Whether from automation or hybrid practices, the results of content optimization hinge on a key decision: What is the metric that is being optimized? Should a news organization optimize for raw volume of attention, engaged attention involving interaction with content, subscription, loyalty, satisfaction, or something else entirely?

The choice of what to optimize is, of course, influenced and enabled by the types of data publishers gather on how users read, share, and otherwise interact with content. At BuzzFeed Lotan told me the organization logs "every interaction that happens on every piece of content that we publish to every platform. . . . We collect a lot of data back about audience, about performance. . . . It's all about data-driven optimization." One reason platforms are able to exert influence over publishers is that they control an important slice of the data publishers use to understand their audiences. As a result, content optimization is determined by the data platforms collect and are willing to share, as well as by the volume, fidelity, and quality of that data. Some platforms make custom Application Programming Interfaces (APIs) available for publishers, while others are less generous. Data limitations drive how much a publisher such as BuzzFeed invests in content on a platform. If there's a paucity of data available, the ability to learn about audience is diminished and so too is the inclination to publish on the platform.

The decision concerning which metrics to optimize should also align with the business orientation and model of the organization.[47] Commercial publishers will orient toward different metrics than nonprofit or publicly funded organizations. For a commercial publisher with an advertising-based revenue model, a focus on the audience as a set of individuals whose attention and engagement can be maximized and measured in terms of traffic makes perfect sense. Part of the financial success of platforms derives from their ability to optimize for individual satisfaction and engagement. Google crafts results to maximize satisfaction by optimizing for individual relevance, and Facebook's newsfeed is a constantly evolving personalized model of interest that heavily emphasizes friend relationships, explicit user interests, and other user-centered behavior in its calculus.[48] The result is increased engagement and the capture of ever more attention that can be sold off to advertisers. News organizations can participate in the advertising market logic of user engagement by optimizing for the most readily available signals of individual attention—the likes, clicks, and shares that are the coin of the social media realm.

Publishers need not necessarily cater to a platform-centric notion of shareability, however. A subscription-oriented business might emphasize user loyalty (as shown in repeat visit patterns, for example) and focus on developing and maintaining a quality brand that is differentiated from commodity news. Subscription represents a growing slice of the revenue pie, perhaps even a way to sustain a viable business for a growing number of publishers.

At some Schibsted publications, such as *Aftenposten*, subscription conversion metrics are available for every article, showing the gender and age breakdown of who decided to buy a subscription after seeing that particular article. This builds visibility for the metric amongst members of the newsroom and enables them to inspect how their articles are performing. Other implementations incorporate more of a predictive element. At the *New York Times* predictive modeling is used at every stage of the user funnel from casual readers, to registered users, to subscribers, and to subscriber renewals.[49] Once such predictions can be made in real-time, the experience of a website can by dynamically adjusted to try to convert users to the next stage of the funnel. Publishers such as Schibsted, the *Wall Street Journal,* and others have data scientists developing paywalls that can predict the propensity that a user will subscribe at any particular moment and which vary how porous the wall is based on the chance a user will convert.[50] So, if a sports fan exhausts his or her free article views looking at Lakers scores, but is then trying to get to a piece of politics coverage, the paywall might give in to allow that view if it seems that it could lead to a subscription down the line.

The choice of metric is also highly context- and content-specific. While a single "God metric" could be useful for a manager to gauge overall business success in aggregate, it may also lead to unfair comparisons when applied to individual articles by an editor thinking about a specific content strategy. Different topics and genres of content are associated with different types of skimming or engaged reading behavior.[51] Consider the national German newspaper *Die Welt,* which computes a single score for each article it publishes. The score takes into account several weighted factors including page views, time spent, video views, social shares, and bounce rate.[52] The issue with this type of score is that if an article lacks a video, perhaps because it's a conceptual essay or other nonvisual story, it would lose out in the overall ranking in comparison to a story that received many video views. Is the goal then to deemphasize any content that isn't well-suited to a video illustration? Some types of stories may naturally deserve and do well with a video, while others are meant to be long reads. Aggregated metrics can frustrate attempts to evaluate content performance according to the most appropriate metric for a specific piece of content. In order to make fair apples-to-apples comparisons of content, aggregated metrics must be broken down into their underlying metrics so performance comparisons can be made along the relevant dimensions.

Different types of content may succeed according to different metrics (or may perform variably even across different channels) and may then play into different value propositions or business objectives for a news organization. "There are certain types of stories that are much more likely to have those viral qualities and inspire passion and excitement in people so that they mark it as interesting or share it. Other types of stories are useful or people are glad they know about it but they're not going to go, 'Oh my God I love that and I'm gonna share it,'" explained Tamar Charney, the managing editor of the NPR One app. It makes sense in some cases to optimize for subscribers, and in others to optimize for reach or advertising revenue—the two don't necessarily go hand in hand. When the *LA Times* published its seven-part Trump piece entitled "Our Dishonest President," the editorial board made a decision not to put ads on the page. "We felt that it was going to do really well with subscribers and was going to resonate with our audience, and we wanted to offer that clean site experience to maximize the subscriber potential," explained Cantarero, who is now VP of data at the *LA Times*. For a broad-audience publication, a portfolio approach may be most effective, such that some content is geared toward building loyalty, other content is meant to drive discussion and dialogue in comment channels, and still other content is geared toward attracting new audience for the first time. Metrics need to be aligned with the editorial priorities of the news organization and its various types of content. Editors should strive to articulate the goal of a *particular* piece of content before they choose what to measure about it and how to evaluate its performance.

In still other scenarios metrics need to be tempered in order to maintain a certain brand expectation. As Kurt Gessler, the deputy editor for Digital at the *Chicago Tribune,* explained, "If you were going to ask me: 'Kurt would you rather publish a Bloomberg story that gets 100,000 reach and 5,000 click-throughs, or would you rather publish one Chicago theater story today that gets a 40,000 reach and 1,000 click-throughs?' I would tell you the latter. It is much more important for the brand that is *Chicago Tribune* to do that. It's not just about 4,000 more page views it's about sustaining the deep brand voice of the *Chicago Tribune* that no one else could do." Staying true to the brand may diminish audience size but at the same time build loyalty within a core audience. This is among the strategic decisions about how metrics are put into dialogue with other editorial priorities of a publisher— strategic decisions an algorithm may struggle with unless those editorial priorities are explicit and measurable.

Clicks, likes, shares, engaged time, subscription: the metrics that currently inform content strategy and optimization are both *convenient* and *plausible* to measure given finite time and resources. These metrics are aligned with the market logic of the content business. But a focus on audience metrics that track individual attention creates a tension with professional values and how professionals think about their impact in the world.[53] Beyond audience traffic, impact can mean everything from awards or financial support for the organization to individual or community awareness and action, public deliberation, and the alteration of public policy.[54] Since the editorial interests of the audience and professionals often diverge, relying too heavily on audience metrics in editorial decision-making can lead to, for instance, less coverage of public affairs topics.[55] Traditional editorial values stress the public interest and civic value of journalism that reports truthfully, strives to build an informed public opinion on matters of shared social significance, and presents a diverse array of voices to support contestation and deliberation. It can be difficult to balance those normative goals with the demands of an audience. Pragmatically this is an issue for content optimization because there are not yet methods to automatically quantify concepts like "public interest." Measuring such a concept will require more than tracking clicks and screen time in a browser. Moreover, the scale of time over which public impact needs to be measured confounds attempts to practically encode that information into news production algorithms and routines.

The *Krakatoa Chronicle* is one of the earliest attempts at a personalized newspaper. It was created by Krishna Bharat, who a few years later went on to build Google News. Already in 1998 he articulated the struggle to algorithmically find the right balance between individual interest and community interest.[56] The community importance algorithm was "still not as effective as having a human editor rate the importance of the articles to the community," he observed. This still largely rings true twenty years later. Given enough manpower, manual methods and schemas can help track and quantify policy changes, hearings, civic engagement, or other institutional responses that are socially significant and affect the public interest.[57] But these have not been operationalized in a way that an algorithm could automatically measure them and thus apply them at scale as part of some other algorithmic optimization routine. This is a fundamental limitation of the algorithmic approach, one that will be alleviated only if factors such as social relevance, importance to a community, or other potential impacts at the level of institutional or individual change can be reliably quantified. The market logic and commercial pressure on news organization to cater to audience demands will continue to heavily influence news distribution.[58] At the same time, new approaches to incorporating editorial logic into algorithmic curation may begin to challenge that dominance.

The Journalistic Newsfeed

By early 2017 *Svenska Dagbladet,* the third largest daily newspaper in Sweden, had already begun experimenting with a set of curation algorithms to run its homepage.[59] Different sections of the page are now driven by differently tuned and oriented algorithmically curated feeds—one for top news, one for long reads, one for traffic winners, and so on. Instead of abusing the page to maximize engagement though, the design goal was to also surface things editors thought their audience *should* read, or that somehow challenged the audience. Hans Martin Cramer, who works on automatic curation tools at parent company Schibsted in Norway, told me that the design goal was to close the gap between what people know and what they should know. That's "the editorial promise of what we do," he explained. In Norwegian this kind of social mission is called a "Samfunnsoppgave"—a sense of responsibility to society.

To realize this sense of responsibility, the Schibsted algorithm, which is also rolling out for *Aftenposten* in Norway, takes several editorial criteria into account when curating content. These include the "news value" of each article, as well as its "time horizon." These are set by reporters and standardized by editors as pieces of metadata that the algorithm then feeds on as it makes its selection and ranking decisions. To make it into the "important news" section of the homepage, which isn't personalized, articles must have a news value of 2.5 or more (on a scale of 1 to 5) and be published within the last forty-eight hours. News values of 1s and 2s are lighter stories about culture, whereas 4s and 5s are big national and international stories; a 3 might be an important opinion piece. The time horizon for a story can be set to "short," "medium," or "long" depending on whether the algorithm should consider the article for one day, for up to a week, or for longer than a week. Important stories that do not have a strict time horizon, such as a major investigation, can be set so the algorithm tries to expose everyone to the story. The setting is quite descriptively called "show to all." Instead of using only simple user-driven metrics such as clicks and engagement, the algorithm puts those into dialog with metadata reflecting the editorial evaluation of the content by journalists. Initial results show that the automated home pages are performing about just as well, or even a little bit better, than the manually curated ones.

Svenska Dagbladet and *Aftenposten* aren't the only ones experimenting with incorporating editorial thinking directly into curation algorithms. There are a range of editorially enlightened possibilities for personalized curation algorithms including showcasing a diversity of articles that can't all make it to a home page, serving underserved audiences with niche interests, and recirculating important stories that didn't find their way to enough people.[60] We are still in the early stages of publishers thinking through how to blend editorial interests into algorithmic distribution.

In the United States, National Public Radio's NPR One app uses algorithmic personalization for its radio and podcast content. It also takes seriously its mission to teach people about important events in the world and to create a common awareness of those events. Personalization is allowed only on certain types of content. If "it's a category that we believe is important for you to be an informed citizen then personalization can't touch it," explained Charney from NPR One. "We have the ability to basically decide this is a big important story and it doesn't really matter what we know about your preferences. You come to us for news and part of our responsibility as a news organization is to bring you the big news of the day, so we do," she elaborated. The content thus tends to lean toward hard news topics. But for some types of content the goal shifts to provide more serendipity and a wider view of the world. Different categories of content have different thresholds for personalization, and identifying those categories and setting those thresholds are new types of editorial decisions that journalists must encode and communicate to the algorithm.

Not all editorial thinking needs to be *explicitly* embedded in algorithms. Sometimes algorithms can implicitly incorporate editorial values by learning them from data sets that reflect editorial decision-making. The Swiss daily *Neue Zürcher Zeitung,* for instance, defines the editorial relevance of an article by quantifying where editors placed it on the website, and for how long.[61] In order to personalize a feed, the quantification of editorial relevance is put into dialogue with a quantification of personal relevance learned from past user interactions. Although this approach reduces the amount of effort needed from reporters or editors, implicitly learning editorial criteria is a tricky business. The semantics of what is measured may change even across different parts of the same site. Editors working on different sections—such as business, sports, or politics—may have different practices for how frequently they turn over content or rotate positions, which could in turn affect the comparability of the editorial relevance metric. Data scientists must therefore ensure machine-learned models take into account the context of the decision as much as possible when training algorithms to implicitly recognize editorial decisions.

In addition to factors such as news value, time horizon, and controlled personalization of content, other editorial goals relating to quality can also be expressed and encoded into algorithms. For the Flipboard news app the editorial team evaluates and labels web domains that they considered spam or low-quality. Engineers use a machine-learned model to label the quality of new never-before-seen URLs by examining the features of those URLs and how people in the app interact with them.[62] The classifier is used to down-rank domains likely to be spam or other low quality sources in making curation decisions for the app. It's worth noting that when values such as "quality" are implemented in algorithms, it can be important to look beneath the surface to understand how "quality" is defined and operationalized. "Quality" to Flipboard may mean something different than it does to the *New York Times,* or to Facebook for that matter.[63]

The SmartNews app tries to take the notion of "originality" into account in its curation algorithm. "Journalistically you want the originator of the story to get credit for it if it's an exclusive story, if it's a scoop," explained Rich Jaroslovsky, the chief journalist at SmartNews. He worked with engineers to look for cues in the text of stories so as to give extra weight to the originator and make the curation algorithm more editorially responsible about picking which version of the story to include in the app. The ability to algorithmically measure editorial dimensions such as "originality" is a key challenge to building journalistically astute curation algorithms. A host of editorially interesting content dimensions are nontrivial to measure computationally. This includes factors such as the evergreen-ness of an article, the depth or density of information it conveys, the coherence or thoughtfulness of its argument, and whether it represents a topic fairly.[64] Moreover, algorithms might take into account dimensions measured over sets of content, such as whether the aggregate consumption of news by an individual is diverse along some dimension of interest such as ideology or perspective.[65]

The journalistic newsfeed of the future will need to find an equilibrium between which editorial values should be embedded in the algorithm and which are technically feasible to actually engineer, as well as decide how to weight those values across a range of scenarios or consumption contexts. There's no "one reader" or "one interest" that an algorithm should optimize. Readers' conceptions of relevance may be different on the weekends when they may have more free time for casual reading, or may even change over the course of a day. Curation algorithms, and the editorial criteria driving them, therefore have to be parameterized. They need to be flexible. *Neue Zürcher Zeitung* accordingly developed three different versions of the personalization algorithm driving three different recommendation channels within its mobile app: an evening reading list, a weekend reading list, and a "catchup" recommender that pushes articles newly published since the last time the user logged in. Each scenario considers a different relationship between the user, the content, and time. For instance, the weekend reading list is weighted toward longer reads due to the expectation of users having more reading time.

I should emphasize that there is no single correct set of values or editorial criteria that *should* be built into curation algorithms. But there are better and worse editorial criteria for achieving different types of value propositions and outcomes for society. Different conceptions of journalism or the media and the role each plays in democracy will necessarily lead to different values being prioritized in any particular algorithm.[66] Not everyone will even agree on how to weight factors as seemingly straightforward as "recency." Some news organizations may develop algorithms that optimize for breaking news, while others may want to encourage "slow journalism," which leaves space for reflection and deliberation.[67] Different actors, with different goals, will embed and prioritize their own values into curation processes, or perhaps parameterize values so that end users can tweak and tune to their own delight.[68]

Expressed in headlines such as "How to Fix Facebook—Before It Fixes us," much of the tension felt between traditional media and the platforms arises because of differences in curatorial values and with how platforms wield those values in influencing audience attention.[69] In 2017, when Facebook adjusted its newsfeed algorithm to prioritize "friends and family" posts that encourage lively debate, critics saw the move as detracting from "serious" posts made by established and trusted media brands.[70] (See again Figure 5.2 for a depiction of the effects.) Curation algorithms become boundary objects mediating between the values of the organization running the algorithm and the values of the organizations producing the media being curated. A diverse algorithmic media system will ultimately need a plurality of values built into competing or complementary algorithmic curation systems.

Asserting Control

By introducing algorithms into news curation, journalists and editors are delegating decision-making about what content to include, where to include it, and when to post it. They are in effect loosening control of key publishing decisions that in the past they have had much more direct power over. Doing so saves time and effort and enables new experiences of personalization. Yet, editorial decisions often require far more contextual information than ratings of "news value" or "time horizon" might provide. Not every situation can fit within the design parameters of any given algorithm. Unlike platforms such as Facebook and Google, editors and reporters may at times be uncomfortable with the loss of control associated with delegating publication and distribution decisions to algorithms. To ensure appropriate editorial oversight, journalistic newsfeeds must be designed to allow editors to control the curation algorithm, to monitor it, and to override it if necessary.

Control of algorithmic curation is indirect. Instead of editors having direct control of where and when content is placed in some publishing medium, they specify metadata that gets weighed against other factors, such as personal relevance, as the algorithm makes its publication decision. At NPR One, for instance, new workflows have cropped up to manage the sorting of content according to the various categories of taste, feel, or aesthetics that are used by the algorithm. Editors have to input the metadata that drives the algorithmic ordering and prioritization of stories. Metadata curation and application—tasks more typically associated with librarians than with journalists—will be of growing importance for operating journalistic newsfeeds.

A focus on metadata as a locus of control over the algorithm creates interesting new dynamics for practice. For instance, metadata like the "news value" applied at *Aftenposten* needs to be standardized, otherwise it becomes an entirely subjective enterprise ruled by gut feelings.[71] "You have to be very strict about what . . . the news value actually represent[s]," explained Cramer

at Schibsted. Reporters and editors need to be trained and social-
ized so that they have a shared understanding of what the metadata means and can apply it consistently. Still, reporters may try
to manipulate the data to gain control of the algorithm. "It hap
pens every once in a while that they start gaming the algorithm
so that they can affect the positioning of the articles by changing
their metadata values," explained Cramer. As Schibsted rolls out
its algorithmic homepage tools to different publishers, it is also
finding that such social processes with respect to the algorithm
can vary from newsroom to newsroom. How journalists control
the algorithm via metadata becomes a new localized expression
of practice. Control and management of metadata in newsrooms
are interesting and evolving areas of practice that will have
implications for how news organizations operate journalistic
newsfeeds.

Another mechanism through which journalists exert control
over algorithmic curation is by deciding the universe of content for
the algorithm to select from—the inputs it's paying attention to.
At SmartNews, editors maintain a carefully curated list of news
sources that they deem to be of acceptable editorial quality from
which their curation algorithm can then select. By starting from a
trusted list and then growing it, SmartNews believes it can
combat some of the issues of misinformation that have plagued
newsfeeds like Facebook's. Input curation is also an important
step for the NPR One app. Someone has to manually select the
"best" version of a story from member stations because the app
should include each story only once. Another task for the editorial team involves reviewing podcasts to find appropriate episodes
to include. This seed content allows the editorial team to gather
data on how people are responding.

Control over algorithmic curation can be supported by providing better monitoring tools that enable editors to see what the
algorithm is doing in aggregate. Recognizing this need, Schibsted
is starting to build some of these tools, allowing editors to monitor the articles in the hopper for the algorithm to choose from,

as well as showing editors article positions and performance. Schibsted felt it was important to design a system in which editors "still feel that they're in control," according to Cramer. Monitoring allows editors to override the algorithm if they have a particular editorial priority they want to emphasize. Hence, the importance of a story may well override performance metrics. Even if it's not doing well, Charney sometimes keeps a story in the lead slot of NPR One if she thinks people really need to know about it. "If they choose to skip it after the first fifteen seconds that's fine because they still found out it's happening," she noted. Monitoring also facilitates quality assurance. At SmartNews, the content operations team is constantly scanning the app for problems such as miscategorized content. The team then fixes these errors directly and manually, while also alerting engineers so that future iterations of the algorithm are improved.

As journalistic newsfeeds evolve and new configurations of algorithms and humans are tested, practices will continue to change. But it is already apparent that shared control, including oversight and monitoring capabilities, are important components that support the integration of algorithmic curation into journalism practice. This is in contrast to major platforms such as Google and Facebook, which have historically taken an overwhelmingly algorithmic-centric approach to curation, underplaying the role that people play in the process and sometimes removing them entirely.[72] But given the limitations of quantification, a dearth of context, and the sometimes fuzzy criteria applied to publication decisions, perhaps the future of algorithmic curation does indeed need to be just a bit more human.

The power to publish is increasingly being delegated to algorithms. Facebook's newsfeed curation and Google's search relevance algorithms direct a large proportion of online attention to news, affecting how people come to know about civic issues, are exposed to diverse perspectives and quality sources of information, build communities, and are informed for the purposes of making important decisions, such as for elections. Platform dominance and power mean that news publishers often have to play by platform rules, optimizing content according to the data and metrics the platforms define. This had led to the use of techniques like headline optimization and content performance prediction. The choice of content optimization metrics is incredibly political though—metrics are an expression of values. While measuring likes, clicks, and shares automatically is easy, measuring social impact is much more challenging. Some news organizations, however, are bucking the dominance of the platform intermediaries to optimize metrics important to their business (such as subscription or loyalty), or even by trying to balance business goals with editorial objectives related to making sure people are informed about important issues in society. As I'll explain further in Chapter 6, this is just the start of how journalists are beginning to push back against the power of algorithms.

6

ALGORITHMIC ACCOUNTABILITY
REPORTING

Imagine you're a young black woman living on Chicago's South Side. In this hypothetical scenario, it's early evening, and you're just back from work, when you hear an unexpected knock on your front door. It's a police officer. "What could he want?" you think to yourself. You did have that brush with the law once—shoplifting—but that was two years ago, and the judge let you go with a warning. The cop hands you a letter that, as you read, explains you're at a high risk for being involved in violent crime. But the thing is, you've never been arrested for violent crime, you're not into drugs, and you stay away from the gangs in the neighborhood.[1] So, what gives?

You've been selected for an intervention by the Chicago Police Department (CPD) based on its Strategic Subjects List (SSL). SSL is a data-driven predictive policing algorithm that assigns a risk score to almost 400,000 people in the Chicago area based on the chance they're going to be the victim or offender in a violent crime. More than 500 notifications were made to people identified as high risk by the algorithm in 2016. In this case, the police visited you because you have a risk score of 499, just one point shy of the maximum score. In the letter you're warned that if you *are* arrested, "The highest possible charges will be pursued." You're on notice, but it's not clear exactly why you had such a high score to begin with.[2]

The promise of predictive policing is quite appealing from a bureaucratic standpoint. Data and algorithms could increase the efficiency of policing and of the justice system, leading to a better management of resources. Predictions can identify people who might benefit from additional social services or early interventions, as well as those who pose less risk and can be released into the community rather than adding to the strain on an already overcrowded prison system. Algorithms can even identify cops with troubling patterns of behavior before they lash out, thereby improving the overall quality of police interactions with the public.[3]

But there are a number of concerns here too. Police can easily abuse risk scores by using them to target individuals as suspects in new crime investigations. Neighborhoods with concentrations of higher risk scores may become overpoliced, creating a pernicious feedback loop leading to more arrests and higher SSL scores in the neighborhood.[4] But perhaps most frustratingly, there is a complete lack of clarity about how the SSL score even works. Is it accurate, unbiased, and fair? The algorithm is entirely opaque, limiting any kind of informed public debate on its merits or shortcomings. That doesn't seem too democratic. Anyone who wants to understand why he or she is on the list and got a particular score is basically in the dark.

At least this was the case until June 2017, when the CPD begrudgingly released data in response to a public records request about SSL.[5] Using the released data, two intrepid reporters were able to reverse-engineer the algorithm and shed light on the importance of various factors in the score.[6] A proxy model—a linear regression fit to the data—showed that the score could be reliably predicted using just eight variables in the public data release.[7] Interestingly, while gang affiliation is often blamed for violence in Chicago, it had a minimally predictive effect on the score (and was in fact later removed by CPD as a contributor to the SSL score). The results illuminate at least some of the factors and their weighting within the calculation of the score (see Figure 6.1).

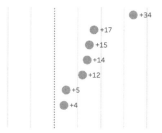

# of assault or battery incidents (as victim)   +34
# of shooting incidents (as victim)   +17
# of arrests for violent offenses   +15
Trend in criminal activity   +14
# of unlawful use of weapon arrests   +12
# of narcotics arrests   +5
Gang affiliation   +4
Age (per decade)   -41

Figure 6.1.   The contribution of each of eight factors in a proxy model predicting the Chicago Police Department's Strategic Subjects List (SSL) scores. The greatest contributor to an increased score is the number of times a person is listed as the victim of an assault or battery, whereas the greatest contributor to a decreased score is age. Source: Original figure by author produced using data derived from a model developed by Rob Arthur using data from the Chicago Police Department.

Predictive policing is of course just one domain where algorithms are being deployed in society. Algorithmic decision-making is now pervasive throughout both the public and private sectors, including in domains such as credit and insurance risk scoring, employment systems that inform hiring and firing, welfare management systems, educational and teacher rankings, and a myriad array of online media ranging from advertising to search engines and curated news feeds.[8] Operating at scale and often affecting large numbers of people, they can make consequential and sometimes contestable calculation, ranking, classification, association, and filtering decisions. Algorithms, and the reams of data driving them, are the new power brokers in society.

But, as the SSL example shows, society largely lacks clarity about how algorithms exercise their decision-making power. Despite their superficial glint of objectivity, algorithms nonetheless reveal mistakes and biases that warrant closer scrutiny.[9] Such mistakes and biases may adversely impact individuals as well as the broader public. How can the public understand the ways in which the power, influence, and bias of an algorithm is refracted through society? This chapter is about the journalistic response to this question. A new strand of computational journalism is emerging to audit and investigate algorithms that have a significant impact on society in order to explain and hold accountable algorithmically informed decisions. I call this "algorithmic accountability reporting," as it is a reorientation of the traditional watchdog function of journalism toward the power wielded through algorithms.[10]

At its core algorithmic accountability is about providing descriptions, explanations, and sometimes even justifications for the behavior of decision-making algorithms, particularly in cases where there was a fault or error. While various forms of algorithmic accountability can take place in diverse forums (political, legal, professional, and so on), the focus here is squarely on algorithmic accountability reporting as an independent journalistic endeavor that contributes to public accountability.[11] The spotlight is on situations of public import and social significance in which a broad array of stakeholders may benefit from additional insight into an algorithm's behavior. This form of public accountability is complementary to other avenues such as by developing regulations, audit institutions, or transparency policies such as algorithmic impact assessments.[12]

An algorithms beat is slowly coalescing as journalistic skills come together with technical skills to provide the scrutiny that many algorithms warrant. In this hybrid endeavor the accountability of algorithms is enabled through the careful, creative, and critical attention of human journalists using computational and data-driven techniques for analysis. The next sections outline the underpinnings of the algorithms beat, including the types of stories it involves, the methodological approaches journalists are applying, and some of the underlying challenges relating to labor, dynamism, and legal access that must be overcome to make the beat thrive. The chapter concludes by examining how journalists can themselves be more accountable with the algorithms they use in news production by building on the norm of transparency.

The Algorithms Beat

Over the last several years algorithms of various ilks have started to garner the attention of inquisitive journalists. Among the most prominent efforts is ProPublica's Machine Bias series, which it began publishing in 2016. This string of investigations into algorithms has included everything from exposing racially biased criminal risk assessment scores used in bail decisions to articulating ad targeting capabilities on Facebook, identifying unfairness in pricing on Amazon.com, locating geographically discriminatory auto insurance rates, and pointing out the lack of transparency in software used in DNA forensics testing for criminal trials.[13] Investigations conducted by my research lab and by me have examined boundaries and mistakes in Google autocomplete filtering that can lead to inappropriate results, as well as identifying unfairness of Uber in terms of lower service quality in neighborhoods where there are greater concentrations of people of color.[14] Other efforts have looked at a diverse array of issues such as price discrimination on e-commerce sites, skewed online rating systems, and the privacy impacts of social recommendation systems. All of these investigations constitute and help characterize the algorithms beat.

What exactly makes an algorithm newsworthy? Oftentimes this boils down to identifying whether it has somehow made a "bad" decision. Violations of an established expectation for how an algorithm ought to be operating are typically interesting to the public. Violations may include an algorithm doing something it wasn't supposed to, as well as *not* doing something it was supposed to. The question of public significance and the consequences of a bad decision are key. What does a failure in any particular decision mean for an individual, or for society? What's the potential for harm? The severity and prevalence of the decision are important factors to consider. An algorithm that recommends a bad movie to watch on Friday night is less newsworthy than one that unjustly contributes to an individual spending more time in prison than is warranted.

The social context of how an algorithmic decision is implemented is crucial. "It's never really just about an algorithm doing harm. It's the context in which the algorithm is being applied and who has power in that position because if it," explained Surya Mattu, the former technical expert on many of ProPublica's Machine Bias investigations. Particularly for the purposes of accountability, it's essential to understand algorithms as sociotechnical assemblages that include not only technical components such as software, models, and data, but also the myriad and dynamic practices and relationships between people and systems that help to enact an overall decision process.[15] These interrelationships complicate and obfuscate who is accountable in an algorithmic system when something goes awry, but at the end of the day there must always be people who are held responsible for an algorithm's behavior. Algorithmic accountability entails understanding how and when people exercise power within and through an algorithmic system, and on whose behalf.[16] The intentions of the people in the system, including those who commissioned, designed, and engineered an algorithmic process, are an important newsworthiness modulator.[17] Even in cases of complete autonomy or those in which the system learns over time from new data, people are responsible for the values embedded in the system, including key components such as the definitions of variables that are optimized, and how algorithms are parameterized. Any investigation into algorithms must recognize and take into account the fact that they are objects of human creation and that their behavior is deeply intertwined in and informed by arrays of people. A blindness to the sociotechnical status of algorithmic systems risks turning algorithms into boogeymen without fully considering the role of humans woven throughout.[18]

In observing the algorithms beat develop over several years, as well as through my own investigations of algorithms, I have identified at least four distinct driving forces that appear to underlie many algorithmic accountability stories: (1) discrimination and unfairness, (2) inaccurate predictions and classifications, (3) violations of laws or social norms, and (4) human misuse of algorithms. While I wouldn't claim that these are exhaustive, they do suggest opportunities for pursuing newsworthy algorithmic accountability stories.

Uncovering discrimination and unfairness is a common theme in algorithmic accountability reporting. Perhaps most striking in this vein is ProPublica's work exposing the racial bias of recidivism risk assessment algorithms in the criminal justice system.[19] Such assessments score individuals on whether they are low risk or high risk for reoffending. Several states use the scores for managing pretrial detention, probation, parole, and even sentencing. ProPublica obtained data via a public records request for thousands of risk scores assessed in Broward County, Florida and then matched these to the criminal histories of defendants to see how the scores lined up with whether they actually recidivated within two years. The investigation found that black defendants tended to be assigned higher risk scores than white defendants and were more likely to be incorrectly labeled as high risk when in fact after two years they hadn't actually been rearrested.[20]

The story sparked a strong rebuttal from Northpointe (since renamed to Equivant), the company that created the risk score, which tried to account for the findings ProPublica published.[21] The company argued that its scores were equally accurate across races and that therefore the scores were fair. But ProPublica pointed out a shortcoming of Northpointe's definition of fairness, which didn't consider the disproportionate volume of mistakes that negatively affect black people.[22] Even with equal prediction accuracy across races (also referred to as predictive parity), if more black people are subjected to errors in the scoring algorithm because they are rated as high risk even though they didn't recidivate, this places an undue burden on a greater number of black people since high risk scores might mean they are incarcerated before trial or given harsher sentences. Stories of discrimination and unfairness hinge on the definitions of fairness applied—and there are a growing number of them[23]—each of which reflects particular political values and suppositions.[24] Ingrained in all the statistics are human decisions about how to define and measure fairness in different contexts. And since it is mathematically impossible to satisfy some alternate definitions of fairness simultaneously, the choice of definition is all the more consequential.[25]

There are typically two kinds of mistakes that classification algorithms make: false positives and false negatives. In criminal risk assessment a false positive is when a person is incorrectly classified as being at high risk for recidivism when in fact he or she is at low risk. A false negative is the reverse, with a person being classified as low risk when in fact he or she is high risk. Developers can tune classification algorithms to have fewer of either type of error, but not fewer of both. Instead, a decrease in false positives typically leads to an increase in false negatives, and vice versa. This adds a political dimension to how developers choose to balance an algorithm's errors, and how that choice impacts different stakeholders. If the balancing favors the interests of powerful business or governmental stakeholders over negative impacts on individuals, that can be an important story to convey to the public.

The significance of both false-positive and false-negative mistakes depends on the semantics surrounding an algorithmic decision. Singling out an individual by some classification decision might lead to either an increase or a decrease in positive or negative treatment for that individual. In other words, sometimes being classified a certain way provides an individual benefit, and other times it is harmful. An error is generally newsworthy when it leads to additional negative treatment for a person, such as when a person is deprived of some right, is denigrated, or has his or her reputation or community standing negatively impacted.[26]

For example, in Massachusetts a man's driver's license was revoked after an antiterrorism facial recognition algorithm incorrectly flagged his image as a fraud.[27] The false positive meant that the man couldn't legally drive, which in turn caused him to lose wages while he waited to have his license restored. Errors are also newsworthy when they lead to a decrease in positive treatment for an individual, such as when an individual misses an opportunity. For instance, a classifier might detect qualified buyers of a niche product for a discount. A false negative in this case would mean a qualified buyer never gets access to the special offer. Such cases are difficult to identify without a bird's eye view of who got what offer. The impacts of errors may also be felt differently by individuals in comparison to the broader society. Consider again the criminal risk assessment case in which a false negative corresponds to falsely labeling a person as low risk when in fact he or she is high risk. While that's great for the individual who evaded additional scrutiny, it creates a greater risk to public safety posed by freeing a person who is more likely to commit a crime again.

Errors in information ranking, association, and filtering can also be newsworthy. Platforms such as Facebook and Google employ a variety of different algorithmic filters (sometimes with humans in the loop) to try to minimize exposure to harmful content including hate speech, violence, or pornography. This can be useful to protect specific vulnerable populations, such as children. For instance, the YouTube Kids app is meant to be a child-friendly source of video material. However, errors in its filtering algorithm mean that sometimes children may encounter inappropriate or violent content.[28] The use of algorithms for filtering out potentially harmful information from view raises the question of the specific criteria and boundaries for that filtering. The type and range of errors will depend on how the algorithm defines and places the filtering boundary. The deployment of filters is complicated by decisions such as how to define "inappropriate" or "hate speech" for which different people or different jurisdictions may have varying opinions about where to draw the line. In other words, errors may not be entirely clear-cut.

An example of a story arising from errors in a filtering algorithm comes from my 2013 study of Google's pornography (and child pornography) filters as implemented in its search autocomplete algorithm, which suggests search queries as soon as the user starts typing.[29] I tested the boundaries of what Google considered to be pornography by automatically inputting 110 different sex-related keywords to see which ones Google would block from being autocompleted. The results showed that many search terms were sensibly blocked (because they clearly lead to pornography), and many were correctly not blocked (such as anatomical terms that people want to be able to search on for medical information). But results also showed some troubling instances in which reasonable people would agree that filtering should take place, such as for cases when the word "child" was added before the pornographic search term. Google should have blocked suggestions for any search terms that led to child pornography, but its algorithm was still letting some through.

There are various other violations of laws or social norms that algorithms can enact, such as taking advantage of human vulnerability or undermining privacy. Since algorithms rely on a narrowly quantified version of reality that only incorporates what is measurable as data, they often miss the social and legal context that would otherwise be essential in rendering an accurate decision. For instance, the state of Florida prohibits price gouging during a state of emergency, but this didn't deter the pricing algorithms of major airlines from ratcheting up the price of a seat more than tenfold for people hoping to escape the path of oncoming Hurricane Irma in 2017.[30] Uber's dynamic pricing algorithm has responded similarly not only to extreme weather events, but also to other situations of public safety such as terrorist attacks. In December 2014, an hours-long hostage situation in Sydney, Australia, initially caused surge pricing on Uber from a rush of people trying to evacuate the immediate area of the incident. A backlash ensued, and Uber instituted a manual override to cap surge pricing later that day.[31] Algorithms that in some way end up exploiting human vulnerability and safety, in these cases by charging exorbitant prices, are oftentimes newsworthy.

Algorithms can impinge on social expectations, such as privacy, too. Predictive algorithms can conjecture a range of sensitive information about someone using just the publicly available information about that individual. A prominent study from 2013 showed that the "likes" that a person makes on Facebook can accurately predict a variety of personal attributes such as sexual orientation, personality traits, political views, and so on.[32] This leads to privacy concerns about the use of inferred attributes without a person's consent or ability to intervene to correct an inaccuracy.[33]

Algorithms can also predict associations between individuals that lead to privacy issues. In one case Facebook's "People You May Know" (PYMK) feature outed the real identity of a sex worker to her clients. PYMK works to algorithmically suggest potential "friends" on the platform. This is problematic not only because of the potential stigma attached to sex work, but also because of the possibility that clients could become stalkers. Despite the woman's care in keeping her real identity separate from her sex-worker identity, the algorithm figured out a connection.[34] PYMK appears to draw on what are sometimes called "shadow profiles," dossiers of information such as phone numbers and email addresses shared with Facebook when people (sometimes just *other* people) upload contacts from their phone address books.[35] If two people have a third person's phone number in the contacts that they've shared with Facebook, they might be suggested to each other in PYMK.

Algorithmic decisions are often embedded in larger decision-making processes that involve other people and algorithms. In some cases, the misuse of an algorithm by a person in the system can be newsworthy. In late 2012 Hurricane Sandy hit the New York City metro area. The storm surge flooded not only many of the train tunnels leading into the city, but also an entire rail yard in New Jersey, leading to the destruction of more than $100 million worth of rail equipment—a substantial economic loss. An investigation showed that much of the damaged equipment could have been safely evacuated if New Jersey Transit had correctly used a software modeling tool to predict the storm surge.[36] Documents acquired via a public records request showed that the modeling software had been misconfigured, leading to specious forecasts for the storm surge. New Jersey could have averted millions of dollars in damage if the software had been used properly.

Bias in algorithmic decisions can often emerge as the result of evolving contexts of use, or simply from a mismatch between the intended or designed-for use and the actual use.[37] Designers can often anticipate a reasonable set of valid contexts for a system's use and thus also articulate constraints on the deployment of the system. If these are ignored in practice, however, they could become interesting stories of negligence, misuse, or obliviousness. The risk assessment scores that were the subject of the story from ProPublica provide a ready example of misuse. "One of the things we found in our reporting is that a lot of people buy this software and then don't ever validate it against their population," explained Jeff Larson, a reporter on the project.[38] Since statistical models can pick up artifacts of bias from whatever data they are trained on, such models must be validated on the population that they are applied to in practice. Broward County in Florida was misusing a risk score designed and calibrated for men by applying it to women as well. Even though Northpointe had validated a scale specifically for a population of women, the county wasn't using it.

Again, the range of examples I've cited are indicative but not exhaustive of algorithmic accountability stories. The beat is still evolving. However, for a summary of the various types of algorithmic accountability stories outlined above, see Table 6.1. Something to keep in mind is that stories about algorithms may not solely relate to algorithmic decisions: how governments procure algorithms and who ultimately owns and controls them may also be worthy angles of coverage.[39] As human inventions algorithms can manifest the entire range of negative human behavior traditionally of interest to investigative journalists, from aiding in theft and corruption to enabling abuse, harassment, fraud, deception, or favoritism. There is a wide territory to cover in

Table 6.1.   Types of algorithmic accountability stories.

Basis for Newsworthiness	Example Impetus for Story
Discrimination or bias	Systematic disparity in the scoring, classification, or ranking of different groups of people (e.g., criminal risk assessments)
	Choice of definitions (e.g., "fairness")
Errors in outputs	Errors leading to an increase in negative treatment or attention (e.g., deprivation of right)
	Errors leading to a decrease in positive treatment (e.g., missed opportunity)
	Errors leading to collective harms (e.g., public safety)
	Errors leading to failure to protect vulnerable populations (e.g., children)
	"Errors" that may be contestable (e.g., people may disagree about what speech is appropriate to filter)
Legal or social norm violations	Exploitation of human vulnerability
	Privacy violations
Misuse within sociotechnical system	Improper configuration or parameterization
	Disregard for appropriate contexts of use

seeking accountability of algorithmic bias, power, and influence in society.

Getting the Story

There is no one method for understanding and exposing how the power of algorithmic decisions is exercised. An exposé of systematic discrimination against an entire class of people needs a different methodological approach than a story reporting on a specific individual deprived of a right, and an investigation into the misuse of an algorithm in a sociotechnical system would call for yet another approach entirely. Some stories will require methods that draw on social science audit techniques, while others benefit from quasi-ethnographic methods, or more casual poking and prodding to understand algorithmic reactions. Many stories will still require traditional journalistic sourcing to find affected individuals or acquire documents via public records requests. Algorithmic accountability will ultimately be best served by a flexible and scrappy methodological inclination. A summary of the methods discussed next is shown in Table 6.2.

Reverse-engineering approaches can help to reveal the nuts and bolts of algorithms, uncovering the specifications of how such technical systems function to arrive at some decision.[40] These specifications might include, for instance, data the system uses, including how that data is defined, measured, and sampled; the variables or features the algorithm is paying attention to and the importance of those features in a statistical model; and the rules or models that describe how the algorithm transforms inputs to outputs. In science and engineering the process of deducing models from observed data is called "system identification" and has been around for more than thirty years.[41] But in journalism the use of these techniques is much more recent, where the goal is less often to reveal some exact mathematical formula than to critically understand the operational logic of the system.[42] For the SSL story mentioned earlier, reporters used publicly released data to create a proxy model that suggested the weighting and importance of the various variables in the actual model. Because the proxy model accounted for a large amount of variance of the SSL score, the reporters became more confident that it was a reasonable facsimile of the model used by the CPD to calculate the scores. Despite the department's claim that it was impossible to reverse engineer the score, additional reporting and discussion with the creator of the algorithm at the Illinois Institute of Technology buttressed the feasibility of the approach.

Auditing techniques have also been fruitfully applied in algorithmic accountability reporting. These techniques have a long history stretching back to the 1940s and 1950s, when they began to be used to study issues not well-suited to standard survey or interview techniques because of social desirability bias.[43] Instead of asking a landlord, "Are you racist against blacks?" which may elicit a perfunctory denial, audit techniques assess questions such as racial discrimination by directly observing behavior. A classic version of an audit study might send two equally qualified applicants of different races to a landlord to inquire about renting an apartment and then observe their subsequent treatment. Repeating this for many landlords could build a picture of racial discrimination in a particular housing market.

Journalists can also use audits to study algorithms,[44] such as by quantifying false positives and negatives and looking for evidence of discrimination. Algorithms always have an ingress and an egress for data: inputs and outputs. Journalists can exploit these to audit the behavior of the algorithm across a wide range of inputs, correlating those inputs to outputs and building a theory of how the algorithm may be functioning. In order for this method to be reliable, an investigator needs access to the algorithm's inputs and outputs. Sometimes Application Programming Interfaces (APIs) allow for direct access to an algorithm, and in other cases algorithmic results are published on web pages from which journalists can scrape outputs. However, in many cases algorithms are hidden behind organizational boundaries, making it impossible to vary inputs and record outputs. For government algorithms public records laws may be used to compel the disclosure of various outputs from the algorithm and evaluate those outputs against some benchmark. This is how ProPublica's criminal risk score audit came about: a public records request for the scores (output) was combined with recidivism data scraped from police websites (benchmark). Journalists joined the datasets and assessed the false positive and false negative rates across races.

Another approach to auditing makes use of so-called "sock puppet" accounts to impersonate real users. This allows the auditor to observing the algorithm from the perspectives of many artificial users. These varied perspectives can then be scraped and analyzed in aggregate to better understand how the algorithm is adapting outputs for users. This approach can be quite useful for the study of online platforms or other personalized systems. For the *Wall Street Journal* it has been effective in studying price discrimination (offering different prices to different people) on e-commerce sites.[45] By polling different websites such as Staples, Home Depot, and Orbitz, reporters found that prices were being adjusted dynamically based on factors such as user geography, browser history, or use of a mobile browser. To get the story the journalists constructed different user profiles and then simulated site visits from different geographics, each time recording the price offered for a particular set of products. They then correlated prices to the relevant aspects of the fake profiles in order to understand how the algorithm was adapting and personalizing prices.

Instead of using fake accounts to study algorithms, journalists can also use crowdsourcing techniques to marshal real people to participate in an audit. This is particularly useful for studying personalized algorithms, since each individual may have a unique "view" of output of the algorithm. Sometimes volunteered user information can provide anecdotal or qualitative evidence of instances when an algorithm has violated expectations. For example, Gizmodo's investigation of Facebook's PYMK involved creating a desktop application that users can download to their

computer to track PYMK results for themselves every six hours
and to store the results on their computer in order to maintain
individual privacy.[46] The reporters who created the app then so-
licited tips from users who thought any of their results were worrisome or surprising.

In Germany a crowdsourcing technique was used to collect
data from more than 4,000 people who contributed to an audit
of Google search results during the 2017 elections. Such activities are sometimes framed as "data donations" and work by re-
cruiting a variety of people to install a browser plugin that can
report data back to the newsroom.[47] Several news outlets have
also used the crowdsourcing approach to help study ad-targeting
on Facebook.[48] In this case the data collected might include details of the ads the person sees or the explanation text of why they
saw those ads. At the *New York Times* the approach resulted in
the collection of about 18,000 ads from approximately 1,000
people in the run-up to the 2016 US election. The downside to
the crowdsourcing approach, in particular in comparison to the
use of fake accounts, is a lack of control in the sampling of the
data. This leads to a sample biased toward a set of self-selected
enthusiastic readers of a particular publication. Moreover, users
may see this approach as somewhat intrusive—they need to be
OK with running the browser plugin software for some period
of time on their own computer. Such concerns might be alleviated by providing independent security audits of the plugin code,
making each instance of data-sharing an opt-in so there is no
sense of illicit surveillance of the user, as well as by making a
plugin open source and open for inspection.

Audits don't always have to be extremely formal endeavors
that rely on data analysis, however. A phenomenological approach
involving casual poking and prodding can sometimes reveal algorithmic reactions that expose a critical or salient weakness evident from a user's experience of the algorithm.[49] One BuzzFeed
story, for instance, was built on the personal experience of a

reporter using Facebook. She was able to illustrate and critique the shift Facebook had made in its newsfeed algorithm to prioritize posts that generate a lot of conversation.[50] By posting something annoying that generated a lot of comments she observed the stickiness of the post in the newsfeeds of friends, whose written ire in turn goaded the algorithm into a loop it couldn't quite escape. The story made the meaning of Facebook's algorithm change more salient and visceral to readers in terms of how it might impact their newsfeed experience.

Yet another method that can be employed for algorithmic accountability reporting is to examine the code of the algorithm. Oftentimes this is neither viable nor feasible, however. Corporations usually view their algorithms as trade secrets and sources of competitive advantage, making it unlikely they would release code for public inspection. And even if that code were to be made public, many complex systems that feed on dynamic data and have feedback loops with other algorithms or people produce outputs that are difficult or even impossible to interpret simply by reading the code. This complexity makes certain types of issues such as discrimination more likely to be emergent from a constellation of interacting code, data, and people. As a result, looking for "smoking gun" discriminatory code may not be as fruitful as considering whether the overall output of the system is discriminatory.[51]

While there are severe limitations to code inspections, they may still be viable in some scenarios, however. In particular, they may be important in cases where complex regulations are difficult to translate into code and warrant verification, or in cases when outcomes are not possible to verify against a ground truth at all and so correctness of intended implementation is essential. For instance, an audit of the Colorado Benefits Management System (CBMS) in 2005 found thousands of erroneous state benefit calculations, many of which were attributable to the incorrect translation of policy rules into computer code.[52] Consider

Table 6.2.   Algorithmic accountability reporting methods and use contexts.

Method	Use Context
Reverse-Engineering	Identify weighting of factors (i.e., input sensitivities)
Auditing	Quantify false positives and false negatives to assess bias
	Characterize associations between inputs and outputs
	Identify boundaries of filtering
Sock Puppets	Systematically collect data on algorithmic adaptation
Crowdsourcing	Collect data on algorithmic personalization
	Collect anecdotal tips of unexpected algorithmic behavior
Phenomenological	Illustration and storytelling around algorithmic reactions to users
Code Inspection	Verification of intended implementation

also something like the algorithms used to assess the probability that an individual's DNA is present in a mixture of DNA swabbed from a crime scene. In some cases there may not be any corroborating evidence of a defendant's presence at a scene of a crime. Because there is no oracle that can provide the absolute truth, it's important to, at the very least, hold accountable how a DNA testing algorithm's outcome was predicted. A code audit could, in some cases, ensure an algorithm was implemented according to the highest professional standards and that its calculations are mathematically correct and implemented fastidiously.[53] Pro-Publica pursued this path when it filed a motion in court to get the code of one particular DNA testing algorithm used in thousands of criminal cases in the state of New York.[54] The code is now publicly available for all to inspect.

Outcomes versus Process

The idea of a source code review makes salient a distinction between two different types of algorithmic accountability: outcome accountability and process accountability. These are, by and large, what they say on the box. Outcome accountability is about monitoring and measuring the outputs of some process—the *what*— whereas process accountability is about adhering to a standard procedure for arriving at a desired outcome—the *how*.[55]

Outcome accountability often takes precedence in the context of journalism. Identifying the presence of algorithmic discrimination has more value to society as an initial step than explaining exactly *how* that discrimination came about. Describing problematic outputs provides a first order diagnostic of algorithmic harms that other actors may then take up as they consider responses and solutions. A journalistic alarm concerning some societal harm might induce congress to hold hearings to compel a more complete accounting from the target, and eventually regulations may be created to mitigate the harm in the future. A focus on outputs and how they impact particular individuals also facilitates more compelling journalistic storytelling, since it not only articulates the harm, but also features specific representative individuals who are the subject of that harm. This provides a more salient and memorable hook than a dry description of some process gone awry. Finally, on a pragmatic note, it's easier to define outcomes that generalize across diverse jurisdictions. Rather than assessing whether an algorithmic process is in adherence to local law, which may vary extensively, auditors can define a single outcome such as "recidivism" once and then apply it uniformly across localities.

There are, however, situations in which eliciting the process really does matter for accountability. These include cases that arouse suspicion of a violation of due process where culpability is exacerbated by ignorance of some accepted process, and for any process where the outcome is *new* knowledge that cannot be assessed against a known expected outcome. Ensuring due

process entails having an opportunity for a "hearing" to examine evidence, which in the case of algorithms entails seeing
the input data and algorithmic logic applied.[56] In situations of
severe deprivation, where for instance liberty may be at stake,
process accountability becomes important for ensuring legitimacy. Process accountability can also be a way for determining
the culpability of people in an algorithmic system. The "culpably
ignorant" are responsible for bad outcomes if they knowingly
avoid adhering to a process, such as an industry best practice,
that would have prevented that bad outcome.[57] Finally, process
accountability is important for any algorithm that creates new
knowledge, and which therefore can't be compared to some expected outcome, such as during DNA mixture testing. In open
science, process accountability is upheld when scientists not only
describe their methods but also disclose their data and code so
that peers can judge whether those methods were a sound way
to arrive at the new piece of knowledge.

Information Deficits

Algorithmic accountability is extraordinarily challenging for
external auditors. Acute information deficits limit auditors' ability
to know where to start and what to ask, to interpret results in
the appropriate context, and to explain why they're seeing the
patterns they're seeing from an algorithm. "A lot of times you
don't even know that they're being used. So you're kind of reliant on knowing that at least before you can even request data,"
explained Rob Arthur, one of the reporters that reverse-engineered
the SSL score.[58]

   Oftentimes all that's available are trickles of information exposed through blog posts, public data releases, interviews, or pat-
ents. For government algorithms, public records requests can
sometimes provide additional information. Such algorithmic
transparency can be invaluable, lowering the barrier to pursuing
an investigation by narrowing information gaps and equipping
stakeholders to monitor, check, criticize, or intervene in an algo-

rithmic decision process.[59] Of course, more information does not automatically equal more accountability. But additional transparency can certainly enable accountability, particularly when actors such as computational journalists are able to make sense of and act on the additional information.[60] Even so, journalists must be wary, as the target may continue to control information disclosure and strategically shape the interpretation of the system. Important elements such as what variables or inputs an algorithm is paying attention to may be incomplete or obfuscated. Even though the CPD released eight of the variables that it said it used to predict SSL scores, it withheld other variables and used that as leverage to undermine confidence in the proxy model results that were ultimately published.

Understanding and explaining *why* an algorithm has made a decision can be extremely difficult using observational audit methods alone.[61] Statistical issues such as omitted variable bias can make it appear as if one variable (for example, race) is more predictive of outcomes than it may actually be, thereby confounding attempts to pin down the source of observed biases.[62] Complementary reporting methods, including interviews and document reviews (or in some cases code reviews), can shed further light on system behavior. Yet even then, the designers of algorithms themselves may not know exactly why a particular variable is predictive of, for instance, a high risk score. Many algorithm audits will be limited to description and characterization of readily observed outcomes and may struggle to explain why a particular result came about.

Expectation Setting

A focus on outcomes means that expectations must be clearly defined and, ideally, agreed upon by stakeholders. But what *should* our collective expectations of an algorithm be in any given situation, and where does that expectation come from? Oftentimes expectations depend on context, and so each scenario where an algorithmic decision is made may spur a different set of expectations. There may be various statistical, moral, social, cultural, and legal standards or norms that create applicable expectations, not to mention that expectations can change over time. To point out just one distinction: the mandate for accountability of algorithms differs between government and private sector usage in that the former is about democratic legitimacy, and the latter is about corporate responsibility or in some cases corporate legal concerns.[63] Different expectations of fairness may be triggered when an algorithm scores someone in the criminal justice system versus when one charges different prices for airline seats.

Clear and well-motivated definitions of outcomes are essential for setting expectations. Sometimes expectations can be set quantitatively by defining a baseline according to some existing and accepted set of outcomes or from a comparable system that provides a point of reference. Consider, for example, my research lab's investigation of bias in the image results of 2016 US presidential candidates on Google. We compared the images selected by the search algorithm for inclusion on the main results page against the entire set of images of each candidate during the same time period as found through Google Image Search.[64] The Google Image Search results provided a data-driven baseline, or statistical expectation, based on the universe of images Google had indexed on each candidate. The images selected for the main results pages could then be meaningfully compared to provide a contrast and help distinguish the bias of the search algorithm from the bias of the input images.

Sometimes it's easy to find a consensus definition for an outcome. It's uncontroversial to claim that an average rating of 4.1 should be rounded down to 4.0 in a ratings interface, whereas a rating of 4.4 could reasonably be rounded up to 4.5 if the interface incorporates half-steps. We expect this because of a common logical understanding of how mathematics defines the rounding of numbers. And so when FiveThirtyEight reported that Fandango was rounding up ratings such as 4.1 to 4.5 in its movie ratings interface, it was an obvious violation of expectations for how that algorithm was functioning. It was systematically inflating the movie ratings people saw on the site.[65]

In many other cases definitions are not universally agreed upon, spurring questions such as "Whose definition is right?" and "Who benefits from this definition?" ProPublica published a story that pointed out a self-serving definition used by the Amazon.com algorithm to determine which items to place in the "buy box" on its site.[66] Amazon's ranking algorithm selects merchants to feature in that lucrative position on the page based on the cost of the product sought plus the cost of shipping. Because products sold by Amazon itself (or its affiliates) are eligible for free shipping (if the order is large enough or if the user is a Prime subscriber) this means that Amazon's own products or those of affiliates that pay to have orders fulfilled by Amazon's warehouses are privileged by the algorithm. This type of definition quickly becomes politically charged, as different stakeholders may not agree that it is a fair and appropriate definition. Nonaffiliate merchants on Amazon struggle to compete because of the way the ranking algorithm is defined.

Common uncontested principles may help set reasonable and acceptable moral expectations for how algorithms treat decision subjects across a variety of contexts.[67] Scholars make a distinction between universal values (such as basic liberty and equality) and doctrinal beliefs (whether they be religious, moral, political, and so on). Universal values are those that reasonable people could be expected to share, without appealing to any kind of controversial claims. They adhere to the democratic ideal of public reason. Investigators might strive to define expectations for algorithms according to such universal public values. This would serve to diminish the ability of a target entity to undermine a call for accountability of its algorithms because an expectation is somehow seen as controversial. A reasonable place to start for widely held public values is the United Nations Universal Declaration of Human Rights which promulgates rights such as freedom, security, expression, and property as well as protections from discrimination, slavery, and arbitrary arrest or detention.[68] At a minimum, society might agree to and expect that algorithmic decisions do not violate these rights and protections.

Whether based on definitions, or on data-driven baselines, setting the outcome expectations for algorithms should always be well-reasoned and rationalized. Given the range of definitions of fairness, for instance, journalists should provide a compelling rationale for how they measure fairness in the particular domain they're investigating. Ultimately, investigators of algorithmic power must convince their audience and other societal stakeholders that the expected outcomes they are holding an algorithm accountable for are appropriate and legitimate and not frivolous or partisan.

Legal Access

Journalists cannot investigate what they don't know about or can't gain access to. Nor can they compare algorithmic outputs to any particular benchmarks or expectations without an ability to observe and measure those outputs. Laws governing access to information about algorithms moderate the ability of journalists to confidently and thoroughly investigate algorithmic power in society. Specific legal implementations and their related concerns will vary, of course, from jurisdiction to jurisdiction, but the focus here is on legal barriers to access within the United States. The legal context is a bit different in public- and private-sector algorithms, and the situation becomes further complicated as privately developed algorithms encroach into the public sector.

For algorithms in use in government, freedom of information laws stipulate the types of information that is compulsory to disclose. At the federal level, the Freedom of Information Act (FOIA) permits members of the public to request access to records from federal agencies. Analogous statutes regulate access to state information. Public records laws, however, suffer from inconsistency in their application to information about algorithms, even across different federal government agencies.[69] Moreover, FOIA requests can be rebuffed on account of any of nine exemptions. For instance, exemption number 4 can be cited to reject a request on the grounds that it would violate the trade secret rights of a corporation whose algorithm is contracted for use by the government.

In 2015 I worked with students to request public records related to algorithms used in criminal justice (such as for parole, probation, bail, or sentencing) from each of the fifty states.[70] We asked for everything we could think of: documents, formulas, data, validation assessments, contracts, and source code.[71] But we didn't get much information back. In one case we received a mathematical description of an algorithm, and from a few other states we received some relevant documents. But in nine cases states refused to supply information on the grounds that the information we requested was owned by a third-party corporation or that the state was contractually prohibited from releasing the requested information. A different analysis of seventy-three FOI requests for algorithms found that 29 percent were granted, with the rest either denied or pending. Denials cited a range of exemptions relating to national security, trade secrets, privacy, and law enforcement.[72] Yet another project made forty-two public records requests across twenty-three states for six different algorithms related to predictive policing, child welfare, and teacher evaluation. Only one jurisdiction was able to produce an actual predictive algorithm with enough detail to describe how it had been developed and validated.[73] Broad assertions related to trade secrecy or confidentiality were a problem, as was a general lack of adequate record keeping by agencies such that they could produce documents explaining how their algorithms worked.

Despite the uneven results, public records requests can still produce useful background information about algorithms in use. Records relating to contracts, software, data, mathematical descriptions, training materials, validation studies, correspondence, or other documentation can all provide rich context for how a system works, what the design goals may have been, what the expectations for outputs may be, and how a third party system was contracted. Because of the inconsistency in responsiveness of some jurisdictions, as well as variability in how different jurisdictions negotiate to retain information rights when contracting algorithms from third parties, requesting information about an algorithm in use across different localities increases the chances for receiving relevant information. Even if most jurisdictions rebuff the requests, one of them might come through.

FOIA laws are applicable only to government use of algorithms and have no power to compel information about private sector use. In the private arena this raises the stakes for methods such as reverse-engineering and auditing. The ability to audit private systems is, however, subject to other legal considerations, such as the Computer Fraud and Abuse Act (CFAA). This law creates a chilling effect on the ability of researchers, journalists, and others who wish to audit algorithms online by implying that a terms of service (ToS) contractual violation may form the basis for liability under CFAA.[74] In visiting and using an online website, we all implicitly accept the site's ToS. And because many ToS prevent scraping or the use of fictitious user accounts, among other things, auditing techniques can potentially be liable under the statute. In order to avoid violation attorneys at the American Civil Liberties Union recommend tactics such as minimizing impacts on the computer systems of targets, and making algorithm audits look like traditional social science audits whose legality have already been upheld by court precedents. In some cases the fear of negative publicity that might result if a large corporation sues a journalist who is trying to audit whether it is discriminatory could provide cover. But this also depends on whether the company is public-facing and sensitized to the threat of boycotts or other social backlash.

Moving Targets

Google typically changes its search algorithm 500–600 times per year, while the city of Chicago is on version five of the SSL algorithm in as many years. As creatures of human design, algorithms can be updated on a whim. An algorithm may stay stable for some period of time or evolve slowly as new training data is used to update a model. But algorithmic behavior can just as well be punctuated by major step changes. And whether it's quick changes or slow evolution, major updates or minor tweaks, those changes may go largely unnoticed.[75] The dynamic and capricious nature of algorithms presents challenges for algorithmic accountability reporting.

Ideally algorithmic systems should be monitored over time. A key underlying question is to first determine how often an algorithm *may* be changing, including the mechanisms for that change, and to pursue a variety of reporting tactics to understand when a technical change that has potentially newsworthy consequences might be rolled out. The expected frequency and significance of changes will inform how often algorithms are audited and whether additional resources for auditing are needed. For instance, periodic public records requests may need to be filed in Chicago every year in order to track changes in the SSL scoring algorithm.

If an algorithm changes as often as the Google search algorithm does, it may even warrant continuous monitoring—something automation may help with. Journalistic data-mining techniques may be useful to alert journalists to substantive differences in algorithm outputs. And the explanation of highly dynamic algorithms can be enabled by the application of automated content production. Static news articles, while they may suffice to describe a snapshot of behavior around an algorithm, may be wholly inadequate to convey information about algorithms that demand routine and ongoing monitoring. More dynamic ways to present the results of algorithm audits will need to be developed, giving rise to new opportunities for journalistic coverage of algorithms. Covering algorithms will require the use of algorithms. All of this is not to suggest that algorithmic accountability can or should be entirely automated using data mining and content generation. What appears abundantly clear is that domain expertise will be essential for contextually defining expectations, interpreting the significance of algorithms, and creatively applying a critical stance on the question of how algorithms may be exerting power.

The Human Resource

Effective algorithmic accountability reporting demands all of the traditional skills journalists need in reporting and interviewing, as well as domain knowledge of a beat, familiarity with public records requests, and ability to write about data-driven results clearly and compellingly, along with a host of new capabilities such as scraping and cleaning data, designing audit studies, and using advanced statistical techniques. Crowdsourcing methods benefit from strong social media engagement skills. Good luck finding a single person who can do all of these things.

In practice, many of the examples cited in this chapter come about through partnerships or teamwork. The work is decomposed into subtasks for which individuals have acquired advanced skills, and the final output is synthesized through iterative collaboration. To take one example, the SSL reverse engineering story came about through a partnership between Jeff Asher, who has deep domain knowledge of crime data from civil and journalistic work, and Rob Arthur who has a PhD in genetics and has advanced expertise in data analysis and modeling. Rob took the lead on the statistical modeling aspect of the project, trying out different models such as random forests or support vector machines and assessing their fit. Using these results, Jeff then worked to evaluate what they meant in terms of what the CPD had claimed publicly. They both have experience as reporters and could divvy-up the tasks of setting up and undertaking interviews, but Jeff's domain knowledge about crime made finding the right people to interview easier. Here we see the value of advanced methodological training coming into play with deep domain knowledge of a particular beat.

A similar story can be told for the way the various investigations in the Machine Bias series at ProPublica came about. Surya Mattu explained how he would often do the heavy lifting in terms of writing scrapers to collect data, but then Jeff Larson would take on more advanced analysis of the data. Lauren Kirchner would do more "email-driven" data collection, including reporting tasks such as asking relevant people for information the team needed. The team's leader, Julia Angwin, had "an amazing ability to understand 'nerd talk,'" explained Mattu. She could parse technical material about the algorithms under investigation in terms of what it meant journalistically for the broader project.

Technologists and methods specialists will have expertise relating to the feasibility and limits of reverse-engineering, auditing, and crowdsourcing techniques for gathering information about algorithms, while nontechnical journalists will have expertise in public records requests, reporting, document analysis, and domain knowledge that enables interpretations revealing the societal significance of algorithms. Expertise in each of these areas may be distributed among a team as long as clear communication, awareness, and leadership are present to make the relevant decisions in delegation and reintegration of work. A senior reporter unaware of what information could be gathered about an algorithm through auditing techniques, for instance, will be limited in what he or she can learn about the algorithm. At the same time, a computer programmer can build an extensive database of political ads, but without the domain knowledge of a politics reporter all but the most obvious leads will go unnoticed. Bringing together technical and nontechnical domain expertise will make algorithmic accountability reporting more robust. Moreover, by operating in teams, methods specialists can partner with *different* domain experts to understand algorithmic power across a variety of social domains.

Accountability of Algorithmic Media

Whether in data mining, automatic content production, newsbots, or the distribution chain, news organizations themselves are rapidly incorporating algorithms that broadly impact how people encounter news media. The various editorial decisions algorithms make to include information or exclude it, highlight it and make it salient are consequential to the flows and pace of online attention, with potential impacts on the convening of publics and the fair and uniform provision of quality information.[76] Biases baked into algorithmic systems can skew public perceptions or guide people astray in ways that undermine democratic ideals. How do we ensure the accountability of the algorithmic media system itself? Absent a costly ad infinitum application of algorithmic accountability reporting by successive layers of news media, other avenues for the accountability of algorithmic media must be explored.

Formal and enforceable media accountability is a difficult proposition in some democracies, when the right to free speech creates an aversion to legislation of the press. The dearth of enforceable accountability via regulation in turn raises the importance of other approaches to media accountability, such as healthy media criticism capable of pointing out failures, clear codes of ethical conduct that engender norms for proper behavior (and contribute to process accountability), and transparency so that stakeholders can have a window into the news production process.[77] Each of these approaches is important on its own and warrants further research and attention, but my focus here is on the concept of transparency and its applicability to algorithms in use in the media. While acknowledging it is not a panacea for all of algorithmic media's misgivings,[78] my goal here is to examine how algorithmic transparency can still contribute to a more accountable media system.

Transparency is an appropriate approach toward the ethical and accountable use of algorithms in the context of journalism because of its growing stature as an important norm for practice in the field.[79] It is now prominently listed as a guiding concept in several ethics codes such as those of the Society for Professional

Journalists and the Radio Television Digital News Association. Journalistic transparency can be defined as the "ways in which people both inside and external to journalism are given a chance to monitor, check, criticize and even intervene in the journalistic process."[80] Disclosing information about the news production process—transparency of method—allows the public to monitor the workings and performance of that process and reinforces the legitimacy of a media outlet as an honest and ethical purveyor of information. Demonstrating adherence to common standards of practice further supports process accountability. There is end-user demand for algorithmic transparency too. In a survey of 120 users of the personalized news app Blendle, 74 percent reported that they wanted to see more information about why articles were selected for them.[81]

Transparency is not a binary concept—it's not all or nothing. Instead, there's a spectrum of information about editorial processes that creators can make transparent. Different degrees and treatments of transparency information will be needed for various stakeholders such as the public, other organizations, or sources. Traditionally transparency in newswork has meant being forthright about the use of evidence and the qualifications or expertise of sources, for instance, as well as about any conflicts related to partners or funders.[82] The normative goal is to offer a window onto editorial decision-making. Creating that window is a bit more challenging for algorithmic transparency, however: technical complexity, sociotechnical intermingling, and machine-learning feedback loops can obscure clear sight lines into the basis for outputs of the system.[83]

Nonetheless, a number of informational dimensions can be disclosed about algorithms. These include aspects of the data, model, and inferencing used by the algorithm.[84] At the data layer, the information quality of the data feeding the algorithms is paramount. Relevant information can be disclosed about data accuracy, uncertainty, timeliness, comprehensiveness, and provenance as well as how data have been transformed, validated, cleaned, and edited. Aspects of the model used, such as the features, variables, and weights, can also be disclosed alongside descriptions of any assumptions, rules, or constraints the model adheres to. Transparency might also include information about the types of inferences made (such as predictions or classifications), as well as providing error analysis and confidence values for inferences. The human influences in algorithmic systems are also essential to articulate in any transparency disclosure. These might include editorial goals, rationale for filtering inputs and outputs, and how governance structures permit adjustments to the system over time. In many cases disclosure of the code itself will be unnecessary.

One situation where transparency crops up is in how news organizations choose to label or byline automatically generated content. At the *Washington Post,* automatically produced articles come with the addendum, "This story may be updated if more information becomes available. It is powered by Heliograf, *The Post*'s artificial intelligence system." The Associated Press similarly labels content that is produced automatically, and modifies the attribution if an article is entirely automatic or is produced in collaboration with a person. Early research examining different byline policies on automated content suggests, however, that there is a lack of consensus on best practices.[85] Yet it seems clear that being forthright with news consumers means that automatically produced content should minimally be labeled as such, possibly bylined to the news organization's software, its third-party software vendor, or individual reporters or software engineers who creatively contributed to what the system outputs.

Transparency is just one component of ethical behavior within journalism and may be weighed against competing norms such as a desire to seek the truth and to minimize harm to the public.[86] For instance, the transparency ideal is routinely violated by the use of anonymous sources. But this violation is deemed legitimate in cases where the source may face a risk of personal harm or reprisal for sharing sensitive information. Similarly, algorithmic transparency may not always "win out" over other important normative goals or external constraints guiding journalistic responsibility.[87] Journalists are less likely to adopt algorithmic transparency that creates harm for individuals or society (because it allows systems to be undermined through gaming or manipulation, violates privacy, or overwhelms end users with superfluous information) or threatens the truth-seeking process. In contrast, journalists are more likely to adopt algorithmic transparency when it mitigates public harm (for example, by alerting people to efforts to attenuate echo chambers) and reinforces the truth-seeking process.

Editorial transparency has gained traction for some news organizations wishing to show their computational and data-driven methods for larger enterprise stories. For instance, ProPublica often publishes white papers describing statistical methodologies used, and organizations such as BuzzFeed News and FiveThirty-Eight maintain repositories on Github, where they open-source data and code used in some of their stories.[88] The Associated Press is transparent about the algorithms and data used in the production of its data journalism so that its members can verify the analysis for themselves.[89] This type of transparency supports basic methodological replicability, as well as buttressing the acceptability of computational evidence for an investigation much as a scientist would. In these cases the value of transparency of method is aligned with the normative goal of truth-seeking: demonstrating the rigor and validity of methods reinforces the stature of evidence for a knowledge claim.

In some cases, however, transparency of computational methods comes into tension with other goals, such as minimizing harm. "The Tennis Racket" published by BuzzFeed News is a nice illustration of how this tension plays out in the context of privacy concerns.[90] The story investigated the issue of fraud in professional tennis by simulating the likelihood that professional tennis players had intentionally lost matches so that confederates could bet against the players and earn windfalls. BuzzFeed News opted not to publish the names of the suspicious players, either in the article or in the accompanying data or code they published. They argued that the statistical evidence provided by their simulations was not definitive and so did not want to cause undue harm by naming individual players. In this case, the desire to minimize harm for individuals in the face of uncertain evidence won out over the desire to be entirely transparent by including names in the published data analysis. Interestingly enough, the source code and detailed methodology published with the story allowed students at Stanford University to figure out the identities relatively quickly, by re-scraping the original data with identities preserved and then repeating the analysis with the code that BuzzFeed had published. While it's not clear that BuzzFeed was *too* transparent in this case, it does raise interesting questions about where to draw the line in enabling reproducibility of journalistic investigations, especially when they bring about statistical indictments of individuals.[91]

In addition to professional norms that compete for priority with transparency in editorial scenarios, there are additional pressures from the business side of news organizations that can impinge on the implementation of transparency. A fairly straightforward business consideration is the cost of producing transparency information. Preparing and periodically updating data, documentation, and benchmark tests incur ongoing expenses that organizations may need to balance against potential benefits. Moreover, as technical innovations, algorithms may offer business advantages in scenarios such as content optimization across various formats and channels, making news organizations reluctant to open up.

A desire to protect the proprietary intellectual property and trade secrets that inhere to algorithms will often diminish attempts at transparency, but it doesn't have to subvert them entirely. For instance, National Public Radio published a written treatise about the use of algorithms to curate and personalize content in its NPR One app.[92] The managing editor of the app, Tamar Charney, explained, "I wanted to divulge enough of it so that people understood what we're doing and have confidence in what we're doing without making it possible for somebody to go 'Oh well I can just do what NPR One does.'" Since there is a spectrum of transparency information that can be disclosed, managing business and proprietary concerns entails striking a balance to ensure that the disclosure isn't compromising the product, but is communicating something of value about the editorial integrity of the product. In this case Charney wanted to ensure that people understood that the personalization practiced by NPR One wouldn't compromise the overarching editorial mission of the organization: to build an informed citizenship with a broader sense of the world. The value of transparency in this case was about communicating the goals of the algorithm and how the algorithm was being responsibly used to support those goals— something that could be accomplished without divulging proprietary details of the algorithm's implementation.

Operating at scale and often affecting large groups of people, algorithms make consequential and sometimes contestable decisions in an increasing range of domains throughout the public and private sectors. In response, a distinct beat in journalism is emerging to investigate the societal power exerted through such algorithms. There are various newsworthy angles on algorithms including discrimination and unfairness, errors and mistakes, social and legal norm violations, and human misuse. Reverse-engineering and auditing techniques can be used to elucidate the contours of algorithmic power. Yet auditing algorithms is not for the faint of heart. Information deficits, expectation setting, limited legal access, and shifting targets can all hamper an investigation. Operating in teams, methods specialists can work with domain experts to overcome these obstacles and publish important stories about algorithms in society. At the same time, journalists themselves must grapple with their own use of algorithms in the production and publication of information. Techniques for algorithmic transparency can enable increased accountability of algorithmic media.

CONCLUSION:

THE FUTURE OF ALGORITHMIC NEWS MEDIA

Algorithms lack animus; they are inert. What animates algorithms are the people who design, develop, operate, and manage them. It is people who define, measure, and sample data to feed and train algorithms. And it is people who consume and are impacted by algorithmic outputs and decisions. I've stressed in this book that as algorithms grow in their capabilities for data mining, automated content production, and curation, journalists and society must not forget the role people will play in the future of algorithmic media. Sometimes that role will be direct—as the writer of a script for a newsbot. But oftentimes there are levels of indirection for human influence in these systems, such as through the data that is defined and sampled to train a machine-learning classifier. We, the people, have agency in—and responsibility for—how these systems ultimately operate and influence the media. The future of algorithmic media must be human-centered.

The main challenges are how to harness the power of algorithms to speed up, scale up, and personalize content while staying true to preferred values, and how to steer toward outcomes that are beneficial to individuals, groups, and society while balancing business concerns. Journalists and other designers of algorithmic media need to be more deliberate about the values they are building into systems, particularly if they want those values to be reflected prominently in the algorithms and artificial intelligence that drive the future of the media. No longer should they be content to say things like "I know news when I see it." Expertise and intuition need to be reified to the greatest extent possible, as rules or as data, if they are to be embodied in technology. A value such as "newsworthiness" comes up again and again in data mining, automated writing, and news curation. But as it is embedded in the technology or reserved for human decision-making, it should be explicitly defined and deliberated and its ramifications considered on outcomes such as diversity, the shape of coverage, and user satisfaction, among others. Unfortunately this won't guarantee positive outcomes, but it will at least make the intentionality of systems more clear and help set expectations for the auditing of outcomes when needed.

Journalistic practices will, of course, continue to change in relation to algorithmic news production. And while algorithms may chip away at some of journalists' daily tasks, their complementarity with people will enable more efficiency and higher quality outputs, too. Algorithmic media may well be more sustainable than traditional media given that the same or even less human effort can drive a larger breadth or greater quality of content. But difficult decisions will need to be made in balancing business models with the quality and variability of media desired, in defining what metrics to use in optimizing content for attention, and in how human effort is reallocated in light of efficiency gains. Particular business models or organizational orientations may benefit in specific ways from algorithms and automation. News wires will benefit from scale and speed, but investigative news outfits will find a boost in the comprehensiveness and output quality that algorithms enable.

It's clear that the future of algorithmic media will involve a coevolution of technology, people, and society. Here I want to outline a few challenges that I think will help define a fruitful yet responsible evolution that reflects the main themes of this book: a meditation on human values in algorithmic news technology, an articulation of how journalism practices are shifting in relation to algorithmic actors, and a considered reflection on what automation may mean for the sustainability of journalism. In particular I want to talk about how advances in artificial intelligence could invade the still human-bound task of information collection, how algorithms, automation, and AI will interact with people in hybrid systems, how professionals will need to be trained and educated differently, and what these changes may entail for the burgeoning algorithmic information environment. These reflect concerns related to (1) the algorithm, (2) the algorithm-human hybrid (3) the human, and (4) the interaction between algorithm and society. I present these as provocations that I hope will stimulate further work by both practitioners and researchers. Together they offer a framework for thinking about, studying, and innovating the continued evolution of computational journalism as a human-centered endeavor.

Artificial Intelligence

"Silicon Valley" is both a geographic region of Northern California that anchors a host of high-tech corporations, and the title of a satirical HBO show that lampoons the corporate culture of the various start-ups and venture capitalists in that region. In one episode of the show, software developer Jian-Yang gets roped into prototyping and demoing a technology for a new venture-backed app called Seefood. The app is supposed to identify the type of food in a photo that a user uploads. Jian-Yang trains an AI system to analyze images and on the demo day shows it to the investor and rest of the team in the start-up group home. To start the demo he snaps a photo of a hotdog he has ready on the kitchen table, suspense builds as an "evaluating" icon spins on the app, and the system comes back with its answer: "Hotdog." The investor and team are overjoyed and relieved. It worked, everyone will be rich! Ok, they want to see it work again. For the next test Jian-Yang snaps a photo of a slice of pizza. The icon spins. The results come back: "Not hotdog." Astonishment. Disbelief. Jian-Yang is nonplussed—the technology is functioning as intended. The investor is dumbfounded. The app can only differentiate between two classes of food, "hotdog" and "not hotdog."

I've described this little scene in some detail because it's quite an on-point critique of the general state of artificial intelligence right now. Data scientists can train classifiers to differentiate between categories such as "hotdog" and "everything else" but training them to understand an open world containing thousands of foods or food combinations is a daunting task. This is a key issue in the domain of automation for news information. Algorithms and artificial intelligence struggle to operate beyond the frontier of their own design. That's not to say engineers can't build useful algorithms and AI in constrained or routine scenarios, just as Jian-Yang did. But to get past these limitations and function in a dynamic world of novel events and news information, AI needs to learn a new trick: to gather its own data and information.

To reach its full potential in the domain of media, AI will need to be able to collect information by asking questions of people, since they are the greatest source of not-already-quantified information in the world. The first step in this direction is training AI to ask and understand responses to questions in constrained domains. In May of 2018 Google launched a new technology called Duplex, which begins to do just that.[1] Duplex is able to undertake seemingly natural conversations with real people and was initially engineered to work for three tasks: making restaurant reservations, scheduling hair salon appointments, and checking holiday business hours. These are targeted tasks in which the conversation is more or less scripted and the dialogue around simple questions such as "Is there a table for two available at 7 p.m.?" can be managed. Asking questions and receiving meaningful answers is the first step toward AI that could contribute directly to information gathering or what journalists would call "reporting." While the technology is still quite limited, it may already be useful in cases where simple information solicitations are required (and where there is an obligation to answer) or where the incentives of an interviewee are aligned with honestly answering a question or providing data. But this represents only a very narrow slice of the conversations that reporters have on a day-to-day basis.

As any reporter will tell you, asking questions is not only about acquiring and gathering new information but also about critiquing and integrating it with already acquired information. Journalists need to be ready to push back on falsehoods, follow up on and clarify facts, or reframe questions to press for responses. AI will need to become a lot more advanced to compete. It needs a model of what it doesn't know, or of what it doesn't know with certainty. Then it needs to be able to identify potential sources to ask, to formulate meaningful and incisive questions, and to parse the answers to those questions in a way that allows it to fill in knowledge gaps that lead to important news stories. This is all not to mention that navigation in the physical world is necessary to capture some types of information; advances in robotics and drones offer yet more opportunities to overcome the physicality or locality of information.[2] These are difficult propositions that will take years of research and experimentation to yield useful advances.

However, if successful, such advances in AI would send a new wave of change through journalism. Let's consider again the information production pipeline consisting of information gathering, sense-making, storytelling, and distribution. Information gathering is the most expensive part of the pipeline, still heavily reliant on people, and largely left to news organizations that invest great amounts of labor to collect, verify, and make sense of information. While social media has lowered the cost of acquiring sensed information from the world, at the same time it has increased the cost of verifying and coming to trust that sensed information. Part of the imbalance of power within the wider media industry is because platforms such as Google and Facebook have been able to automate content distribution. If information gathering were to become more susceptible to automation due to advances in AI and drones, this in turn could cause another shift in the news and information industry as the capital-rich platforms vertically integrate down the content production pipeline using technical advances.

"Organize the world's information and make it universally accessible and useful," reads Google's mission statement. Whether the news industry likes it or not it, it shares a lot with that mission, though journalism layers a particular ideology on top of the knowledge production processes it practices. If news organizations want to compete in the future of media they need to be more like Google, and they need to start investing heavily in developing their own competitive strains of algorithms and AI for knowledge production.

Designing Hybrid Journalism

Notwithstanding major breakthroughs in artificial intelligence, the expert thinking and complex communication skills of journalists will ensure the use of hybrid systems throughout much of journalistic practice. Such systems need to be designed so that algorithms and people complement each other. This will boost the productivity, quality, and scope of journalistic efforts, while ensuring human autonomy and agency in what is ultimately produced. A key to that design process will be in articulating aspects of domain expertise and news values such that algorithms can help cope with the scale of the modern information environment. Once articulated, this knowledge can be reflected in the algorithms and interfaces that become the computational power tools of news production. But how should we go about tapping into this knowledge?

Because of journalists' ready access to domain knowledge in news information production, a vital source for innovation in the development of hybrid practices will come from experimenting with when and how they might delegate pieces of their work to algorithms that can calculate analytic criteria and then prioritize, classify, associate, and filter information. Computational thinking skills, and indeed programming abilities, will permit a level of tinkering that will encourage exploration of this frontier of human-machine symbiosis in a way that reflects the nuance, context, and constraints of the existing task. While noncoding collaborators will be essential for understanding tasks and workflow constraints, it is only with programming skills that the full palette of opportunity can be explored.

Another approach is to embed other types of computational thinkers in the middle of newsrooms so that they can rub shoulders with editorial thinkers. The Knight-Mozilla Open News program explored this model between 2011 and 2016, when it stationed fellows with a background in open source development (but not necessarily with any editorial experience) in the middle of a newsroom environment. One fellow innovated a new video-editing workflow by leveraging automated speech-to-text transcription, making it more efficient to edit the types of subtitled videos demanded by social platforms.[3] The proximity of computational skill to existing practice allows such a fellow to imagine new processes in their appropriate context. An important component of this model is that the fellow needs to be proximate to context but not entirely constrained by it, not bogged down in the day-to-day staid workflow. Management structures, existing workflow routines, or organizational expectations may hamper more novel ways of reformatting the work. This model could also work the other way around: by bringing editorial thinkers into highly computational environments. Institutions should consider establishing journalism fellowship programs that invite editorial thinkers into collaborative university or industry hubs of computing.

Yet another approach to innovating hybrid workflows is based on user-centered design (UCD), which may involve a host of user research methods. Techniques such as contextual inquiry, ethnography, focus groups, or interviews can be used to elicit the needs of experienced journalists and understand how technology can enhance their work or take over for repetitive, rule-bound tasks. Task analysis can then help decompose high-level tasks into subtasks that might be amenable to automation. Let's say we want to redesign the workflow for fact-checking. We might first interview and observe fact-checkers at organizations such as PolitiFact, FactCheck.org, or FullFact to understand the overall goals, subtasks, and contingencies of the work. In this particular case others have already done this research and identified tasks including claim spotting, verifying claims by comparing them to existing fact-checks, and disseminating corrections.[4] Claim spotting can in turn be broken down into subtasks such as detecting whether a claim in a text is new or a repeat and prioritizing claims for human fact-checkers. At some point in the task decomposition, we can start asking whether an automated calculation, prioritization, classification, association, or filtering decision would produce a competitive result to an existing workflow, or if human complex communication or expert thinking capabilities would need to be coupled to the algorithmic decision. UCD techniques are well suited to developing new tools and workflows when it's not practical for people like fellows to be embedded within a newsroom environment for an extended period of time. Moreover, user research methods can help articulate durable design criteria that can inform other designers seeking to innovate workflows to meet particular user needs.[5]

As people come to interact with and become entwined in computational news production, a host of challenging human-computer interaction (HCI) challenges become apparent. The workflows and processes that define how information work is decomposed, delegated to algorithms, and recomposed will need to be designed and evaluated, not only so that they are efficient, but also so that editors feel confident in the outputs. Whereas automation will clearly enhance the scale of activity, whether surfacing news leads or outputting content, maintaining the quality of content at scale will require new computational tools, visual analytic methods, and interfaces to enable human oversight and *editing* at scale. The idea of "editing at scale" captures the central idea that an editorial thinker will need to supervise, manage, and provide feedback to a massive breadth of computational outputs via some interface. A challenging question for the future of hybrid media, then, is how to design such interfaces so that editors are empowered to control the automation, directly or indirectly, while maintaining human agency. Mechanisms will be needed for editors to communicate feedback to algorithms so that changes are intuitive but reflect concretely on how content outputs are impacted.

Another aspect of the human-computer interface for algorithmic media, one that I have barely touched on in this book, is how news audiences will come to interact with, perceive, and consume algorithmic media.[6] Research has only just begun to illuminate how readers perceive automatically written news, how they react to information agents on social media, and whether and how they understand algorithmic curation. Additional work will need to examine affective factors of satisfaction with automated media, as well as how typical content performance metrics such as clicks, time spent, and engagement are impacted when users consume algorithmically produced media. Whether it's the proliferation of semi-automatically produced video or the roll-out of automatically produced localized content, much is still to be learned from field experiments examining user interaction with real algorithmic media outputs in the course of typical information consumption patterns.

Algorithmic Media Literacy

Newsworkers will, without a doubt, need new skills and training to be successful collaborators in a hybrid media system. Above all they will need algorithmic media literacy. The broader public will also benefit from developing this literacy as they come into increasing contact with algorithmic media systems. Computational thinking, data thinking, and advanced methods training will all play a role in developing this broader literacy.

Computational thinking, again, is about being able to formulate problems and their solutions so those solutions can be carried out programmatically. Computational thinkers will be able to exploit the capabilities of automation and algorithms to find news leads, tell stories in unique ways, and creatively apply algorithmic approaches to new tasks and challenges as they arise. A capacity for computational thinking may emerge as people work with algorithms and automation and develop abilities to anticipate how an algorithm will react and "see" the world. In a way, people need to develop some form of "empathy" for algorithms so they can see a problem through computational eyes. This in turn will help head off errors and missteps due to algorithmic limitations and lead to a more robust hybrid system. For future designers of algorithmic media systems, computational thinking offers ways to approach problems through parameterization, modeling, and decomposition, which can further unlock the power of computing for new products and innovations.

Developing data thinking will likewise be essential for journalists and other practitioners working with algorithmic media. If algorithms are the verbs, then data are the nouns, and without both you can't have a complete computational sentence. In other words, to really achieve algorithmic media literacy you have to be able to think both computationally and with data. This involves every stage of data manipulation from collecting, sampling, and cleaning to transforming, querying, and validating. Understanding and connecting how data reflect and represent the world, mix with algorithms, and interact with human psychology when they are presented as media are all essential components. Data are an important indirect control mechanism and learning how to manage algorithmic behavior via data, either by selecting training data or by setting metadata parameters, is a necessary skill for any algorithmic media editor.

Finally, in order to have the best chance to use algorithms and data to produce sound evidence and knowledge, journalists need training in advanced statistical techniques. We're closing in on almost fifty years since Philip Meyer wrote his landmark book *Precision Journalism,* which advocated for the use of social scientific and statistical research methods in the journalistic enterprise.[7] With the world awash in data, the need is more crucial now than ever. Statistical inferences, interpretations, and uncertainty are often difficult for human minds to grasp, but are essential to more advanced and rigorous uses of machine learning and data mining within journalism. Not every journalist necessarily needs advanced statistical methods training, but data journalists who want to push the envelope of computational possibilities will benefit greatly.

How should journalists go about developing algorithmic media literacy? Almost 50 percent of journalism programs accredited by the Accrediting Council on Education in Journalism and Mass Communications (ACEJMC) that were surveyed in a recent study in the United States had no class in basic data journalism.[8] Of the programs examined 16 percent had three or more classes, some of which are advanced courses on topics such as data visualization and programming. These statistics expose a wide gap that needs to be bridged to integrate data thinking (let alone computational thinking and advanced statistical methods) into traditional educational curricula. Indeed, the Global Data Journalism Survey conducted in early 2017 showed that 81 percent of the 206 surveyed professionals would be "very interested" in advancing their data journalism capabilities, ideally in nontraditional educational settings.[9] Massive Open Online Courses (MOOCs) are one approach that can help draw in large numbers of students and expose them to basics, but they struggle to convey in-depth knowledge and experience. The level of training in relevant skills such as statistics, coding, data science, data visualization, and machine learning languish despite a healthy demand expressed by professionals.

Part of the problem is a lack of qualified instructors for these topics. Whether in formal academic programs or in the form of editors shepherding newbie reporters in the newsroom, society needs more people who can teach technical approaches to news production in a highly contextualized way that aligns with the values and constraints of journalism. It's my contention that a separate graduate degree in Computational and Data Journalism is needed in order to teach a new breed of educator-practitioner-scholar. A separate degree would allow more curricular space to be devoted to the skills needed to become highly competent in the field. A handful of masters degrees are heading in this direction, such as the dual Computer Science and Journalism program at Columbia University. But this can be extended further. For practitioners we might imagine a Doctorate of Professional Practice in Computational Journalism, comparable to advanced professional degrees in clinical fields such as Psychology and Physical Therapy. We might also imagine a PhD in Computational Journalism, with an emphasis on how to practically (yet generalizably) apply computational thinking, data thinking, and advanced statistical methods to issues in journalism, not just in reporting but throughout the algorithmic media production pipeline. By training academics with doctoral degrees in these areas a new generation of teachers and educators would be prepared to bring these skills to other journalism programs. While some have decried the excessive price tag of graduate education in journalism, the program in Computational Journalism I envision would leverage the STEM-oriented funding model in which research grants are used to fund students.[10] Education would thus be subsidized from research productivity, which would not only lead to better trained computational journalists but also produce new knowledge that advances the field.

Algorithms, Authenticity, and Society

Throughout this book I've emphasized the positive potential of technical advances for the production of news information. In responsible hands and with carefully embedded prosocial values that reflect the public interest, automation and algorithms can be a powerful force for enhancing the efficiency, sustainability, and quality of news media. At times, though, I've also pointed out how bad actors can misuse and abuse automated content.

Newsbots, for instance, can manipulate the credibility of people or issues, they can amplify and spread propaganda and junk news, they can dampen or suppress opposition and debate, and they can intimidate or deny access to authentic people who want to participate in discussion. Simply put, in the wrong hands, the same technologies that can enhance the production of *news information* can also be employed for the sake of *disinformation*.

Society will need to come to grips with an inability to rely on the authenticity of mediated communication and interaction—on social media, and on the Internet more broadly. Advanced forms of algorithmic media synthesis can generate fictitious yet compelling images of faces, puppeteered video of politicians, synthesized voices, and indistinguishable text comments. Any of these techniques might fabricate subversive information that challenges the truth-finding process.[11] Sure, photos have been manipulated almost since photographic technology was originally invented. And the media itself is a simulacrum of reality, in which each selection, edit, highlight, or turn of phrase shapes the audience's interpretation of events. What's new here is that media synthesis algorithms further fracture the expectation of authenticity for recorded media while enabling a whole new scale, pervasiveness, potential for personalization, and ease of use. What happens when the public can no longer trust any media they encounter online? Or when even professionals will struggle to distinguish the authentic from the inauthentic? How will we have the debates and dialogues we need to run a democracy when automation creates so much potential for information corruption?

Major investments will be needed in the domain of media forensics, both in developing core techniques and algorithms and in designing interfaces for making those algorithms available within hybrid workflows.[12] Forensics techniques look at pixel statistics, recompression artifacts, geometric aberrations, and sensor noise among other signals to try to certify an image or video as unadulterated. One recent approach looks for blood flow in video of a person's face in order to see if pixels periodically get redder when the heart pumps blood.[13] Another layer of media forensics will need to consider the context of media in determining authenticity. If an image can be so easily synthesized, metadata about the time, place, social setting, or other context will be increasingly important for proper verification. Journalists will need to develop expertise and tooling that helps them make sense of that context.[14] Advances in technology are being driven by government agencies such as the Defense Advanced Research Projects Agency (DARPA), with its MediFor project, the National Institute of Standards and Technology (NIST), which runs the Media Forensics Challenge, and by the European Union with investments in projects such as InVid.[15] But much of this technology is still several steps away from the kind of cheap public availability that would make it practical in reporting. More translational work needs to be done to get research into practice. And like information security, media forensics will need ongoing and sustained support, attention, and resources from industry and civil society.

In the online environment of machine-altered reality, professional media should double-down on process transparency in order to maintain the trust of information consumers. Developing and communicating standardized and robust processes for media forensics and verification could help end users come to trust that professionals are adhering to careful and exhaustive processes.[16] Such transparency necessarily includes algorithmic transparency for any computational tools in the verification process. If we can't trust our eyes on the Internet, perhaps we can trust that a media outlet is following a rigorous process to ensure that whatever it does publish is authentic. Few intermediaries are better placed to function as trusted validators and assessors of mediated reality than professionally trained journalists with access to advanced computational forensics tools. Synthesized media of questionable authenticity could be just the thing that drives the public back into the arms of mainstream news organizations.

NOTES

1. HYBRIDIZATION: COMBINING ALGORITHMS, AUTOMATION, AND PEOPLE IN NEWSWORK

1. Bastian Obermayer and Frederik Obermaier, *The Panama Papers: Breaking the Story of How the Rich and Powerful Hide Their Money* (London, UK: Oneworld Publications, 2017).

2. Mar Cabra, "How We Built the Data Team behind the Panama Papers," *Source*, November 2017, https://source.opennews.org/articles /how-we-built-data-team-behind-panama-papers/.

3. Mar Cabra and Erin Kissane, "Wrangling 2.6TB of Data: The People and the Technology behind the Panama Papers," April 26, 2016, https://panamapapers.icij.org/blog/20160425-data-tech-team-ICIJ .html; the actual tool is open sourced and can be found at https://github .com/ICIJ/extract, accessed October 21, 2018.

4. James Manyika et al., "Harnessing Automation for a Future That Works," McKinsey Global Institute, 2017, https://www.mckinsey.com /featured-insights/digital-disruption/harnessing-automation-for-a -future-that-works.

5. Mary (Missy) Cummings, "Man Versus Machine or Man + Machine?" *IEEE Intelligent Systems* 29, no. 5 (2014).

6. Peter Denning, "Is Computer Science Science?" *Communications of the ACM* 48, no. 4 (2005).

7. Raja Parasuraman, Thomas Sheridan, and Christopher Wickens, "A Model for Types and Levels of Human Interaction with Automation," *IEEE Transactions on Systems, Man, and Cybernetics—Part A: Systems and Humans,* 30, no. 3 (2000).

8. Mark Hansen et al., *Artificial Intelligence: Practice and Implications for Journalism* (New York: Tow Center for Digital Journalism, 2017).

9. Erik Brynjolfsson and Andrew McAfee, *The Second Machine Age: Work, Progress, and Prosperity in a Time of Brilliant Technologies* (New York: W. W. Norton, 2014).

10. H. P. Luhn, "The Automatic Creation of Literature Abstracts," *IBM Journal of Research and Development* 2, no. 2 (1958).

11. Susan Straus, "Testing a Typology of Tasks: An Empirical Validation of McGrath's (1984) Group Task Circumplex," *Small Group Research* 30, no. 2 (1999).

12. Sarah Cohen, James T. Hamilton, and Fred Turner, "Computational Journalism," *Communications of the ACM* 54, no. 10 (2011).

13. Geoffrey Bowker et al., *Sorting Things Out: Classification and Its Consequences* (Cambridge, MA: MIT Press, 2000).

14. Reuben Binns et al., "Like Trainer, Like Bot? Inheritance of Bias in Algorithmic Content Moderation," presented at the International Conference on Social Informatics (SocInfo), Oxford, UK, 2017.

15. Michael Schudson, *The Sociology of News,* 2nd. ed. (New York: W.W. Norton, 2011).

16. Pierre Bourdieu, "The Political Field, The Social Science Field and the Journalistic Field," in *Bourdieu and The Journalistic Field,* ed. Rodney Benson and Erik Neveu (Cambridge, UK: Polity, 2005).

17. Matt Carlson, "The Many Boundaries of Journalism," in *Boundaries of Journalism Professionalism, Practices and Participation,* ed. Seth C. Lewis and Matt Carlson (London: Routledge, 2015).

18. Mark Deuze, "What Is Journalism?: Professional Identity and Ideology of Journalists Reconsidered," *Journalism* 6, no. 4 (2005).

19. David Ryfe, *Journalism and the Public (Key Concepts in Journalism)* (Cambridge, UK: Polity, 2017); Jane Singer, "Out of Bounds: Professional Norms as Boundary Markers," in *Boundaries of Journalism Professionalism, Practices and Participation,* ed. Seth C. Lewis and Matt Carlson (London: Routledge, 2015).

20. Bob Kovach and Tom Rosenstiel, *The Elements of Journalism,* 3rd ed. (New York: Three Rivers Press, 2014); Ryfe, *Journalism and the Public.*

21. Society of Professional Journalists (SPJ) Code of Ethics, September 2014, https://www.spj.org/ethicscode.asp.

22. For an example of this model applied to the context of newswire services, see: Barbara Czarniawska, *Cyberfactories: How News Agencies Produce News* (Cheltenham, UK: Edward Elgar, 2011).

23. Robert S. Taylor, *Value-Added Processes in Information Systems* (Norwood, NJ: Ablex Publishing Corporation, 1986).

24. Nicholas Diakopoulos, *Cultivating the Landscape of Innovation in Computational Journalism* (New York: Tow-Knight Center for Entrepreneurial Journalism, 2012).

25. Sašo Slaček Brlek, Jurij Smrke, and Igor Vobič, "Engineering Technologies for Journalism in the Digital Age," *Digital Journalism* 5, no. 8 (2017).

26. Mary Lynn Young and Alfred Hermida, "From Mr. and Mrs. Outlier to Central Tendencies," *Digital Journalism* 3, no. 3 (2014); James T. Hamilton and Fred Turner, "Accountability through Algorithm: Developing the Field of Computational Journalism," Report from the Center for Advanced Study in the Behavioral Sciences Summer Workshop, 2009, https://web.stanford.edu/~fturner/Hamilton%20Turner%20Acc%20 by%20Alg%20Final.pdf; Nicholas Diakopoulos, "A Functional Roadmap for Innovation in Computational Journalism," January 2010, http://www.nickdiakopoulos.com/2011/04/22/a-functional-roadmap-for-innovation-in-computational-journalism/; James T. Hamilton, *Democracy's Detectives* (Cambridge, MA: Harvard University Press, 2016); C. W. Anderson and David Caswell, "Computational Journalism," in *The International Encyclopedia of Journalism Studies,* ed. Tim Vos and Folker Hanusch (London: Sage, 2018). For a description of the emergence and various facets of the field over its first dozen years see Neil Thurman, "Computational Journalism," in *The Handbook of Journalism Studies,* Second Edition, ed. Karin Wahl-Jorgensen and Thomas Hanitzsch (New York: Routledge, 2019).

27. Matt Carlson, "Automating Judgment? Algorithmic Judgment, News Knowledge, and Journalistic Professionalism," *New Media & Society* 8, no. 4 (2017); Wendy Espeland and Mitchell Stevens, "A Sociology of Quantification," *European Journal of Sociology* 49, no. 3 (2009).

28. Sergio Splendore, "Quantitatively Oriented Forms of Journalism and Their Epistemology," *Sociology Compass* 10, no. 5 (2015); Nikki Usher, *Interactive Journalism: Hackers, Data, and Code* (Urbana: University of Illinois Press, 2016); Mark Coddington, "Clarifying Journalism's Quantitative Turn," *Digital Journalism* 3, no. 3 (2014), does an excellent job parsing out some of the nuances of these terms.

29. John Pavlik, "The Impact of Technology on Journalism," *Journalism Studies* 1, no. 2 (2000); Henrik Örnebring, "Technology and Journalism-as-Labour: Historical Perspectives," *Journalism* 11, no. 1 (2010).

30. Matthew Powers, "'In Forms That Are Familiar and Yet-to-Be Invented': American Journalism and the Discourse of Technologically Specific Work," *Journal of Communication Inquiry* 36, no. 1 (2011).

31. Building computer systems becomes a form of "engineering activism": Helen Nissenbaum, "How Computer Systems Embody Values," *Computer* 34, no. 3 (2001).

32. Coddington, "Clarifying Journalism's Quantitative Turn."

33. For a treatment of ethics with respect to automated journalism, see Konstantin Dörr and Katharina Hollnbuchner, "Ethical Challenges of Algorithmic Journalism," *Digital Journalism* 5, no. 4 (2017).

34. Ryfe, *Journalism and the Public.*

35. Leo Leppänen et al., "Finding and Expressing News from Structured Data," presented at AcademicMindtrek, Helsinki, Finland, 2017.

36. Batya Friedman et al., "Value Sensitive Design and Information Systems," in *Human-Computer Interaction and Management Information Systems,* ed. Ping Zhang, and Denis Galletta (Oxford, UK: Routledge, 2006).

37. In terms of ethical implications Kirsten Martin argues that "developers make a moral choice as to the delegation of who-does-what between algorithms and individuals" because design determines where in the system careful human consideration of a decision is employed, and where potentially inferior automated decisions may inadequately substitute for humans in uneven ways. For more detail, see Kirsten Martin, "Ethical Implications and Accountability of Algorithms," *Journal of Business Ethics,* published ahead of print (2018).

38. Frank Levy and Richard J. Murnane, *The New Division of Labor* (Princeton, NJ: Princeton University Press, 2004).

39. Nathalie Riche et al., eds., *Data-Driven Storytelling* (Boca Raton, FL: CRC Press, 2018); Karin Assmann and Nicholas Diakopoulos, "Negotiating Change: Audience Engagement Editors as Newsroom Intermediaries," *#ISOJ Journal* 7, no. 1 (2017).

40. For a clear comparison of the relative capabilities of humans and machines, see section 3.3.6 of Ben Shneiderman et al., *Designing the User Interface: Strategies for Effective Human-Computer Interaction,* 6th ed. (Boston: Pearson, 2017). For a comparison that is explicitly applied to automated content creation, see Arjen van Dalen, "The Algorithms behind the Headlines," *Digital Journalism* 6, nos. 5–6 (2012).

41. Noam Lemelshtrich Latar, *Robot Journalism: Can Human Journalism Survive?* (Singapore: World Scientific Publishing Company, 2018).

42. Erik Brynjolfsson and Tom Mitchell, "What Can Machine Learning Do? Workforce Implications," *Science* 358, no. 6370 (2017).

43. Jeanette Wing, "Computational Thinking," *Communications of ACM* 49, no. 3 (2006).

44. Peter Denning, "Remaining Trouble Spots with Computational Thinking," *Communications of the ACM* 60, no. 6 (2017).

45. Nicholas Diakopoulos, "Computational Journalism and the Emergence of News Platforms," in *The Routledge Companion to Digital Journalism Studies,* ed. Bob Franklin and Scott Eldridge II (London: Routledge, 2016).

46. Gregor Aisch, "Seven Features You'll Want in Your Next Charting Tool," *Vis4.net* (blog), 2015, http://vis4.net/blog/posts/seven-features-youll-wantin-your-next-charting-tool/.

47. Carl-Gustav Linden, "Algorithms for Journalism: The Future of News Work," *Journal of Media Innovations* 4, no. 1 (2017).

48. Mark Ackerman, "The Intellectual Challenge CSCW—The Gap Between Social Requirements and Technical Feasibility," *Human-Computer Interaction* 15, no. 2 (2000).

49. Thomas B. Sheridan, "Function Allocation: Algorithm, Alchemy or Apostasy?" *International Journal of Human-Computer Studies,* 52, no. 2 (2000); Richard Patton and Peter Patton, "What Can Be Automated? What Cannot Be Automated?" in *Springer Handbook of Automation,* ed. Shimon Y. Nof (Heidelberg: Springer, 2009).

50. Robert Picard, "The Economics of Journalism and News Provision," in *Journalism (Handbooks of Communication Science),* ed. Tim Vos (Berlin, Boston: Mouton De Gruyter, 2018).

51. Seth C. Lewis and Oscar Westlund, "Actors, Actants, Audiences, and Activities in Cross-Media News Work," *Digital Journalism* 3, no. 1 (2014).

52. Matthew Weber and Allie Kosterich, "Coding the News," *Digital Journalism* 6, no. 3 (2018).

53. Brynjolfsson and McAfee, *The Second Machine Age.*

54. Michael Bernstein et al., "Soylent: A Word Processor with a Crowd Inside," *Communications of the ACM* 58, no. 8 (2015); Aniket Kittur et al., "CrowdForge: Crowdsourcing Complex Work," *Proceedings of the Symposium on User Interface Software and Technology (UIST)* (New York: ACM, 2011); Elena Agapie, Jaime Teevan, and Andrés Monroy-Hernández, "Crowdsourcing in the Field: A Case Study Using Local Crowds for Event Reporting," presented at the third AAAI Conference on Human Computation and Crowdsourcing, San Diego, CA, 2015.

55. Tanja Aitamurto, "Crowdsourcing in Open Journalism," in *The Routledge Companion to Digital Journalism Studies,* ed. Bob Franklin and Scott Eldridge II (London: Routledge, 2016); Tanja Aitamurto, "Crowdsourcing as a Knowledge-Search Method in Digital Journalism," *Digital Journalism* 4, no. 2 (2015); Elliot Higgins, "Crowdsourcing

Conflict and Beyond," in *Data Journalism Past, Present, Future,* ed. John Mair, Richard Lance Keeble, and Megan Lucero (Bury St Edmunds, UK: Abramis, 2017).

56. Aniket Kittur et al., "The Future of Crowd Work," *Proceedings of the Conference on Computer Supported Cooperative Work and Social Computing (CSCW)* (New York: ACM, 2013).

57. Gianluca Demartini, "Hybrid Human–Machine Information Systems: Challenges and Opportunities," *Computer Networks* 90, no. 29 (2015).

58. Daniela Retelny, Michael Bernstein, and Melissa Valentine, "No Workflow Can Ever Be Enough: How Crowdsourcing Workflows Constrain Complex Work," *Proceedings on the ACM on Human Computer Interaction* 1 (2017).

59. Ackerman, "The Intellectual Challenge of CSCW."

60. Laura Hazard Owen, "How 7 News Organizations Are Using Slack to Work Better and Differently," Nieman Lab, July 30, 2015, http://www.niemanlab.org/2015/07/how-7-news-organizations-are-using-slack-to-work-better-and-differently/.

61. Agapie, Teevan, and Monroy-Hernández, "Crowdsourcing in the Field."

62. Ibid.

63. Steven Rich, "What I Learned by Submitting the Same FOIA 1,033 Times (and Counting)," presented at the National Institute for Computer Assisted Reporting (NICAR) Conference, Jacksonville, FL, 2017, http://slides.com/stevenrich/allofthefoias#/.

64. Kittur et al., "The Future of Crowd Work"; Daniel Weld et al., "Artificial Intelligence and Collective Intelligence," presented at the Association for the Advancement of Artificial Intelligence (AAAI) Workshop on Human Computation, San Francisco, CA, 2011.

65. John Micklethwait, "The Future of News," Bloomberg, May 3, 2018, https://www.bloomberg.com/news/articles/2018-05-03/john-micklethwait-the-future-of-news.

2. JOURNALISTIC DATA MINING

1. Carrie Teegardin et al., "Doctors & Sex Abuse," *Atlanta Journal Constitution,* July 6, 2016, http://doctors.ajc.com/doctors_sex_abuse.

2. "How the Doctors & Sex Abuse Project Came About," *Atlanta Journal Constitution,* 2016, http://doctors.ajc.com/about_this_investigation/.

3. Jeff Ernsthausen, "Doctors & Sex Abuse," presented at the National Institute for Computer Assisted Reporting (NICAR) Conference, Jack-

sonville, FL, 2017, https://docs.google.com/presentation/d/1keGeDk_w
pBPQgUOOhbRarPPFbyCculTObGLeAhOMmEM/edit#slide=id.p.

4. Usama Fayyad, Gregory Piatetsky-Shapiro, and Padhraic Smyth, "The KDD Process for Extracting Useful Knowledge from Volumes of Data," *Communications of the ACM* 39, no. 11 (1996); Mehmed Kantardzic, *Data Mining: Concepts, Models, Methods, and Algorithms,* 2nd ed. (Hoboken, NJ: Wiley, 2011).

5. Usama Fayyad, Gregory Piatetsky-Shapiro, and Padhraic Smyth, "From Data Mining to Knowledge Discovery in Databases," *AI Magazine* 17, no. 3 (1996).

6. Mary Branscombe, "Artificial Intelligence's Next Big Step: Reinforcement Learning," *New Stack,* January 2017, https://thenewstack.io/reinforcement-learning-ready-real-world/.

7. Zorroa, https://zorroa.com/core-features/, accessed October 28, 2018, and Snapstream, https://www.snapstream.com/, accessed October 28, 2018 are both companies that offer such archive tagging services to media companies.

8. Martha Stone, *Big Data for Media* (Oxford: Reuters Institute for the Study of Journalism, 2014), https://reutersinstitute.politics.ox.ac.uk/our-research/big-data-media.

9. Matt Lindsay and Patrick Tornabene, "Newsday Data Analytics Boost Subscriber Retention," *Ideas Blog* (blog), September 2016, http://www.inma.org/blogs/ideas/post.cfm/newsday-data-analytics-boost-subscriber-retention.

10. Bob Kovach and Tom Rosenstiel, *The Elements of Journalism,* 3rd ed. (New York: Three Rivers Press, 2014).

11. Pamela Shoemaker and Tim Vos, *Gatekeeping Theory* (New York: Routledge, 2009); Pamela Shoemaker and Stephen Reese, *Mediating the Message in the 21st Century: A Media Sociology Perspective* (New York: Routledge, 2013). For additional background on the economic forces that shape news content, see Robert Picard, "The Economics of Journalism and News Provision," in *Journalism (Handbooks of Communication Science),* ed. Tim Vos (Berlin, Boston: Mouton De Gruyter, 2018).

12. Tony Harcup and Deirdre O'Neill, "What Is News?: News Values Revisited (Again)," *Journalism Studies* 18, no. 12 (2017).

13. Franziska Badenschier and Holger Wormer, "Issue Selection in Science Journalism: Towards a Special Theory of News Values for Science News?," in *The Sciences' Media Connection—Public Communication and Its Repercussions. Sociology of the Sciences Yearbook,* ed. Simone Rödder, Martina Franzen, and Peter Weingart (Dordrecht: Springer Netherlands, 2011).

14. Heidi Blake and John Templon, "The Tennis Racket," *BuzzFeed News,* January 2016, https://www.buzzfeed.com/heidiblake/the-tennis -racket. For a critique of the methods used, see Nicholas Diakopoulos, "Enabling Accountability of Algorithmic Media: Transparency as a Constructive and Critical Lens," in *Towards Glass-Box Data Mining for Big and Small Data,* ed. Tania Cerquitelli, Daniele Quercia, and Frank Pasquale (Cham, Switzerland: Springer, 2017). Another example of statistical anomaly detection (Monte Carlo simulation) to find a story is in Susan Pulliam and Rob Barry, "Executives' Good luck in Trading Own Stock," *Wall Street Journal,* November 27, 2012, https://www.wsj.com /articles/SB10000872396390444100404577641463717344178.

15. Matt Shearer, Basile Simon, and Clément Geiger, "Datastringer: Easy Dataset Monitoring for Journalists," presented at the Computation + Journalism Symposium, New York, 2014.

16. Måns Magnusson, Jens Finnäs, and Leonard Wallentin, "Finding the News Lead in the Data Haystack: Automated Local Data Journalism Using Crime Data," presented at the Computation + Journalism Symposium, Palo Alto, CA, 2016. To try out the Newsworthy service, see http://www.newsworthy.se/en/, accessed October 28, 2018; for examples of output, see https://www.europeandatajournalism.eu/eng/Tools-for -journalists/Stats-Monitor, accessed October 28, 2018.

17. Titus Plattner, Didier Orel, and Olivier Steiner, "Flexible Data Scraping, Multi-Language Indexing, Entity Extraction and Taxonomies: Tadam, a Swiss Tool to Deal with Huge Amounts of Unstructured Data," presented at the Computation + Journalism Symposium, Palo Alto, CA, 2016.

18. Derek Willis, "Seeing the Real Campaign with ProPublica's Election DataBot," ProPublica, September 2016, https://www.propublica.org /article/seeing-the-real-campaign-with-propublica-election-databot.

19. Robert Faturechi and Derek Willis, "'On Like Donkey Kong': How a Dubious Super PAC Boosted a Questionable Penny Stock," ProPublica, May 2016, https://www.propublica.org/article/how-a-dubious -super-pac-boosted-a-questionable-penny-stock.

20. William Perrin, "Local News Engine: Can the Machine Help Spot Diamonds in the Dust?" in *Data Journalism Past, Present, Future,* ed. John Mair, Richard Lance Keeble, and Megan Lucero (Bury St Edmunds, UK: Abramis, 2017).

21. Peter Aldhous, "BuzzFeed News Trained a Computer to Search for Hidden Spy Planes. This Is What We Found," *BuzzFeed News,* August 2017, https://www.buzzfeed.com/peteraldhous/hidden-spy-planes.

22. Vlad Herasymenko et al. "Leprosy of the Land," Texty.org.ua, March 2018, http://texty.org.ua/d/2018/amber_eng/; for the methods for the project, see Amber Methodology, https://github.com/texty/amber -methodology.

23. Ryan J. Foley, Larry Fenn, and Nick Penzenstadler, "Chronicle of Agony: Gun Accidents Kill at Least 1 Kid Every Other Day," *USA Today*, October 14, 2016, https://www.usatoday.com/story/news/2016/10/14/ap -usa-today-gun-accidents-children/91906700/.

24. William Lyon, "Combining the BuzzFeed Trumpworld Graph with Government Contracting Data in Neo4j," *William Lyon* (blog), January 2017, http://www.lyonwj.com/2017/01/30/trumpworld-us-cont racting-data-neo4j/.

25. Jonathan Stray, "Network Analysis in Journalism: Practices and Possibilities," presented at the Knowledge Discovery and Data Mining (KDD) Workshop on Data Science + Journalism, Halifax, CA, 2017.

26. "The Russian Laundromat Exposed," Organized Crime and Corruption Reporting Project (OCCRP), March 2017, https://www.occrp .org/en/laundromat/the-russian-laundromat-exposed.

27. The corpint library is open sourced and available here, https:// github.com/alephdata/corpint, accessed August 7, 2018.

28. For an example of how Dedupe is interactively trained, see https:// dedupe.io/#demo, accessed October 28, 2018.

29. Bedfellows, accessed August 7, 2018, https://github.com/The Upshot/Bedfellows/blob/master/introduction.md.

30. Derek Willis, "Campaign Donations Reflect the Sharp Split in Congress among Republicans," ProPublica, January 2016, https://www .propublica.org/article/campaign-donations-reflect-the-sharp-split-in -congress-among-republicans.

31. Joan Biskupic, Janet Roberts, and John Shiffman, "The Echo Chamber," Reuters, December 8, 2014, http://www.reuters.com/investigates /special-report/scotus/.

32. Peter Tolmie et al., "Supporting the Use of User-Generated Content in Journalistic Practice," *Proceedings of the Conference on Human Factors in Computing Systems* (New York: ACM, 2017).

33. Matthew Brehmer et al., "Overview: The Design, Adoption, and Analysis of a Visual Document Mining Tool for Investigative Journalists," *IEEE Transactions on Visualization and Computer Graphics (TVCG)* 20, no. 12 (2014).

34. Overview News Stories, accessed August 7, 2018, https://github .com/overview/overview-server/wiki/News-stories.

35. Cristian Felix et al., "RevEx: Visual Investigative Journalism with a Million Healthcare Reviews," presented at the Computation + Journalism Symposium, New York, 2015; Charles Ornstein, "On Yelp, Doctors Get Reviewed like Restaurants—And It Rankles," National Public Radio, August 6, 2015, https://www.npr.org/sections/health-shots /2015/08/06/429624187/on-yelp-doctors-get-reviewed-like-restaurants -and-it-rankles.

36. Seid Muhie Yimam et al., "new/s/leak—Information Extraction and Visualization for Investigative Data Journalists," presented at the Association for Computational Linguistics—Systems Demonstrations, Berlin, Germany, 2016.

37. Takeshi Sakaki, Makoto Okazaki, and Yutaka Matsuo, "Earth-quake Shakes Twitter Users: Real-Time Event Detection by Social Sensors," *Proceedings of the World Wide Web Conference* (New York: ACM, 2010).

38. Neil Thurman, "Social Media, Surveillance, and News Work," *Digital Journalism* 6, no. 1 (2018).

39. Xiaomo Liu et al., "Reuters Tracer: Toward Automated News Production Using Large Scale Social Media Data," *Proceedings of the IEEE Big Data* (2017); Xiaomo Liu et al., "Reuters Tracer—A Large Scale System of Detecting & Verifying Real-Time News Events from Twitter," *Proceedings of the Conference on Information and Knowledge Management* (New York: ACM, 2016).

40. Tom Reilly (Cloudera) and Khalid Al-Kofahi (Thomson Reuters), "Becoming Smarter about Credible News," presented at Strata + Hadoop World, San Francisco, CA, March 2017, https://www.youtube.com/watch ?v=1rwYOiWZmzc.

41. "Timeliness Analysis of 31 Breaking News," accessed August 7, 2018, https://docs.google.com/document/d/1iECb9y9aKRe0z58Fz0Sqd qhTOMEQU2pLZ4yQ6PUvgAw/edit#heading=h.yve85j9jv4qw.

42. Xiaomo Liu, et al., "Real-time Rumor Debunking on Twitter," *Proceedings of the International Conference on Information and Knowledge Management* (New York: ACM, 2015).

43. Raz Schwartz, Mor Naaman, and Ranny Theordoro, "Editorial Algorithms: Using Social Media to Discover and Report Local News," *Proceedings of the International Conference on Web and Social Media* (Palo Alto: The AAAI Press, 2015).

44. An example of video monitoring is Face-O-Matic, which can alert users when the faces of the president or congressional leaders appear on major TV news channels: Nancy Watzman, "Internet Archive TV News Lab: Introducing Face-O-Matic, Experimental Slack Alert System

Tracking Trump & Congressional Leaders on TV News," *Internet Archive* (blog), July 19, 2017, https://blog.archive.org/2017/07/19/intro ducing-face-o-matic.

45. Kalev Leetaru and Philip A. Schrodt, "GDELT: Global Data on Events, Location, and Tone," presented at the International Studies Association meeting, San Francisco, CA, April 2013.

46. Konstantina Papanikolaou et al., "'Just the Facts' with PALOMAR: Detecting Protest Events in Media Outlets and Twitter," presented at the Workshop on Social Media in the Newsroom, Cologne, Germany, 2016; Elizabeth Boschee, Premkumar Natarajan, and Ralph Weischedel, "Automatic Extraction of Events from Open Source Text for Predictive Forecasting," in *Handbook of Computational Approaches to Counterterrorism*, ed. V. S. Subrahmanian (New York: Springer New York, 2012).

47. "Documenting Hate News Index," ProPublica, August 2017, https://projects.propublica.org/hate-news-index/; Simon Rogers, "A New Machine Learning App for Reporting on Hate in America," *Google* (blog), August 2017, https://www.blog.google/topics/journalism-news /new-machine-learning-app-reporting-hate-america/.

48. Katherine Keith et al., "Identifying Civilians Killed by Police with Distantly Supervised Entity-Event Extraction," *Proceedings of the Conference on Empirical Methods in Natural Language Processing* (Association for Computational Linguistics, 2017).

49. See, for example, "2017 NFL Predictions," FiveThirtyEight, accessed August 7, 2018, https://projects.fivethirtyeight.com/2017-nfl -predictions/; "2016 U.S. Open Predictions," FiveThirtyEight, accessed August 7, 2018, https://projects.fivethirtyeight.com/2016-us-open-tennis -predictions/; "CARMELO NBA Player Projections," FiveThirtyEight, accessed August 7, 2018, https://projects.fivethirtyeight.com/carmelo/.

50. Jeff Ernsthausen, "Predict-a-Bill: How It Works," *Atlanta Journal Constitution* (blog), February 2014, http://ajcnewsapps.tumblr.com/post /77008124090/predict-a-bill-how-it-works; Jeff Ernsthausen, "Predict-a-Bill Goes Real-Time (More or Less)," *Atlanta Journal Constitution* (blog), February 2015, http://ajcnewsapps.tumblr.com/post/112039443036 /predict-a-bill-goes-real-time-more-or-less.

51. For a solid critique of this and related problems, see Nate Silver, "The Media Has a Probability Problem," FiveThirtyEight, September 2017, https://fivethirtyeight.com/features/the-media-has-a-probability-problem/.

52. For a treatment of how probabilistic horse race coverage may impact voter perceptions and turnout, see Sean Westwood, Solomon Messing, and Yphtach Lelkes, "Projecting Confidence: How the Probabilistic

Horse Race Confuses and Demobilizes the Public," Social Science Research Network (*SSRN*), 2018, https://papers.ssrn.com/sol3/papers.cfm?abstract_id=3117054.

53. Nate Silver, "A User's Guide to FiveThirtyEight's 2016 General Election Forecast," FiveThirtyEight, June 2016, https://fivethirtyeight.com/features/a-users-guide-to-fivethirtyeights-2016-general-election-forecast/.

54. Nate Silver, "The Real Story of 2016," FiveThirtyEight, January 2017, http://fivethirtyeight.com/features/the-real-story-of-2016/.

55. Tolmie et al., "Supporting the Use of User Generated Content in Journalistic Practice."

56. Steve Schifferes et al., "Identifying and Verifying News through Social Media," *Digital Journalism* 2, no. 3 (2014).

57. Ben Posten, Joel Rubin, and Anthony Pesce, "LAPD Underreported Serious Assaults, Skewing Crime Stats for 8 Years," *LA Times,* October 15, 2015, http://www.latimes.com/local/cityhall/la-me-crime-stats-20151015-story.html.

58. Freia Nahser, "Three Examples of Machine Learning in the Newsroom," *Global Editors Network* (blog), March 2018, https://medium.com/global-editors-network/three-examples-of-machine-learning-in-the-newsroom-1b47d1f7515a.

59. Alfred Hermida, Seth C. Lewis, and Rodrigo Zamith, "Sourcing the Arab Spring: A Case Study of Andy Carvin's Sources on Twitter during the Tunisian and Egyptian Revolutions," *Journal of Computer-Mediated Communication,* 19, no. 3 (2014).

60. For details on the development of one score that considers Twitter activity of a user, see Richard Fletcher, Steve Schifferes, and Neil Thurman, "Building the 'Truthmeter': Training Algorithms to Help Journalists Assess the Credibility of Social Media Sources," *Convergence: The International Journal of Research into New Media Technologies,* published ahead of print (2017).

61. Nicholas Diakopoulos, Munmun De Choudhury, and Mor Naaman, "Finding and Assessing Social Media Information Sources in the Context of Journalism," *Proceedings of the Conference on Human Factors in Computing Systems* (New York: ACM, 2012).

62. Rui Fang et al., "Witness Identification in Twitter," presented at the Fourth International Workshop on Natural Language Processing for Social Media, Austin, TX, 2016.

63. Claire Wardle, "Fake News. It's Complicated," *First Draft News* (blog), February 2017, https://medium.com/1st-draft/fake-news-its-complicated-d0f773766c79.

64. Arkaitz Zubiaga et al., "Analysing How People Orient to and Spread Rumours in Social Media by Looking at Conversational Threads," *PloS one* 11, no. 3 (2016).

65. Klas Backholm et al., "Crises, Rumours and Reposts: Journalists' Social Media Content Gathering and Verification Practices in Breaking News Situations," *Media and Communication* 5, no. 2 (2017).

66. Carlos Castillo, Marcelo Mendoza, Barbara Poblete, "Information Credibility on Twitter," *Proceedings of the World Wide Web Conference* (New York ACM, 2011).

67. Christina Boididou et al., "Learning to Detect Misleading Content on Twitter," *Proceedings of the International Conference on Multimedia Retrieval* (New York: ACM, 2017).

68. The efforts are part of an EU-funded project called "InVid." See "InVID Verification Plugin Open Beta Release," accessed August 7, 2018, http://www.invid-project.eu/invid-verification-plugin-open-beta-release/.

69. See the MediaEval Benchmarking Initiative for Multimedia evaluation http://www.multimediaeval.org/, accessed October 28, 2018; for a summary of RumourEval results from 2017, see Leon Derczynski et al., "SemEval-2017 Task 8: RumourEval: Determining Rumour Veracity and Support for Rumours," presented at the Workshop on Semantic Evaluation, Vancouver, Canada, 2017, https://arxiv.org/abs/1704.059/2v1.

70. Sarah Harrison Smith, *The Fact Checker's Bible: A Guide to Getting It Right* (New York: Anchor, 2004); Lucinda Southern, "Inside Spiegel's 70-Person Fact-Checking Team," Digiday, August 2017, https://digiday.com/media/inside-spiegels-70-person-fact-checking-team/.

71. Elizabeth Jensen, "Behind the Scenes: NPR Fact Checks First Debate in Near Real Time," National Public Radio, October 3, 2016, http://www.npr.org/sections/ombudsman/2016/09/27/495654679/behind-the-scenes-npr-fact-checks-first-debate-in-near-real-time; Shan Wang, "How NPR Factchecked the First Presidential Debate in Real-time, on Top of a Live Transcript," Nieman Lab, September 2016, http://www.niemanlab.org/2016/09/how-npr-factchecked-the-first-presidential-debate-in-realtime-on-top-of-a-live-transcript/.

72. Brooks Jackson and Kathleen Hall Jamieson, *unSpun: Finding Facts in a World of Disinformation* (New York: Random House, 2007).

73. Mevar Babakar and Will Moy, "The State of Automated Fact-checking," FullFact, August 2016, https://fullfact.org/media/uploads/full_fact_the_state_of_automated_factchecking_aug_2016.pdf.

74. Nicholas Diakopoulos, "Scaling Fact-Checking," *Tow-Knight Center for Entrepreneurial Journalism* (blog), June 2012, http://towknight

.org/research/thinking/scaling-fact-checking/. See also a summary of automated fact checking initiatives which reinforces the need for a hybrid approach in Lucas Graves, *Understanding the Promise and Limits of Automated Fact-Checking* (Oxford, UK: Reuters Institute for the Study of Journalism, 2018).

75. Naeemul Hassan et al., "Toward Automated Fact-Checking: Detecting Check-Worthy Factual Claims by ClaimBuster," *Proceedings of the Conference on Knowledge Discovery and Datamining* (New York: ACM, 2017).

76. ClaimBuster is available online and you can enter your own text to score it: http://idir-server2.uta.edu/claimbuster/demo, accessed October 28, 2018.

77. Daniel Funke, "This Washington Post Fact Check Was Chosen by a Bot," Poynter, January 2018, https://www.poynter.org/news/washington -post-fact-check-was-chosen-bot.

78. Lev Konstantinovskiy et al. "Towards Automated Factchecking: Developing an Annotation Schema and Benchmark for Consistent Automated Claim Detection," presented at The First Workshop on Fact Extraction and Verification (FEVER), Brussels, Belgium, 2018.

79. For demos, see Will Moy and Mevan Babakar, "Automated Factchecking in the Era of Fake News," presented at PyData, London, 2017, https://www.youtube.com/watch?v=VPtfezx8WSg. See also Daniel Funke, "In a Step toward Automation, Full Fact Has Built a Live Fact-Checking Prototype," Poynter, November, 2017, https://www.poynter.org /news/step-toward-automation-full-fact-has-built-live-fact-checking -prototype.

80. James Thorne and Andreas Vlachos, "An Extensible Framework for Verification of Numerical Claims," presented at the European Chapter of the Association for Computational Linguistics, Valencia, Spain, 2017.

81. Nathalie Jomini Stroud, Joshua Scacco, Alexander Curry, "The Presence and Use of Interactive Features on News Websites," *Digital Journalism* 4, no. 3 (2016).

82. Nicholas Diakopoulos and Mor Naaman, "Towards Quality Discourse in Online News Comments," *Proceedings of the Conference on Computer Supported Cooperative Work* (New York: ACM, 2011).

83. Ashley A. Anderson et al., "The 'Nasty Effect': Online Incivility and Risk Perceptions of Emerging Technologies," *Journal of Computer-Mediated Communication* 19, no. 3 (2014).

84. AutoModerator, Reddit, accessed August 7, 2018, https://www .reddit.com/wiki/automoderator.

85. For more details on the performance of the system, see Shailesh Prakash, "Journalism & Technology: Big Data, Personalization & Automation," keynote presented at the Computation + Journalism Symposium, Evanston, IL, 2017, https://youtu.be/PqMvxo89AQ4?list=PL3k jMDQ990L556im9F1qozenDo2rMpccH&t=2737.

86. Jillian York, "Google's Anti-Bullying AI Mistakes Civility for Decency," Motherboard, August 2017, https://motherboard.vice.com/en_us /article/qvvv3p/googles-anti-bullying-ai-mistakes-civility-for-decency.

87. Nicholas Diakopoulos, "The Editor's Eye: Curation and Comment Relevance on the New York Times," *Proceedings of the Conference on Computer Supported Cooperative Work* (New York: ACM, 2015).

88. Nicholas Diakopoulos, "Picking the NYT Picks: Editorial Criteria and Automation in the Curation of Online News Comments," *#ISOJ Journal* 6, no. 1 (2016).

89. Deok Gun Park et al., "Supporting Comment Moderators in Identifying High Quality Online News Comments," *Proceedings of the Conference on Human Factors in Computing Systems* (New York: ACM, 2016).

90. James T. Hamilton, *Democracy's Detectives* (Cambridge, MA: Harvard University Press, 2016).

91. For statistics on the average time spent on an investigative report, see Hamilton, *Democracy's Detectives,* 159.

92. Ariana Giorgi, "An Analysis of Methods for Information Retrieval," MA thesis, Columbia Journalism School, 2015, https://github .com/arianagiorgi/masters-proj/blob/master/Giorgi_MP2015.pdf.

93. Meredith Broussard, "Artificial Intelligence for Investigative Reporting," *Digital Journalism* 3, no. 6 (2015).

94. Shoemaker and Vos, *Gatekeeping Theory.*

95. François Heinderyckx and Tim Vos, "Reformed Gatekeeping," *Communication and Media* 11, no. 38 (2016).

96. Shoemaker and Vos, *Gatekeeping Theory.*

97. Nicholas Diakopoulos, "Diversity in the Robot Reporter Newsroom," *Tow Center for Digital Journalism* (blog), July 2014, https:// towcenter.org/diversity-in-the-robot-reporter-newsroom/.

98. See for instance the ClaimRank system, which is trained on and can be adapted based on data from nine different fact-checking organizations: Israa Jaradat et al., "ClaimRank: Detecting Check-Worthy Claims in Arabic and English," presented at the Annual Conference of the North American Chapter of the Association for Computational Linguistics:

Human Language Technologies (NAACL-HLT) Demonstrations, New Orleans, LA, 2018.

99. Eirik Stavelin, "Computational Journalism. When Journalism Meets Programming," PhD diss., University of Bergen, 2014, http:// stavelin.com/uib/ComputationalJournalism_EirikStavelin.pdf.

100. Neil Thurman et al., "Giving Computers a Nose for News," *Digital Journalism* 4, no. 7 (2016).

101. Jens Finnäs and Måns Magnusson, "Marple: 'We Tried to Automate Story Finding in Data—This Is What We Learnt,'" *Data Driven Journalism,* August 2017, http://datadrivenjournalism.net/featured _projects/marple_we_tried_to_automate_story_finding_in_data_this_is _what_we_learnt#.WZLWkcDXK9Y.twitter.

102. Schwartz, Naaman, and Theordoro, "Editorial Algorithms: Using Social Media to Discover and Report Local News"; and Thurman, "Social Media, Surveillance, and News Work."

103. Hamilton, *Democracy's Detectives.*

104. For a survey, while not applied in the domain of journalism, see Richard J. Bolton and David J. Hand, "Statistical Fraud Detection: A Review," *Statistical Science* 17, no. 3 (2002).

105. For a review of the evolution in journalism, see Stephen Ward, "Epistemologies of Journalism," in *Journalism (Handbooks of Communication Science),* ed. Tim Vos (Berlin, Boston: Mouton De Gruyter, 2018).

106. Seth Lewis and Oscar Westlund, "Big Data and Journalism," *Digital Journalism* 3, no. 3 (2015); Sylvain Parasie, "Data-Driven Revelation?" *Digital Journalism* 3, no. 3 (2015).

107. James Ettema and Theodore Glasser, *Custodians of Conscience: Investigative Journalism and Public Virtue* (New York: Columbia University Press, 1998).

108. For an example of a public-facing decision tree in journalism, see Stefano Ceccon, "The Election Explained by the Times Data Team," *Digital Times* (blog), May 18, 2015, https://medium.com/digital-times /the-election-explained-by-the-times-data-team-482d3ab95f5c.

109. Jennifer Stark and Nicholas Diakopoulos, "Towards Editorial Transparency in Computational Journalism," presented at the Computation + Journalism Symposium, Palo Alto, CA, 2016.

110. For a more thorough treatment of "the dial" and its relationship to the understanding of certainty and uncertainty in journalism, see C. W. Anderson, *Apostles of Certainty: Data Journalism and the Politics of Doubt* (Oxford: Oxford University Press, 2018).

3. AUTOMATED CONTENT PRODUCTION

1. Neil Thurman, Konstantin Dörr, and Jessica Kunert, "When Reporters Get Hands-On with Robo-Writing: Professionals Consider Automated Journalism's Capabilities and Consequences," *Digital Journalism* 5, no. 10 (2017).

2. Dongwan Kim, "An Algorithmic Approach to Personalized and Interactive News Generation," PhD diss., Seoul National University, 2017, http://s-space.snu.ac.kr/bitstream/10371/120411/1/000000141346.pdf.

3. Ehud Reiter and Robert Dale, *Building Natural Language Generation Systems* (Cambridge, UK: Cambridge University Press, 2000); Ehud Reiter, "Natural Language Generation," in *The Handbook of Computational Linguistics and Natural Language Processing*, ed. Alexander Clark, Chris Fox, and Shalom Lappin (Oxford, UK: Wiley-Blackwell, 2010); Amanda Stent and Srinivas Bangalore, eds., *Natural Language Generation in Interactive Systems* (New York: Cambridge University Press, 2014).

4. Eli Goldberg, Norbert Driedger, and Richard Kittredge, "Using Natural-Language Processing to Produce Weather Forecasts," *IEEE Expert* 9, no. 2 (1994).

5. Leo Leppänen et al., "Finding and Expressing News From Structured Data," presented at AcademicMindtrek, Helsinki, Finland, 2017.

6. Bastian Haarmann and Lukas Sikorski, "Natural Language News Generation from Big Data," *International Journal of Computer, Electrical, Automation, Control and Information Engineering* 9, no. 6 (2015).

7. Nicholas D. Allen et al., "StatsMonkey: A Data-Driven Sports Narrative Writer," presented at the Association for the Advancement of Artificial Intelligence (AAAI) Fall Symposium, Arlington, VA, 2010.

8. Lawrence A. Birnbaum et al., System and Method for Using Data to Automatically Generate a Narrative Story, US Patent, US8688434B1, filed May 13, 2010, and issued April 1, 2014, https://www.google.com/patents/US8688434.

9. Espen Waldal, "Building a Robot Journalist," *B&B Stories* (blog), November 18, 2016, https://medium.com/bakken-b%C3%A6ck/building-a-robot-journalist-171554a68fa8.

10. Albert Gatt and Ehud Reiter, "SimpleNLG: A Realisation Engine for Practical Applications," presented at the European Workshop on Natural Language Generation, Athens, Greece, 2009; Al Johri, Eui-Hong Han, and Dhrumil Mehta, "Domain Specific Newsbots," presented at the Computation + Journalism Symposium, Palo, Alto, CA, 2016.

11. Regina Barzilay and Mirella Lapata, "Collective Content Selection for Concept-to-Text Generation," *Proceedings of the Human Language Technology Conference and Conference on Empirical Methods in Natural Language Processing* (Stroudsburg, PA: Association for Computational Linguistics, 2005).

12. Joy Mahapatra, Sudip Naskar, and Sivaji Bandyopadhyay, "Statistical Natural Language Generation from Tabular Non-Textual Data," *Proceedings of the International Natural Language Generation Conference* (2016).

13. Ravi Kondadadi, Blake Howald, and Frank Schilder, "A Statistical NLG Framework for Aggregated Planning and Realization," *Proceedings of the Association for Computational Linguistics* (Stroudsburg, PA: Association for Computational Linguistics, 2013).

14. Freddy Chong Tat Chua and Sitaram Asur, "Automatic Summarization of Events from Social Media," *Proceedings of the Conference on Weblogs and Social Media* (Palo Alto: The AAAI Press, 2013); Philip J. McParlane, Andrew J. McMinn, Joemon M. Jose, "Picture the Scene . . .: Visually Summarising Social Media Events," *Proceedings of the International Conference on Information and Knowledge Management* (New York: ACM, 2014); Jeffrey Nichols, Jalal Mahmud, and Clemens Drews, "Summarizing Sporting Events Using Twitter," *Proceedings of the Conference on Intelligent User Interfaces* (New York: ACM, 2012).

15. Elena Lloret and Manuel Palomar, "Towards Automatic Tweet Generation: A Comparative Study from the Text Summarization Perspective in the Journalism Genre," *Expert Systems with Applications* 40, no. 16 (2013); Kristian Woodsend and Mirella Lapata, "Automatic Generation of Story Highlights," *Proceedings of the Annual Meeting of the Association for Computational Linguistics* (Stroudsburg, PA: Association for Computational Linguistics, 2010); Bonnie Dorr, David Zajic, and Richard Schwartz, "Hedge Trimmer: A Parse-and-Trim Approach to Headline Generation,"(presented at the Human Language Technologies - North American Chapter of the Association for Computational Linguistics (HLT-NAACL) Workshop on Text Summarization, Edmonton, Canada, 2003; Yonatan Oren, "Flipboard's Approach to Automatic Summarization," *Flipboard* (blog), October 2014, https://about.flipboard.com /engineering/flipboards-approach-to-automatic-summarization/.

16. Ani Nenkova and Kathleen McKeown, "A Survey of Text Summarization Techniques," in *Mining Text Data*, ed. Charu C. Aggarwal and ChengXiang Zhai (Boston: Springer, 2012).

17. Stefano Bocconi, Frank Nack, and Lynda Hardman, "Automatic Generation of Matter-of-Opinion Video Documentaries," *Web Seman-*

tics: Science, Services and Agents on the World Wide Web 6, no. 2 (2008); Diogo Delgado, Joao Magalhaes, and Nuno Correia, "Assisted News Reading with Automated Illustration," *Proceedings of the International Conference on Multimedia* (New York: ACM, 2010); Jack Jansen et al., "Just-in-Time Personalized Video Presentations," *Proceedings of the Symposium on Document Engineering* (New York: ACM, 2012); Nate Nichols and Kristian Hammond, "Machine-Generated Multimedia Content," presented at the Conference on Advances in Computer-Human Interactions, Washington, DC, 2009.

18. Nathalie Riche, Christophe Hurter, Nicholas Diakopoulos, and Sheelagh Carpendale, eds. *Data-Driven Storytelling* (Boca Raton, FL: CRC Press, 2018).

19. Jessica Hullman, Nicholas Diakopoulos, and Eytan Adar, "Contextifier: Automatic Generation of Annotated Stock Visualizations," *Proceedings of the Conference on Human Factors in Computing Systems [CHI]* (New York: ACM, 2013).

20. Stephen Feiner and Kathleen McKeown, "Automating the Generation of Coordinated Multimedia Explanations," *Computer* 24 no. 10 (1991); Nancy Green et al., "Autobrief—An Experimental System for the Automatic Generation of Briefings in Integrated Text and Information Graphics," *International Journal of Human-Computer Studies* 61, no. 1 (2004); Rola Alhalaseh et al., "Towards Data-Driven Generation of Visualizations for Automatically Generated News Articles" presented at Academic Mindtrek, Tampere, Finland, 2018.

21. Vibhu Mittal et al., "Describing Complex Charts in Natural Language: A Caption Generation System," *Computational Linguistics* 24, no. 3 (1998).

22. Hullman, Diakopoulos, and Adar, "Contextifier"; Tong Gao et al., "NewsViews: An Automated Pipeline for Creating Custom Geovisualizations for News," *Proceedings of the Conference on Human Factors in Computing* (New York: ACM, 2014).

23. Patrick Stotz and Danial Montazeri, "Taktiktafeln: You've Never Seen Soccer Like This Before!" ("SPON-Taktiktafeln—So Haben Sie Fußball Noch Nie Gesehen!") *Spiegel Online,* January 27, 2017, http://www.spiegel.de/sport/fussball/bundesliga-taktiktafeln-paesse-und-formationen-der-bundesligateams-a-1131647.html. Reuters has experimented with automatically including visualizations produced by Graphiq, see: Lora Kolodny, "Reuters Is the Latest Large News Agency to Embrace Content Automation," *Tech Crunch,* September 13, 2016, https://techcrunch.com/2016/09/13/reuters-is-the-latest-large-news-agency-to-embrace-content-automation/.

24. For an example of voice generation see Vocal Avatar, Lyrebird, accessed August 9, 2018, https://lyrebird.ai/demo.

25. Mattias Niessner, "Face2Face: Real-Time Face Capture and Reenactment of RGB Videos," YouTube, March 2016, https://www.youtube.com/watch?v=ohmajJTcpNk.

26. Kevin Roose, "Here Come the Fake Videos, Too," *New York Times,* March 4, 2018, https://www.nytimes.com/2018/03/04/technology/fake-videos-deepfakes.html.

27. See video linked here: Karen Hao, "Researchers Have Figured Out How to Fake News Video with AI," *Quartz,* July 2017, https://qz.com/1031624/researchers-have-figured-out-how-to-fake-news-video-with-ai/; Supasorn Suwajanakorn, Steven Seitz, and Ira Kemelmacher-Shlizerman, "Synthesizing Obama: Learning Lip Sync From Audio," *ACM Transactions On Graphics* 36, no. 4 (2017).

28. Tero Karras et al., "Progressive Growing of GANs for Improved Quality, Stability, and Variation," presented at the International Conference on Learning Representations, Vancouver, Canada, 2018.

29. Yuanshun Yao, "Automated Crowdturfing Attacks and Defenses in Online Review Systems," *Proceedings of Computer and Communications Security* (New York: ACM, 2017).

30. James Vincent, "Artificial Intelligence Is Going to Make It Easier than Ever to Fake Images and Video," *Verge,* December 20, 2016, https://www.theverge.com/2016/12/20/14022958/ai-image-manipulation-creation-fakes-audio-video.

31. Valentina Conotter et al., "Physiologically-Based Detection of Computer Generated Faces in Video," *Proceedings of the IEEE International Conference on Image Processing* (2014); Andreas Rössle et al., "FaceForensics: A Large-Scale Video Dataset for Forgery Detection in Human Faces," ArXiv pre-print, https://arxiv.org/abs/1803.09179. See also Hany Farid, "How to Detect Faked Photos," *American Scientist* 105, no. 2 (March–April, 2017).

32. Goldberg, Driedger, and Kittredge, "Using Natural-Language Processing to Produce Weather Forecasts."

33. "Robots at 'Le Monde' During the Departmental Elections? Yes and No" ("Des robots au 'Monde' pendant les élections départementales? Oui . . . et non") *Back Office* (blog), March 23, 2015, http://makingof.blog.lemonde.fr/2015/03/23/des-robots-au-monde-pendant-les-elections-departementales-oui-et-non/; Johanna Vehkoo, "News Robots Finally Arrived in Finland," "Uutisrobotit Tulivat Vihdoin Suomeen," Jornalisti, March 2017, https://www.journalisti.fi/artikkelit/2017/4/uutisrobotit-tulivat-vihdoin-suomeen/; Leo Leppänen et al., "Data-

Driven News Generation for Automated Journalism," *Proceedings of the International Conference on Natural Language Generation* (Stroudsburg, PA: Association for Computational Linguistics, 2017).

34. Andreas Graefe, *Computational Campaign Coverage* (New York: Tow Center for Digital Journalism, 2017), https://www.cjr.org/tow_center_reports/computational-campaign-coverage.php/.

35. Alexander Fanta, *Putting Europe's Robots on the Map: Automated Journalism in News Agencies* (Oxford: Reuters Institute for the Study of Journalism, 2017), https://reutersinstitute.politics.ox.ac.uk/our-research/putting-europes-robots-map-automated-journalism-news-agencies.

36. Allen et al., "StatsMonkey"; see http://statsmonkey.infolab.north western.edu/baseball/ for sample output. For information on Yle's open source hockey story writer, see https://github.com/Yleisradio/avoin-voitto, accessed October 31, 2018; Rich McCormick, "AP's 'Robot Journalists' Are Writing about Minor League Baseball Now," *Verge*, July 4, 2016, https://www.theverge.com/2016/7/4/12092768/ap-robot-journa lists-automated-insights-minor-league-baseball.

37. "The Washington Post to Use Artificial Intelligence to Cover Nearly 500 Races on Election Day," *Washington Post*, October 19, 2016, https://www.washingtonpost.com/pr/wp/2016/10/19/the-washington-post-uses-artificial-intelligence-to-cover-nearly-500-races-on-election-day; "The Washington Post Leverages Automated Storytelling to Cover High School Football," *Washington Post*, September 1, 2017, https://www.washingtonpost.com/pr/wp/2017/09/01/the-washing ton-post-leverages-heliograf-to-cover-high-school-football/.

38. Scott Klein, "How to Edit 52,000 Stories at Once," ProPublica, January 2013, https://www.propublica.org/nerds/item/how-to-edit-52000-stories-at-once; Mary Lynn Young and Alfred Hermida, "From Mr. and Mrs. Outlier to Central Tendencies," *Digital Journalism* 3, no. 3 (2014); Will Oremus, "The First News Report on the L.A. Earthquake Was Written by a Robot," *Slate*, March 17, 2014, http://www.slate.com/blogs/future_tense/2014/03/17/quakebot_los_angeles_times_robot_journalist_writes_article_on_la_earthquake.html.

39. Li L'Estrade, "MittMedia Homeowners Bot Boosts Digital Subscriptions with Automated Articles," *INMA* (blog), June 2018, https://www.inma.org/blogs/ideas/post.cfm/mittmedia-homeowners-bot-boosts-digital-subscriptions-with-automated-articles.

40. Shuguang Wang, Eui-Hong (Sam) Han, and Alexander Rush, "Headliner: An Integrated Headline Suggestion System," presented at the Computation+Journalism Symposium, Palo Alto, CA, 2016.

41. Rob Hotakainen, Lindsay Wise, Frank Matt, and Samantha Ehlinger, "Irradiated," McClatchy, 2016, http://media.mcclatchydc.com/static/features/irradiated/.

42. Andreas Graefe, *Guide to Automated Journalism* (New York: Tow Center for Digital Journalism, 2016), https://www.cjr.org/tow_center_reports/guide_to_automated_journalism.php/.

43. Nikki Usher, "Breaking News Production Processes in US Metropolitan Newspapers: Immediacy and Journalistic Authority," *Journalism* 19, no. 1 (2017); and Justin Lewis and Stephen Cushion, "The Thirst to Be First," *Journalism Practice* 3, no. 3 (2009).

44. Gaye Tuchman, "Making News by Doing Work: Routinizing the Unexpected," *American Journal of Sociology,* 79, no. 1 (1973).

45. Jonathan Bright, "The Social News Gap: How News Reading and News Sharing Diverge," *Journal of Communication* 66, no. 3 (2016).

46. Matt Carlson, "Automated Journalism: A Posthuman Future for Digital News?" in *The Routledge Companion to Digital Journalism Studies,* ed. Bob Franklin and Scott Eldridge II (London: Routledge, 2016).

47. Elizabeth Blankespoor, Ed deHaan, and Christina Zhu, "Capital Market Effects of Media Synthesis and Dissemination: Evidence from Robo-Journalism," *Review of Accounting Studies* 21, no. 2 (2016).

48. Oremus, "The First News Report on the L.A. Earthquake."

49. Graefe, *Computational Campaign Coverage.*

50. Ben Ashwell, "How Automated Financial News Is Changing Quarterly Earnings Coverage," *IR Magazine,* June 2018, https://www.irmagazine.com/reporting/how-automated-financial-news-changing-quarterly-earnings-coverage.

51. Daniel Billsus and Michael Pazzani, "Adaptive News Access," in *The Adaptive Web: Lecture Notes in Computer Science* (Heidelberg: Springer, 2007); Neil Thurman, "Making 'The Daily Me': Technology, Economics, and Habit in the Mainstream Assimilation of Personalized News," *Journalism* 12, no. 4 (2011).

52. Krishna Bharat, Tomonari Kamba, and Michael Albers, "Personalized, Interactive News on the Web," *Multimedia Systems* 6, no. 5 (1998).

53. Eytan Adar et al., "PersaLog: Personalization of News Article Content," *Proceedings of Human Factors in Computing Systems* (New York: ACM, 2017).

54. Billsus and Pazzani, "Adaptive News Access."

55. Kim, "An Algorithmic Approach to Personalized and Interactive News Generation."

56. Somayajulu Sripada et al., "A Case Study: NLG Meeting Weather Industry Demand for Quality and Quantity of Textual Weather Forecasts," *Proceedings of the International Conference on Natural Language Generation* (New York: ACM, 2014).

57. "Google Funds Automated News Project," *BBC News*, July 6, 2017, http://www.bbc.com/news/technology-40517420. See also the RADAR website: http://radarai.com/, accessed October 31, 2018.

58. David Sharman, "Four Journalists Join PA Robot Reporting Unit as Scheme Expands," *HoldTheFrontPage*, June 18, 2018, https://www.holdthefrontpage.co.uk/2018/news/four-journalists-join-pa-robot-reporting-unit-as-scheme-expands/.

59. Shan Wang, "This Hyperlocal News Site in San Francisco Is Reinventing Itself with an Automated Local News Wire," Nieman Lab, February 2018, http://www.niemanlab.org/2018/02/this-hyperlocal-news-site-in-san-francisco-is-reinventing-itself-with-an-automated-local-news-wire/. For an example article, see: "Explore These 5 New Montrose Businesses," February 2018, http://abc13.com/food/explore-these-5-new-montrose-businesses/3039818/.

60. Gregor Aisch et al., "Where the Poor Live Longer: How Your Area Compares," *New York Times*, April 11, 2016, https://www.nytimes.com/interactive/2016/04/11/upshot/where-the-poor-live-longer-how-your-area-compares.html; Gregor Aisch et al., "The Best and Worst Places to Grow Up: How Your Area Compares," *New York Times*, May 4, 2015, https://www.nytimes.com/interactive/2015/05/03/upshot/the-best-and-worst-places-to-grow-up-how-your-area-compares.html; Kevin Quealy and Margot Sanger-Katz, "The Experts Were Wrong about the Best Places for Better and Cheaper Health Care," *New York Times*, December 15, 2016, https://www.nytimes.com/interactive/2015/12/15/upshot/the-best-places-for-better-cheaper-health-care-arent-what-experts-thought.html; Ted Mellnik et al., "America's Great Housing Divide: Are You a Winner or Loser?" *Washington Post*, April 28, 2016, https://www.washingtonpost.com/graphics/business/wonk/housing/overview/; Sarah Kliff, Soo Oh, and Sarah Frostenson, "Today's Teens . . . Less Than You Did," *Vox*, June 2016, https://www.vox.com/a/teens.

61. Lucia Moses, "The Washington Post's Robot Reporter Has Published 850 Articles in the Past Year," *Digiday*, September 2017, https://digiday.com/media/washington-posts-robot-reporter-published-500-articles-last-year/.

62. L'Estrade, "MittMedia Homeowners."

63. Thurman, Dörr, and Kunert, "When Reporters Get Hands-On with Robo-Writing."

64. Katherine Fink and C. W. Anderson, "Data Journalism in the United States," *Journalism Studies* 16, no. 4 (2014).

65. Fanta, *Putting Europe's Robots on the Map.*

66. Fergus Pitt, *Sensors and Journalism* (New York: Tow Center for Digital Journalism, 2014), http://towcenter.org/wp-content/uploads/2014 /05/Tow-Center-Sensors-and-Journalism.pdf; Sarah Cohen, James T. Hamilton, and Fred Turner, "Computational Journalism," *Communications of the ACM* 54, no. 10 (2011).

67. For instance, many of the quality heuristics available in "The Quartz Guide to Bad Data" required human attention; see https://github .com/Quartz/bad-data-guide, accessed October 31, 2018. For a framework for assessing data quality for automated journalism developed, see Laurence Dierickx, "News Bot for the Newsroom: How Building Data Quality Indicators Can Support Journalistic Projects Relying on Real-Time Open Data," presented at the Global Investigative Journalism Conference, Johannesburg, South Africa, 2017, http://ijec.org/2018/02/02 /research-news-bot-for-the-newsroom-how-building-data-quality -indicators-can-support-journalistic-projects-relying-on-real-time-open -data/.

68. David Caswell and Konstantin Dörr, "Automated Journalism 2.0: Event-Driven Narratives," *Journalism Practice* 12, no. 4 (2018); David Caswell, "Computable News Ecosystems: Roles for Humans and Machines," presented at the Second Workshop on Computing News Storylines, Austin, TX, 2016.

69. Matt Carlson, "The Robotic Reporter," *Digital Journalism* 3, no. 3 (2015).

70. Tarleton Gillespie, "The Relevance of Algorithms," in *Media Technologies: Essays on Communication, Materiality, and Society,* ed. Tarleton Gillespie, Pablo Boczkowski, and Kirstin Foot (Cambridge, MA: MIT Press, 2014). See also the case study of structured journalism presented in C. W. Anderson, *Apostles of Certainty: Data Journalism and the Politics of Doubt* (Oxford: Oxford University Press, 2018).

71. Carl-Gustav Linden, "Algorithms for Journalism: The Future of News Work," *Journal of Media Innovations* 4, no. 1 (2017); Konstantin Dörr and Katharina Hollnbuchner, "Ethical Challenges of Algorithmic Journalism," *Digital Journalism* 5, no. 4 (2017).

72. Aylin Caliskan, Joanna Bryson, and Arvind Narayanan, "Semantics Derived Automatically from Language Corpora Contain Human-Like Biases," *Science,* 356, no. 6334 (2017).

73. Fink and Anderson, "Data Journalism in the United States"; Dörr and Hollnbuchner, "Ethical Challenges of Algorithmic Journalism."

74. Cohen, Hamilton, and Turner, "Computational Journalism."

75. Zvi Reich, "The Impact of Technology on News Reporting: A Longitudinal Perspective," *Journalism & Mass Communication Quarterly* 90, no. 3 (2013).

76. Noam Lemelshtrich Latar, "The Robot Journalist in the Age of Social Physics: The End of Human Journalism?" in *The New World of Transitioned Media. The Economics of Information, Communication, and Entertainment,* ed. Gali Einav (Cham, Switzerland: Springer International Publishing, 2015).

77. Eric Horvitz, "Reflections on Challenges and Promises of Mixed-Initiative Interaction," *AI Magazine,* Summer 2007.

78. Jeffrey Nichols and Jeon-Hyung Kang, "Asking Questions of Targeted Strangers on Social Networks," *Proceedings of the Conference on Computer Supported Cooperative Work* (New York: ACM, 2012).

79. Dan Berkowitz, "Non-Routine News and Newswork: Exploring a What-a-Story," *Journal of Communication* 42, no. 1 (1992).

80. Raja Parasuraman, Thomas Sheridan, and Christopher Wickens, "A Model for Types and Levels of Human Interaction with Automation," *IEEE Transactions on Systems, Man, and Cybernetics—Part A: Systems and Humans,* 30, no. 3 (2000).

81. Fanta, *Putting Europe's Robots on the Map.*

82. Leppänen et al., "Data-Driven News Generation for Automated Journalism."

83. Rong-Gong Lin II, "Revenge of Y2K? A Software Bug Might Have Caused False Alert for Big (and Very Old) Earthquake," *LA Times,* June 22, 2017, http://www.latimes.com/local/lanow/la-me-earthquakesa -earthquake-68-quake-strikes-near-isla-vista-calif-jyhw-htmlstory.html.

84. Graefe, *Guide to Automated Journalism.*

85. Alexander Fanta, "Robots Can Save Local Journalism. But Will They Make It More Biased?" *Data Driven Journalism,* March 2018, http://datadrivenjournalism.net/news_and_analysis/robots_can_save _local_journalism._but_will_they_make_it_more_biased.

86. Carlson, "Automated Journalism."

87. Nicholas Diakopoulos, "Algorithmic Defamation: The Case of the Shameless Autocomplete," *Tow Center* (blog), August 2013, https:// towcenter.org/algorithmic-defamation-the-case-of-the-shameless -autocomplete/. For a definition of "defamation," see Digital Media Law Project, http://www.dmlp.org/legal-guide/defamation, accessed October 31, 2018.

88. For a more international perspective on the laws governing automatic speech, see Meg Leta Jones, "Silencing Bad Bots: Global, Legal and

Political Questions for Mean Machine Communication," *Communication Law and Policy* 23, no. 2 (2018).

89. Meg Leta Ambrose and Ben Ambrose, "When Robots Lie: A Comparison of Auto-Defamation Law," presented at the IEEE Workshop on Advanced Robotics and its Social Impacts (ARSO), Evanston, IL, 2014.

90. Seth C. Lewis, Amy Kristin Sanders, and Casey Carmody, "Libel by Algorithm? Automated Journalism and the Threat of Legal Liability," *Journalism & Mass Communication Quarterly* 80, no. 1 (2018).

91. Dan Ring, "Natural Language Generation Software Turns Data into Plain English," *Tech Target,* September 2016, http://searchfinancial applications.techtarget.com/feature/Natural-language-generation -software-turns-data-into-plain-English.

92. Andreas Graefe et al., "Readers' Perception of Computer-Generated News: Credibility, Expertise, and Readability," *Journalism* 7, no. 6 (2017); Christer Clerwall, "Enter the Robot Journalist," *Journalism Practice* 8, no. 5 (2014); Jaemin Jung et al., "Intrusion of Robots into Journalism: The Public's and Journalists' Perceptions of News Written by Robots and Human Journalists," *Computers in Human Behavior* 71 (2017); Hilla van der Kaa and Emiel Krahmer, "Journalist versus News Consumer: The Perceived Credibility of Machine Written News," presented at the Computation+Journalism Symposium, New York, 2014.

93. Clerwall, "Enter the Robot Journalist."

94. Graefe et al., "Readers' Perception of Computer-Generated News."

95. Anja Wölker and Thomas Powell, "Algorithms in the Newsroom? News Readers' Perceived Credibility and Selection of Automated Journalism," *Journalism* 70, no. 14 (2018).

96. Magnus Melin et al., "No Landslide for the Human Journalist - An Empirical Study of Computer-Generated Election News in Finland," *IEEE Access*, published ahead of print, (2018).

97. Romain Paulus, Caiming Xiong, and Richard Socher, "A Deep Reinforced Model for Abstractive Summarization," arXiv.org, 2017, https://arxiv.org/abs/1705.04304.

98. Fanta, *Putting Europe's Robots on the Map.*

99. "Artificial Intelligence, Automation, and the Economy," Executive Office of the President of the United States, 2016.

100. Konstantin Dörr, "Mapping the Field of Algorithmic Journalism," *Digital Journalism* 4, no. 6 (2016).

101. Ken Schwencke, "How to Break News while You Sleep," *Source,* March 24, 2014, https://source.opennews.org/en-US/articles/how-break -news-while-you-sleep/.

102. Bocconi, Nack, Hardman, "Automatic Generation of Matter-of-Opinion Video Documentaries."

103. Graefe, *Computational Campaign Coverage.*

104. Ben Shneiderman, et al., *Designing the User Interface: Strategies for Effective Human-Computer Interaction,* 6th ed. (Boston: Pearson, 2017); John Lee and Katrina See, "Trust in Automation: Designing for Appropriate Reliance," *Human Factors* 46 no. 1 (2016); Horvitz, "Reflections on Challenges and Promises of Mixed-Initiative Interaction"; Daniel Repperger and Chandler Phillips, "The Human Role in Automation," in *Springer Handbook of Automation,* ed. Shimon Y. Nof (Heidelberg: Springer, 2009).

105. "Artificial Intelligence, Automation, and the Economy."

106. Klein, "How to Edit 52,000 Stories at Once."

107. Sripada et al., "A Case Study: NLG Meeting Weather Industry Demand."

108. Franco Moretti, *Distant Reading* (London: Verso, 2013).

109. Adar et al., "PersaLog."

110. Henrik Örnebring, "Technology and Journalism-as-Labour: Historical Perspectives," *Journalism* 11, no. 1 (2010); Young and Hermida, "From Mr. and Mrs. Outlier to Central Tendencies."

111. Hanna Tuulonen, "A Possibility, a Threat, a Denial? How News Robots Affect Journalists' Work Practices and Professional Identity," MA thesis, University of Gothenburg, 2017.

112. Caswell, "Computable News Ecosystems: Roles for Humans and Machines."

113. Peter Bro, Keneth Reinecke Hansen, and Ralf Andersoon, "Improving Productivity in the Newsroom?" *Journalism Practice* 10, no. 8 (2016); Chang-de Liu, "De-Skilling Effects on Journalists: ICTs and the Labour Process of Taiwanese Newspaper Reporters," *Canadian Journal of Communication* 31, no. 3 (2006).

114. Caswell and Dörr, "Automated Journalism 2.0."

115. Robert O. Wyatt and David Badger, "A New Typology for Journalism and Mass Communication Writing," *Journalism Educator,* Spring 1993.

116. Bocconi, Nack, and Hardman, "Automatic Generation of Matter-of-Opinion Video Documentaries"; Michael Mateas, Paul Vanouse, and Steffi Domike, "Generation of Ideologically-Biased Historical Documentaries," *Proceedings of the Association for the Advancement of Artificial Intelligence (AAAI) Conference on Artificial Intelligence* (2000).

117. Stotz and Montazeri, "Taktiktafeln: You've Never Seen Soccer Like This Before!" ("SPON-Taktiktafeln—So Haben Sie Fußball Noch Nie Gesehen!").

4. NEWSBOTS: AGENTS OF INFORMATION

1. Nicholas Diakopoulos, "Picking the NYT Picks: Editorial Criteria and Automation in the Curation of Online News Comments," #*ISOJ Journal* 6, no. 1 (2015).

2. Nicholas Diakopoulos, "Enabling Accountability of Algorithmic Media: Transparency as a Constructive and Critical Lens," in *Transparent Data Mining for Big and Small Data*, ed. Tania Cerquitelli, Daniele Quercia, and Frank Pasquale (Cham, Switzerland: Springer International Publishing, 2017).

3. AnecbotalNYT (@AnecbotalNYT), Twitter, January 22, 2017, https:// twitter.com/AnecbotalNYT/status/823351538198446080.

4. Tim Hwang, Ian Pearce, and Max Nanis, "Socialbots: Voices from the Fronts," *Interactions*, March / April, 2012; Timothy Graham and Robert Ackland, "Do Socialbots Dream of Popping the Filter Bubble?," in *Socialbots and Their Friends: The Role of Socialbots in Promoting Deliberative Democracy in Social Media*, ed. Robert W. Gehl and Maria Bakardjieva (New York: Routledge, 2017).

5. Nicholas Confessore et al., "The Follower Factory," *New York Times*, January 27, 2018, https://www.nytimes.com/interactive/2018/01 /27/technology/social-media-bots.html.

6. Stefan Wojcik et al., *Bots in the Twittersphere* (Washington, DC: Pew Research Center, 2018), http://www.pewinternet.org/2018/04/09 /bots-in-the-twittersphere/.

7. Onur Varol et al., "Online Human-Bot Interactions: Detection, Estimation, and Characterization," *Proceedings of the International Conference on Web and Social Media* (Palo Alto: The AAAI Press, 2017).

8. Norah Abokhodair, Daisy Yoo, and David W. McDonald, "Dissecting a Social Botnet," *Proceedings of the Conference on Computer Supported Cooperative Work and Social Computing* (New York: Association for Computing Machinery, 2015); Hwang, Pearce, and Nanis, "Socialbots"; Claudia Wagner et al., "When Social Bots Attack: Modeling Susceptibility of Users in Online Social Networks," presented at the second Workshop on Making Sense of Microposts, Lyon, France, 2012; Robert W. Gehl and Maria Bakardjieva, eds., *Socialbots and their Friends* (New York: Routledge, 2017). For a thorough review of definitions of and distinctions between crawlers, chatbots, spambots, social bots, sock puppets, and cyborgs, see Robert Gorwa and Douglas Guilbeault,

"Understanding Bots for Policy and Research: Challenges, Methods, and Solutions," presented at the International Communication Association (ICA) Conference, Prague, Czechia, 2018.

9. Christian Grimme et al., "Social Bots: Human-Like by Means of Human Control?" *Big Data* 5, no. 4 (2017).

10. Robert Dale, "The Return of the Chatbots," *Natural Language Engineering* 22, no. 5 (2016).

11. "Bad Bot Report," Distil Networks, 2017, https://resources.distilnetworks.com/white-paper-reports/2017-bad-bot-report.

12. Emilio Ferrara, et al., "The Rise of Social Bots," *Communications of the ACM* 59, no. 7 (2016).

13. Ewa Luger and Abigail Sellen, "Like Having a Really Bad PA: The Gulf between User Expectation and Experience of Conversational Agents," *Proceedings of the Conference on Human Factors in Computing Systems [CHI]* (New York: Association for Computing Machinery, 2016).

14. Kedar Dhamdhere, "Analyza—Exploring Data with Conversation," *Proceedings of International Conference on Intelligent User Interfaces* (New York: Association for Computing Machinery, 2017).

15. Amanda Stent and Srivinas Bangalore, "Introduction," in *Natural Language Generation in Interactive Systems,* eds. Amanda Stent and Srivinas Bangalore (Cambridge, UK: Cambridge University Press, 2014); Dale, "The Return of the Chatbots"; Justine Cassell, "Embodied Conversational Interface Agents," *Communications of the ACM* 43, no. 4 (2000); Robert Moore et al., "Conversational UX Design," presented at the Conversational UX Design CHI Workshop, Denver, CO, 2017.

16. Al Johri, Eui-Hong (Sam) Han, and Dhrumil Mehta, "Domain Specific Newsbots," presented at the Computation + Journalism Symposium, Palo Alto, CA, 2016.

17. Marisa Vasconcelos, Heloisa Candello, and Claudio Pinhanez, "Bottester: Testing Conversational Systems with Simulated Users," presented at the Conversational UX Design CHI Workshop, Denver, CO, 2017.

18. For a light treatment, see Alex Hern, "Please, Facebook, Don't Make Me Speak to Your Awful Chatbots," April 29, 2016, *Guardian,* https://www.theguardian.com/technology/2016/apr/29/please-facebook-dont-make-me-speak-to-your-awful-chatbots. For a more rigorous comparison between GUIs and CUIs, see Michael Lewis, "Designing for Human-Agent Interaction," *AI Magazine* 19, no. 2 (1998); and Ben Shneiderman, "Direct Manipulation versus Agents: Paths to Predictable, Controllable, and Comprehensible Interfaces," in *Software Agents,* ed. Jeffrey M. Bradshaw (Menlo Park, CA: AAAI Press, 1997).

19. "Meet Our Experimental Guardian Sous-Chef Facebook Messenger Bot," *Guardian,* June 9, 2016, https://www.theguardian.com/technology /2016/jun/09/meet-our-experimental-guardian-sous-chef-facebook -messenger-bot; "Want to Join the Vogue Club?" *Vogue,* February 2017, http://www.vogue.co.uk/article/vogue-daily-update-messaging-service.

20. For an overview of the emerging area of human-machine communication which considers the "creation of meaning among humans and machines," see Andrea L. Guzman, "What Is Human-Machine Communication, Anyway?" in *Human-Machine Communication: Rethinking Communication, Technology, and Ourselves,* ed. Andrea L. Guzman (New York: Peter Lang, 2018).

21. For a full description of the sample and our methodology for analysis, see Tanya Lokot and Nicholas Diakopoulos, "News Bots: Automating News and Information Dissemination on Twitter," *Digital Journalism* 4 no. 6 (2016).

22. Chad Edwards et al., "Is That a Bot Running the Social Media Feed? Testing the Differences in Perceptions of Communication Quality for a Human Agent and a Bot Agent on Twitter," *Computers in Human Behavior* 33 (2014).

23. Max Willens, "Bots Are the New Apps, only They Suck (for Now)," *Digiday,* October 2016, https://digiday.com/media/bots-new -apps-suck-now/.

24. The BBC is experimenting heavily with bots for many different purposes; see "Bots," BBC News Labs, http://bbcnewslabs.co.uk/projects /bots/, accessed October 26, 2018.

25. Keith Collins, "The Injuries Most Likely to Land You in an Emergency Room in America," Quartz, February 2016, https://qz.com/609255 /the-injuries-most-likely-to-land-you-in-an-emergency-room-in-america/.

26. Jia Zhang, "Introducing censusAmericans, a Twitter Bot for America," FiveThirtyEight, July 2015, https://fivethirtyeight.com/features /introducing-censusamericans-a-twitter-bot-for-america/.

27. Eduardo Suarez, "How We Created Politibot, the Bot Who Reports on Telegram Messenger about the Spanish Election Campaign," *Medium* (blog), June 2016, https://nohacefaltapapel.com/how-we-created -politibot-the-bot-who-reports-on-telegram-messenger-about-the -spanish-election-bb21242f6b4f; Mădălina Ciobanu, "More than 6,000 People are Talking to Politibot about the Upcoming Elections in Spain," Journalism.co.uk, June 2016, https://www.journalism.co.uk/news/thous ands-of-people-are-talking-to-politibot-about-the-upcoming-elections /s2/a649186/.

28. Amanda Zamora, "T-Squared: Meet Paige, Our New Facebook Messenger Bot," *Texas Tribune*, March 20, 2017, https://www.texastribune .org/2017/03/20/meet-paige-our-new-facebook-messenger-bot/.

29. Jennifer Nelson, "What the Coloradoan Staff Is Learning while Experimenting with Bots," Reynolds Journalism Institute, April 2017, https://www.rjionline.org/stories/what-the-coloradoan-staff-is-learning -while-experimenting-with-bots.

30. Superkühe, *Westdeutscher Rundfunk*, 2017, https://superkuehe .wdr.de/. see also Bertram Weiß and Jakob Vicari, "Sensor Journalism: Combining Reporting with the Internet of Things," presented at the Algorithms, Automation, and News Conference, Munich, Germany, 2018.

31. In fact, Al Jazeera Interactive has a prototype of tool called "InterviewJS" that could enable such an experience; see "InterviewJS," AJInteractive, April 2018, https://github.com/AJInteractive/InterviewJS.

32. Julia Angwin, Ariana Tobin, and Madeleine Varner, "Have You Experienced Hate Speech on Facebook? We Want to Hear from You," ProPublica, August 2017, https://www.propublica.org/article/have-you -experienced-hate-speech-on-facebook-we-want-to-hear-from-you.

33. Ricardo Bilton, "With Its First Facebook Messenger Bot, ProPublica Is Collecting Reader Stories about Hate Speech," Nieman Lab, August 2017, http://www.niemanlab.org/2017/08/with-its-first-facebook -messenger-bot-propublica-is-collecting-reader-stories-about-hate -speech/.

34. Ariana Tobin, Madeleine Varner, and Julia Angwin, "Facebook's Uneven Enforcement of Hate Speech Rules Allows Vile Posts to Stay Up," ProPublica, December 2017, https://www.propublica.org/article/facebook -enforcement-hate-speech-rules-mistakes.

35. Teddy Amenabar et al., "We Made a Facebook Messenger Bot to Track People's Feelings about the Election. Here's What We Learned," *Washington Post* (blog), December 2016, https://medium.com/thewashing tonpost/we-made-a-facebook-messenger-bot-to-track-peoples-election -feeling-here-s-what-we-learned-1752a889a849.

36. Valerie Belair-Gagnon, Colin Agur, and Nicholas Frisch, "Mobile Sourcing: A Case Study of Journalistic Norms and Usage of Chat Apps," *Mobile Media & Communication* 3, no. 33 (2017).

37. Amanda Hickman and Westley Hennigh-Palermo, "Buzz Bot: What We Learned," Buzzfeed, September 2016, https://www.buzzfeed .com/amandahickman/buzz-bot-what-we-learned.

38. Keith Collins, "Watch as These Bitcoin Wallets Receive Ransomware Payments from the Ongoing Global Cyberattack," Quartz, May 2017,

https://qz.com/982993/watch-as-these-bitcoin-wallets-receive
-ransomware-payments-from-the-ongoing-cyberattack/.

39. For examples from environmental monitoring, see Weiß and Vicari, "Sensor Journalism."

40. Amar Toor, "This Twitter Bot Is Tracking Dictators' Flights in and out of Geneva," *Verge,* October 13, 2016, https://www.theverge.com /2016/10/13/13243072/twitter-bot-tracks-dictator-planes-geneva-gva -tracker.

41. Margaret Sullivan, "No, I Haven't Given Up on Anonymous Sources," *New York Times,* January 13, 2015, https://publiceditor.blogs .nytimes.com/2015/01/13/new-york-times-public-editor-anonymous -sources/; Steve Buttry, "New York Times Takes a Tougher Approach on Unnamed Sources," *The Buttry Diary* (blog), March 16, 2016, https:// stevebuttry.wordpress.com/2016/03/16/new-york-times-takes-a -tougher-approach-on-unnamed-sources/.

42. Nicholas Diakopoulos, "Bots and the Future of Automated Accountability," *Columbia Journalism Review,* September 11, 2018. https:/ /www.cjr.org/tow_center/prepare-to-welcome-our-accountability-bot -overlords.php.

43. Heather Ford, Elizabeth Dubois, and Cornelius Puschmann, "Keeping Ottawa Honest, One Tweet at a Time? Politicians, Journalists, Wikipedians and Their Twitter Bots," *International Journal of Communication* 10 (2016).

44. Mark Sample, "A Protest Bot Is a Bot So Specific You Can't Mistake It for Bullshit," *Medium* (blog), May 2014, https://medium.com /@samplereality/a-protest-bot-is-a-bot-so-specific-you-cant-mistake-it -for-bullshit-90fe10b7fbaa.

45. "United States Foreign Intelligence Surveillance Court," Wikipedia, accessed September 16, 2017, https://en.wikipedia.org/wiki /United_States_Foreign_Intelligence_Surveillance_Court.

46. Jeremy B. Merrill, "What Is the Sound of PunditBot Yapping," *Source,* April 2016, https://source.opennews.org/articles/punditbot-yapping/.

47. Annalisa Merelli, "Introducing Quartz's Newest Bot: @TrumpOfYore," *Quartz,* June 2017, https://qz.com/1006391/introducing-quartzs -new-bot-trump-of-yore/.

48. "Automation Rules," Twitter, April 2017, https://support.twitter .com/articles/76915.

49. Amber Madison, "When Social-Media Companies Censor Sex Education," *Atlantic,* March 2015, http://www.theatlantic.com/health /archive/2015/03/when-social-mediacensors-sex-education/385576/.

50. Colin Lecher, "Twitter Shuts Down a Site that Saved Politicians' Deleted Tweets," *Verge*, June 4, 2016, https://www.theverge.com/2015 /6/4/8731387/politwoops-sunlight-foundation-twitter.

51. David Murphy, "Politicians Beware: Twitter Has Reinstated Politwoops," *PCMag*, December 2015, http://www.pcmag.com/article2 /0,2817,2497304,00.asp.

52. For a critical perspective, see Shneiderman, "Direct Manipulation versus Agents."

53. Cassell, "Embodied Conversational Interface Agents."

54. Luger and Sellen, "Like Having a Really Bad PA."

55. Elizabeth Dwoskin, "The Next Hot Job in Silicon Valley Is for Poets," *Washington Post*, April 7, 2016, https://www.washingtonpost .com/news/the-switch/wp/2016/04/07/why-poets-are-flocking-to-silicon-valley/; John Paul Titlow, "Google Enlists Artists to Make Bots Feel like Friends," *Fast Company*, May 2016, https://www.fastcompany .com/3060180/google-enlists-artists-to-make-bots-feel-like-friends.

56. Gene Ball and Jack Breese, "Emotion and Personality in a Conversational Agent," in *Embodied Conversational Agents*, ed. Justine Cassell et al. (Cambridge, MA: MIT Press, 2000).

57. Jennifer Hill, W. Randolph Ford, and Ingrid G. Farreras, "Real Conversations with Artificial Intelligence: A Comparison between Human–Human Online Conversations and Human–Chatbot Conversations," *Computers in Human Behavior* 49 (2015).

58. Kevin Munger, "Tweetment Effects on the Tweeted: Experimentally Reducing Racist Harassment," *Political Behavior* 39, no. 3 (2017); Amir Shevat, "Hard Questions about Bot Ethics," *Techcrunch*, September 16, 2016, https://techcrunch.com/2016/09/16/hard-questions-about -bot-ethics/.

59. Henriette Cramer and Jennifer Thom, "Moving Parts Surrounding Conversational UX," presented at the Conversational UX Design CHI Workshop, Denver, CO, 2017.

60. "Scripting Chatbots Is Hard. Here's How We Made It Easier for BBC Journalists," *BBC News Lab* (blog), June 2018, https://medium.com /bbc-news-labs/bbc-botbuilder-ba8e09b6a2e9.

61. Mark Stephen Meadows, "I'll Be Bot: Give 'Em Frikkin' License Plates," *Medium*, June 2016, https://medium.com/@meadovian/ill-be-bot -give-em-frikkin-license-plates-343e05f82a24.

62. Samuel Woolley and Philip Howard, "Political Communication, Computational Propaganda, and Autonomous Agents—Introduction," *International Journal of Communication* 10 (2016).

63. Alessandro Bessi and Emilio Ferrara, "Social Bots Distort the 2016 US Presidential Election Online Discussion," *First Monday* 21 no. 11 (2016); Samuel Woolley and Douglas Guilbeault, *Computational Propaganda in the United States of America: Manufacturing Consensus Online* (Oxford, UK: Computational Propaganda Research Project, Oxford Internet Institute, 2017).

64. Bence Kollanyi, Philip Howard, and Samuel Woolley, "Bots and Automation over Twitter during the Third US Presidential Debate," Oxford Internet Institute, 2016, https://www.oii.ox.ac.uk/blog/bots-and-automation-over-twitter-during-the-third-u-s-presidential-debate/.

65. Douglas Guilbeault and Samuel Woolley, "How Twitter Bots Are Shaping the Election," *Atlantic,* November 11, 2016, https://www.theatlantic.com/technology/archive/2016/11/election-bots/506072/.

66. Ryan Bort, "Nearly Half of Donald Trump's Twitter Followers Are Fake Accounts and Bots," *Newsweek,* May 2017, http://www.newsweek.com/donald-trump-twitter-followers-fake-617873.

67. Geoff Goldberg, "When Bots Attack," *Medium,* March 2018, https://medium.com/@geoffgolberg/when-bots-attack-af7f9f87b612.

68. Luis Daniel, "Rise of the Peñabots," *Points* (blog), February 2016, https://points.datasociety.net/rise-of-the-pe%C3%B1abots-d35f9fe12d67.

69. Lisa-Maria Neudert, Bence Kollanyi, and Philip Howard, "Junk News and Bots during the German Parliamentary Election: What Are German Voters Sharing over Twitter?" Computational Propaganda Project, 2017, http://comprop.oii.ox.ac.uk/research/junk-news-and-bots-during-the-german-parliamentary-election-what-are-german-voters-sharing-over-twitter/.

70. "Robotrolling," NATO Stratcom Centre for Excellence, 2017, http://stratcomcoe.org/download/file/fid/75496.

71. Panagiotis Takis Metaxas and Eni Mustafaraj, "Social Media and the Elections," *Science* 338, no. 6106 (2012).

72. For an example of bots used for prosocial activism, see Saiph Savage, Andrés Monroy-Hernández, and Tobias Höllerer, "Botivist: Calling Volunteers to Action Using Online Bots," *Proceedings of Computer Supported Cooperative Work & Social Computing [CSCW]* (New York: ACM, 2016).

73. Isaac Arnsdorf, "Pro-Russian Bots Take Up the Right-Wing Cause after Charlottesville," ProPublica, August 2017, https://www.propublica.org/article/pro-russian-bots-take-up-the-right-wing-cause-after-charlottesville.

74. Chengcheng Shao et al., "The Spread of Fake News by Social Bots," arXiv.org, 2017, http://arxiv.org/abs/1707.07592.

75. Metaxas and Mustafaraj, "Social Media and the Elections."

76. Shao et al., "The Spread of Fake News by Social Bots."

77. Bjarke Mønsted et al., "Evidence of Complex Contagion of Information in Social Media: An Experiment Using Twitter Bots," *PloS one* 12, no. 9 (2017).

78. Woolley and Guilbeault, *Computational Propaganda in the United States*.

79. Bessi and Ferrara, "Social Bots Distort the 2016 US Presidential Election Online Discussion."

80. Klint Finley, "Pro-Government Twitter Bots Try to Hush Mexican Activists," *Wired,* August 2015, https://www.wired.com/2015/08/pro-government-twitter-bots-try-hush-mexican-activists/.

81. Abokhodair, Yoo, and McDonald, "Dissecting a Social Botnet."

82. Henk van Ess and Jane Lytvynenko, "This Russian Hacker Says His Twitter Bots Are Spreading Messages to Help Germany's Far Right Party in the Election," *Buzzfeed News,* September 2017, https://www.buzzfeed.com/henkvaness/these-russian-hackers-say-theyre-using-twitter-bots-to-help.

83. "#BotSpot: The Intimidators," *Digital Forensic Research Lab* (blog), August 2017, https://medium.com/dfrlab/botspot-the-intimidators-135244bfe46b.

84. Fenwick McKelvey and Elizabeth Dubois, *Computational Propaganda in Canada: The Use of Political Bots* (Oxford, UK: Computational Propaganda Research Project, Oxford Internet Institute, 2017), http://comprop.oii.ox.ac.uk/wp-content/uploads/sites/89/2017/06/Comprop-Canada.pdf.

85. Woolley and Guilbeault, *Computational Propaganda in the United States*.

86. "Fakes, Bots, and Blockings in Armenia," *Digital Forensic Research Lab* (blog), April 2017, https://medium.com/dfrlab/fakes-bots-and-blockings-in-armenia-44a4c87ebc46; Brian Krebs, "Twitter Bots Use Likes, RTs for Intimidation," *Krebs on Security* (blog), August 2017, https://krebsonsecurity.com/2017/08/twitter-bots-use-likes-rts-for-intimidation/. For details on how Twitter approaches bots on the platform, see Colin Crowel, "Our Approach to Bots & Misinformation," *Twitter* (blog), June 2017, https://blog.twitter.com/official/en_us/topics/company/2017/Our-Approach-Bots-Misinformation.html.

87. John Herrman, "Not the Bots We Were Looking For," *New York Times,* November 1, 2017, https://www.nytimes.com/2017/11/01

/magazine/not-the-bots-we-were-looking-for.html; Meg Heckman, "Used Carefully, Chatbots Can Be an Asset to Newsrooms," *Columbia Journalism Review,* March 2018, https://www.cjr.org/innovations/chatbots .php.

88. Carolina Alves de Lima Salge and Nicholas Berente, "Is That Social Bot Behaving Unethically?" *Communications of the ACM* 60, no. 9 (2017).

89. Jacob Ratkiewicz et al., "Detecting and Tracking Political Abuse in Social Media," *Proceedings of the International Conference on Web and Social Media [ICWSM]* (Palo Alto: The AAAI Press, 2011).

90. V. S. Subrahmanian et al., "The DARPA Twitter Bot Challenge," *Computer* 49, no. 6 (2016).

91. Ferrara et al., "The Rise of Social Bots."

92. Grimme et al., "Social Bots."

93. Nic Dias, "The Era of Whatsapp Propaganda Is upon Us," *Foreign Policy,* August 17, 2017, http://foreignpolicy.com/2017/08/17/the -era-of-whatsapp-propaganda-is-upon-us/.

94. Jen Weedon, William Nuland, and Alex Stamos, "Information Operations and Facebook," Facebook, 2017, https://fbnewsroomus.files .wordpress.com/2017/04/facebook-and-information-operations-v1.pdf. see also: "Update on Twitter's Review of the 2016 U.S. Election," *Twitter* (blog), January 2018, https://blog.twitter.com/official/en_us/topics /company/2018/2016-election-update.html.

95. Nicholas Diakopoulos, "The Bots Beat: How Not to Get Punked by Automation," *Columbia Journalism Review,* April 2018, https://www .cjr.org/tow_center/bots-manipulate-trends.php.

96. See Botometer, https://botometer.iuni.iu.edu/#!/, accessed October 26, 2018.

97. Schweizer Radio und Fernsehen (SRF) used a bot classifier to quantify fake followers on Instagram: "Fake It 'til You Make It: Influencer in der Schweiz," Schweizer Radio und Fernsehen, October 2017, https://www.youtube.com/watch?v=K90QjwjSZXY.The New York Times identified patterns in followers of various "influencers" suggesting influencers had bought fake followers; see Nicholas Confessore et al., "The Follower Factory," *New York Times,* January 27, 2018, https://www .nytimes.com/interactive/2018/01/27/technology/social-media-bots.html.

5. DIGITAL PAPERBOYS: ALGORITHMS IN NEWS DISTRIBUTION

1. Source concentration is well-documented for Google News as well; see Mario Haim, Andreas Graefe, and Hans-Bernd Brosius, "Burst of the Filter Bubble?" *Digital Journalism* 6, no. 3 (2018); Roland Schroeder and

Moritz Kralemann, "Journalism ex Machina—Google News Germany and Its News Selection Processes," *Journalism Studies* 6, no. 2 (2006).

2. Although accounting for 3 percent of all links observed, it was really just one story from the *Buffalo News* that gained any exposure from the search engine: Jerry Zremski, "Tax Reform Bill Could Cost Buffalo Schools $12.2 Million, Cut Medicare," *Buffalo News*, November 18, 2017, http://buffalonews.com/2017/11/18/tax-reform-bill-could-cost-buffalo-schools-12-2-million/.

3. Daniel Trielli and Nicholas Diakopoulos, "How Google Shapes the News You See about the Candidates," *Slate*, November 2016, http://www.slate.com/articles/technology/future_tense/2016/11/how_google_shapes_the_news_you_see_about_the_candidates.html.

4. Panagiotis Takis Metaxas and Yada Pruksachatkun, "Manipulation of Search Engine Results during the 2016 US Congressional Elections," presented at the International Conference on Internet and Web Applications and Services, Venice, Italy, 2017.

5. "The Personal News Cycle: How Americans Choose to Get Their News," Media Insight Project, March 2017, https://www.americanpressinstitute.org/publications/reports/survey-research/how-americans-get-news/.

6. Nic Newman et al., *Reuters Digital News Report* (Oxford, UK: Reuters Institute for the Study of Journalism, 2017), https://reutersinstitute.politics.ox.ac.uk/sites/default/files/Digital%20News%20Report%202017%20web_0.pdf.

7. Jeffrey Gottfried and Elisa Shearer, "News Use across Social Media Platforms 2017," Pew Research Center, September 7, 2017, http://www.journalism.org/2017/09/07/news-use-across-social-media-platforms-2017/.

8. Referrer Dashboard for Parse.ly Customers, https://www.parse.ly/resources/data-studies/referrer-dashboard/#google__search,facebook.com__social, accessed January 15, 2018.

9. Efrat Nechushtai, "Could Digital Platforms Capture the Media through Infrastructure?" *Journalism* 89, no. 1 (2017); Emily Bell, "The Dependent Press: How Silicon Valley Threatens Independent Journalism," in *Digital Dominance: Implications and Risks*, ed. Martin Moore and Damian Tambini (Oxford: Oxford University Press, 2018).

10. Will Oremus, "The Great Facebook Crash," *Slate*, June 2018. https://slate.com/technology/2018/06/facebooks-retreat-from-the-news-has-painful-for-publishers-including-slate.html.

11. Shan Wang, "When a Facebook Test Moves News Stories to a Separate Feed, Traffic—and Public Discourse—Are at Stake," Nieman

Lab, October 2017, http://www.niemanlab.org/2017/10/when-a-facebook
-test-moves-news-stories-to-a-separate-feed-traffic-and-public-discourse
-are-at-stake/.

12. "The Strange Tale of USA Today's Facebook Page," EzyInsights,
May 2017, https://ezyinsights.com/the-strange-tale-of-usa-todays-facebook
-page/.

13. Emily Bell and Taylor Owen, *The Platform Press: How Silicon
Valley Reengineered Journalism* (New York: Tow Center for Digital Journalism, 2017).

14. Philip Napoli and Robyn Caplan, "Why Media Companies Insist
They're Not Media Companies, Why They're Wrong, and Why It
Matters," *First Monday* 22, no. 5 (2017).

15. Tarleton Gillespie, *Custodians of the Internet: Platforms, Content Moderation, and the Hidden Decisions that Shape Social Media*
(New Haven, CT: Yale University Press, 2018).

16. Tarleton Gillespie, "Regulation of and by Platforms," in *The
SAGE Handbook of Social Media,* ed. Jean Burgess, Alice Marwick, and
Thomas Poell (London: Sage, 2018).

17. "Expanding Our Work against Abuse of Our Platform," You-
Tube Blog, December 2017, https://youtube.googleblog.com/2017/12
/expanding-our-work-against-abuse-of-our.html; "More Information,
Faster Removals, More People–An Update on What We're Doing to Enforce YouTube's Community Guidelines," YouTube Blog, April 2018,
https://youtube.googleblog.com/2018/04/more-information-faster
-removals-more.html; Annalee Newitz, "The Secret Lives of Google
Raters," Ars Technica, April 2017, https://arstechnica.com/features/2017
/04/the-secret-lives-of-google-raters/.

18. Amanda Hess, "How YouTube's Shifting Algorithms Hurt Independent Media," *New York Times,* April 17, 2017, https://www.nytimes
.com/2017/04/17/arts/youtube-broadcasters-algorithm-ads.html.

19. Amber Madison, "When Social-Media Companies Censor Sex
Education," *Atlantic,* March 2015, http://www.theatlantic.com/health
/archive/2015/03/when-social-media- censors-sex-education/385576/.

20. Nicholas Diakopoulos et al., "I Vote For—How Search Informs
Our Choice of Candidate," in *Digital Dominance: Implications and
Risks,* ed. Martin Moore and Damian Tambini (Oxford: Oxford Uni-
versity Press, 2018).

21. Micah Sifry, "Facebook Wants You to Vote on Tuesday. Here's
How It Messed with Your Feed in 2012," *Mother Jones,* October 2014,
http://www.motherjones.com/politics/2014/10/can-voting-facebook
-button-improve-voter-turnout/.

22. Bing Pan et al., "In Google We Trust: Users' Decisions on Rank, Position, and Relevance," *Journal of Computer-Mediated Communication* 12, no. 3 (2007); Eugene Agichtein et al., "Learning User Interaction Models for Predicting Web Search Result Preferences," *Proceedings of the Conference on Research and Development in Information Retrieval (SIGIR)* (New York: ACM, 2006).

23. Robert Epstein and Ronald Robertson, "The Search Engine Manipulation Effect (SEME) and Its Possible Impact on the Outcomes of Elections," *Proceedings of the National Academy of Sciences* 112, no. 33 (2015).

24. Taina Bucher, "Want to Be on the Top? Algorithmic Power and the Threat of Invisibility on Facebook," *New Media & Society* 14, no. 7 (2014); Tarleton Gillespie, "The Relevance of Algorithms," in *Media Technologies: Essays on Communication, Materiality, and Society,* ed. Tarleton Gillespie, Pablo Boczkowski, and Kirstin Foot (Cambridge, MA: MIT Press, 2014); Martin Moore, *Tech Giants and Civic Power* (London: Centre for the Study of Media Communication & Power, 2016), https://www.kcl.ac.uk/sspp/policy-institute/cmcp/tech-giants-and-civic-power.pdf.

25. Zeynep Tufekci, "Algorithmic Harms beyond Facebook and Google: Emergent Challenges of Computational Agency," *Colorado Technology Law Journal* 13 (2015).

26. Engin Bozdag and Jeroen van den Hoven, "Breaking the Filter Bubble: Democracy and Design," *Ethics and Information Technology* 17, no. 4 (2015).

27. Motahhare Eslami et al., "I Always Assumed that I Wasn't Really that Close to [Her]: Reasoning about Invisible Algorithms in News Feeds," *Proceedings of the Conference on Human Factors in Computing Systems* (New York: ACM, 2015); Elia Powers, "My News Feed Is Filtered?" *Digital Journalism* 5, no. 10 (2017).

28. Engin Bozdag, "Bias in Algorithmic Filtering and Personalization," *Ethics and Information Technology* 15, no. 3 (2013).

29. Philip Napoli, "Social Media and the Public Interest: Governance of News Platforms in the Realm of Individual and Algorithmic Gatekeepers," *Telecommunications Policy* 39, no. 9 (2015); Mike Ananny and Kate Crawford, "A Liminal Press," *Digital Journalism* 3, no. 2 (2015); Matthew Weber and Allie Kosterich, "Coding the News," *Digital Journalism* 6, no. 3 (2018); Matt Carlson, "Facebook in the News," *Digital Journalism* 6, no. 1 (2018).

30. Rasmus Kleis Nielsen and Sarah Anne Ganter, "Dealing with Digital Intermediaries: A Case Study of the Relations between Publishers and Platforms," *New Media & Society* 20, no. 4 (2017).

31. Robyn Caplan and Danah Boyd, "Isomorphism through Algorithms: Institutional Dependencies in the Case of Facebook," *Big Data & Society* 5, no 1 (2018).

32. Caitlin Petre, *The Traffic Factories: Metrics at Chartbeat, Gawker Media, and the New York Times* (New York: Tow Center for Digital Journalism, 2015), https://academiccommons.columbia.edu/catalog/ac:kd51c59zxv.

33. Hong Tien Vu, "The Online Audience as Gatekeeper: The Influence of Reader Metrics on News Editorial Selection," *Journalism* 15, no. 8 (2013).

34. Philip Napoli, "Automated Media: An Institutional Theory Perspective on Algorithmic Media Production and Consumption," *Communication Theory* 24, no. 3 (2014).

35. Eun-Ju Lee and Edson Tandoc, "When News Meets the Audience: How Audience Feedback Online Affects News Production and Consumption," *Human Communication Research* 43, no. 4 (2017); Kasper Welbers et al., "News Selection Criteria in the Digital Age: Professional Norms versus Online Audience Metrics," *Journalism* 17, no. 8 (2015).

36. Alicja Piotrkowicz et al., "Headlines Matter: Using Headlines to Predict the Popularity of News Articles on Twitter and Facebook," *Proceedings of the International Conference on Web and Social Media* (Palo Alto, CA: AAAI, 2017).

37. Shailesh Prakash, "Journalism & Technology: Big Data, Personalization & Automation," keynote presented at the Computation + Journalism Symposium, Evanston, IL, 2017, https://www.youtube.com/watch?v=PqMvxo89AQ4&index=1&list=PL3kjMDQ990L556im9F1qozenDo2rMpccH.

38. Shuguang Wang, Eui-Hong (Sam) Han, and Alexander M. Rush, "Headliner: An Integrated Headline Suggestion System," presented at the Computation + Journalism Symposium, Palo Alto, CA, 2016.

39. Yaser Keneshloo et al., "Predicting the Shape and Peak Time of News Article Views," presented at the International Conference on Big Data, Washington, DC, 2016.

40. Shan Wang, "The New York Times Built a Slack Bot to Help Decide which Stories to Post to Social Media," Nieman Lab, August 2015, http://www.niemanlab.org/2015/08/the-new-york-times-built-a-slack-bot-to-help-decide-which-stories-to-post-to-social-media/.

41. Carlos Castillo et al., "Characterizing the Life Cycle of Online News Stories Using Social Media Reactions," *Proceedings of the Con-*

ference on Computer Supported Cooperative Work & Social Computing (New York: ACM, 2014).

42. Alexander Spangher, "Building the Next New York Times Recommendation Engine," *New York Times*, August 11, 2015, https://open .blogs.nytimes.com/2015/08/11/building-the-next-new-york-times -recommendation-engine/.

43. Prakash, "Journalism & Technology."

44. Jiahui Liu, Peter Dolan, Elin Rønby Pedersen, "Personalized News Recommendation Based on Click Behavior," *Proceedings of the International Conference on Intelligent User Interfaces* (New York: ACM, 2010).

45. Shan Wang, "The New York Times Is Trying to Narrow the Distance between Reporters and Analytics Data," *Nieman Lab*, July, 2016, http://www.niemanlab.org/2016/07/the-new-york-times-is-trying-to -narrow-the-distance-between-reporters-and-analytics-data/.

46. Sheila Doshi, "How Buzzfeed Uses Real-Time Machine Learning to Choose Their Viral Content," *Domino Data Lab* (blog), October 2016, https://blog.dominodatalab.com/buzzfeed-uses-real-time-machine -learning-choose-viral-content/.

47. Federica Cherubini and Rasmus Kleis Nielson, *Editorial Analytics: How News Media Are Developing and Using Audience Data and Metrics* (Oxford, UK: Reuters Institute for the Study of Journalism, 2016).

48. Michael A. DeVito, "From Editors to Algorithms," *Digital Journalism 5*, no. 6 (2017); Kelly Cotter, Janghee Cho, and Emilee Rader, "Explaining the News Feed Algorithm: An Analysis of the 'News Feed FYI' Blog," *Proceedings of the 2017 CHI Conference Extended Abstracts on Human Factors in Computing Systems* (New York: ACM, 2017).

49. Chris Wiggins, "Data Science @ The New York Times," keynote presented at the Computation + Journalism Symposium, New York, 2015, https://youtu.be/jgurTtnCyAA?t=22231.

50. Shan Wang, "After Years of Testing, The Wall Street Journal Has Built a Paywall That Bends to the Individual Reader," Nieman Lab, February 2018, http://www.niemanlab.org/2018/02/after-years-of-testing -the-wall-street-journal-has-built-a-paywall-that-bends-to-the -individual-reader/; Liam Corcoran, "Not All News Site Visitors Are Created Equal. Schibsted is Trying to Predict the Ones Who Will Pay Up," Nieman Lab, February 2018, http://www.niemanlab.org/2018/02/not-all -news-site-visitors-are-created-equal-schibsted-is-trying-to-predict-the

-ones-who-will-pay-up/; Lucinda Southern, "How Swiss News Publisher NZZ Built a Flexible Paywall Using Machine Learning," *Digiday*, June 2018, https://digiday.com/media/swiss-news-publisher-nzz-built -flexible-paywall-using-machine-learning.

51. Nir Grinberg, "Identifying Modes of User Engagement with On-line News and Their Relationship to Information Gain in Text," *Proceedings of the World Wide Web Conference* (New York: ACM, 2018).

52. Shan Wang, "Die Welt's Analytics System De-Emphasizes Clicks and Demystifies What It Considers a 'Quality' Story," Nieman Lab, May 2016, http://www.niemanlab.org/2016/05/die-welts-analytics -system-de-emphasizes-clicks-and-demystifies-what-it-considers-a -quality-story/.

53. Edson Tandoc and Ryan Thomas, "The Ethics of Web Analytics," *Digital Journalism* 3, no. 2 (2014).

54. Elia Powers, "Selecting Metrics, Reflecting Norms," *Digital Journalism* 6, no. 4 (2018).

55. Pablo Boczkowski and Eugenia Mitchelstein, *The News Gap: When the Information Preferences of the Media and the Public Diverge* (Cambridge, MA: MIT Press, 2013).

56. Krishna Bharat, Tomonari Kamba, and Michael Albers, "Personalized, Interactive News on the Web," *Multimedia Systems* 6, no. 5 (1998).

57. See work from the Center for Investigative Reporting on their Impact Tracker: Lindsay Green-Barber, "CIR's Impact Tracker: How to Use It and Why You Need It," Center for Investigative Reporting, September 2016, https://www.revealnews.org/article/cirs-impact-tracker -how-to-use-it-and-why-you-need-it/.

58. Michael Schudson, *The Sociology of News,* 2nd ed. (New York: W. W. Norton, 2011).

59. Felippe Rodrigues, "Meet the Swedish Newspaper Editor Who Put an Algorithm in Charge of His Homepage," Storybench, March 2017, http://www.storybench.org/meet-swedish-newspaper-editor-put -algorithm-charge-homepage/.

60. Balázs Bodó, "Means, Not an End (of the World)—The Customization of News Personalization by European News Media," presented at the Algorithms, Automation, and News Conference, Munich, Germany, 2018.

61. René Pfitzner, "Data Science for a Smart News Experience," *Medium,* October 2017, https://medium.com/@RenePfitznerZH/data-science -for-a-smart-news-experience-35d316846d04.

62. Mike Vlad Cora, "Detecting Trustworthy Domains," *Flipboard Engineering* (blog), April 2017, http://engineering.flipboard.com/2017/04 /domainranking.

63. For instance, Facebook relies on user surveys to help define what it sees as a "high-quality" post. See Varun Kacholia, "News Feed FYI: Showing More High Quality Content," *Facebook News Feed FYI* (blog), August 2013, https://www.facebook.com/business/news/News-Feed-FYI -Showing-More-High-Quality-Content.

64. See Nicholas Diakopoulos, "Picking the NYT Picks: Editorial Criteria and Automation in the Curation of Online News Comments," *#ISOJ Journal* 6, no. 1 (2015); Yinfei Yang and Ani Nenkova, "Combining Lexical and Syntactic Features for Detecting Content-Dense Texts in News," *Journal of Artificial Intelligence Research* 60, no. 1 (2017); and Frederic Filloux, "Scoring Stories to Make Better Recommendation Engines for News," *Monday Note (blog),* October 2017, https://mondaynote .com/scoring-stories-to-make-better-recommendation-engines-c3c73 a596893.

65. Souneil Park et al., "NewsCube: Delivering Multiple Aspects of News to Mitigate Media Bias," *Proceedings of the Conference on Human Factors in Computing Systems* (New York: ACM, 2009).

66. C. W. Anderson, "Deliberative, Agonistic, and Algorithmic Audiences: Journalism's Vision of Its Public in an Age of Audience Transparency," *International Journal of Communication* 5 (2011); Bozdag and van den Hoven, "Breaking the Filter Bubble."

67. Mike Ananny, "Networked News Time," *Digital Journalism* 4 no. 4 (2016).

68. Kjerstin Thorson and Chris Wells, "Curated Flows: A Framework for Mapping Media Exposure in the Digital Age," *Communication Theory* 26, no. 3 (2015); Adrienne LaFrance, "What If You Could Subscribe to Somebody Else's Facebook Feed?" *Atlantic,* August 2014, https://www.theatlantic.com/technology/archive/2014/08/what-if -people-could-subscribe-to-different-facebook-algorithms/378925/.

69. Roger McNamee, "How to Fix Facebook—Before It Fixes Us," *Washington Monthly,* January–March 2018, https://washingtonmonthly .com/magazine/january-february-march-2018/how-to-fix-facebook -before-it-fixes-us/.

70. Jonah Engel Bromwich and Matthew Haag, "Facebook Is Changing. What Does That Mean for Your News Feed?" *New York Times,* January 12, 2018, https://www.nytimes.com/2018/01/12/tech nology/facebook-news-feed-changes.html.

71. See an early study of the rollout of the technology at Omni in Taina Bucher, "'Machines Don't Have Instincts': Articulating the Computational in Journalism," *New Media & Society* 12, no. 5 (2016).

72. Carlson, "Facebook in the News."

6. ALGORITHMIC ACCOUNTABILITY REPORTING

1. This scenario is fictitious, but informed by real data from an individual who was scored by the Chicago Police Department.

2. Chicago Police Department, *Custom Notifications in Chicago,* October 2015, http://directives.chicagopolice.org/directives/data/a7a57bf0 -1456faf9-bfa14-570a-a2deebf33c56ae59.html.

3. Rob Arthur, "We Now Have Algorithms to Predict Police Misconduct," FiveThirtyEight, March 2016, https://fivethirtyeight.com/features /we-now-have-algorithms-to-predict-police-misconduct/.

4. Matt Stroud, "Chicago's Predictive Policing Tool Just Failed a Major Test," *Verge,* August 19, 2016, https://www.theverge.com/2016/8 /19/12552384/chicago-heat-list-tool-failed-rand-test; Yana Kunichoff and Patrick Sier, "The Contradictions of Chicago Police's Secretive List," *Chicago Magazine,* August 2017, http://www.chicagomag.com /city-life/August-2017/Chicago-Police-Strategic-Subject-List/. For more on how predictive policing can create feedback loops, see Kristian Lum and William Isaac, "To Predict and Serve?" *Significance* 13, no. 5 (2015).

5. Mick Dumke and Frank Main, "A Look Inside the Watch List Chicago Police Fought to Keep Secret," *Chicago Sun Times,* May 18, 2017, https://chicago.suntimes.com/chicago-politics/what-gets-people-on -watch-list-chicago-police-fought-to-keep-secret-watchdogs/.

6. Jeff Asher and Rob Arthur, "Inside the Algorithm that Tries to Predict Gun Violence in Chicago," *New York Times,* June 13, 2017, https://www.nytimes.com/2017/06/13/upshot/what-an-algorithm -reveals-about-life-on-chicagos-high-risk-list.html.

7. The code for the model was supplied to the author upon request, and the results were replicated. A generalized linear model (GLM) with eight variables explained 94.6 percent of the variance in the SSL score; in statistical terms $R^2 = 0.946$.

8. Cathy O'Neil, *Weapons of Math Destruction: How Big Data Increases Inequality and Threatens Democracy* (New York: Crown, 2016); Frank Pasquale. *The Black Box Society: The Secret Algorithms that Control Money and Information* (Cambridge, MA: Harvard University Press, 2015); Virginia Eubanks, *Automating Inequality: How High-Tech*

Tools Profile, Police, and Punish the Poor (New York: St. Martin's Press, 2018).

9. Batya Friedman and Helen Nissenbaum, "Bias in Computer Systems," *ACM Transactions on Information Systems* 14, no. 3 (1996); Peter Neumann, *Computer-Related Risks* (New York: ACM Press, 1995).

10. Nicholas Diakopoulos, *Algorithmic Accountability Reporting: On the Investigation of Black Boxes* (New York: Tow Center for Digital Journalism, January, 2014). The phrase "algorithmic accountability" was originally coined in Nicholas Diakopoulos, "Sex, Violence, and Autocomplete Algorithms," *Slate*, August 2013, http://www.slate.com/articles/technology/future_tense/2013/08/words_banned_from_bing_and_google_s_autocomplete_algorithms.html, and elaborated in Nicholas Diakopoulos, "Rage against the Algorithms," *Atlantic*, October 2013, https://www.theatlantic.com/technology/archive/2013/10/rage-against-the-algorithms/280255/.

11. Mark Bovens, Thomas Schillemans, and Robert E. Goodin, "Public Accountability," in *The Oxford Handbook of Public Accountability*, ed. Mark Bovens, Robert. E. Goodin, and Thomas Schillemans (Oxford: Oxford University Press, 2014).

12. Dillon Reisman et al., *Algorithmic Impact Assessments: A Practical Framework for Public Agency Accountability* (New York, AI Now Institute, 2018), https://ainowinstitute.org/aiareport2018.pdf.

13. For stories in this series, see "Machine Bias: Investigating Algorithmic Injustice," *ProPublica*, https://www.propublica.org/series/machine-bias, accessed October 26, 2018.

14. Diakopoulos, "Sex, Violence, and Autocomplete Algorithms"; Jennifer Stark and Nicholas Diakopoulos, "Uber Seems to Offer Better Service in Areas with More White People. That Raises Some Tough Questions," *Washington Post*, March 10, 2016, https://www.washingtonpost.com/news/wonk/wp/2016/03/10/uber-seems-to-offer-better-service-in-areas-with-more-white-people-that-raises-some-tough-questions/.

15. Nick Seaver, "Algorithms as Culture: Some Tactics for the Ethnography of Algorithmic Systems," *Big Data & Society* 4, no. 2 (2017); *Algorithmic Accountability: Applying the Concept to Different Country Contexts*, World Wide Web Foundation, 2017, http://webfoundation.org/docs/2017/07/WF_Algorithms.pdf; Mike Ananny, "Toward an Ethics of Algorithms," *Science, Technology & Human Values* 41, no. 1 (2015).

16. Taina Bucher, *If . . . Then: Algorithmic Power and Politics* (New York: Oxford University Press, 2018).

17. In March 2014 researchers in the United States uncovered discrepancies in the output emissions of certain Volkswagen diesel engines when tested under normal road conditions. But this only turned into national news about eighteen months later, when it became clear that VW had used a software algorithm to deceive emissions testing and that engineers had tried to cover their tracks to evade regulators. This *intentional* deception made the story much more powerful than had the explanation been "it was a bug" or "it emerged from unanticipated contexts of use."

18. The notion of sociotechnical blindness comes from Deborah Johnson and Mario Verdicchio, "AI Anxiety," *Journal of the Association for Information Science and Technology* 68, no. 9 (2017).

19. Julia Angwin et al., "Machine Bias," ProPublica, May 2016, https://www.propublica.org/article/machine-bias-risk-assessments-in-criminal-sentencing.

20. Jeff Larson et al., "How We Analyzed the COMPAS Recidivism Algorithm," ProPublica, May 2016, https://www.propublica.org/article/how-we-analyzed-the-compas-recidivism-algorithm/.

21. William Dieterich, Christina Mendoza, and Tim Brennan, "COMPAS Risk Scales: Demonstrating Accuracy Equity and Predictive Parity," Northpointe Research Report, July 2016.

22. Ongoing research has further critiqued the algorithm by pointing out that crowd workers were able to predict recidivism at the same accuracy level, and that a simplified linear model using two features (age and total number of previous convictions) performs just as well as the algorithm. See Julia Dressel and Hany Farid, "The Accuracy, Fairness, and Limits of Predicting Recidivism," *Science Advances* 4, no. 1 (2018).

23. Mirror Mirror: Reflections on Quantitative Fairness, accessed August 2, 2018, https://speak-statistics-to-power.github.io/fairness/. See also Arvind Narayanan, "21 Fairness Definitions and Their Politics," tutorial presented at the Fairness, Accountability, and Transparency Conference, New York, 2018, https://www.youtube.com/watch?v=jIXIuYdnyyk.

24. Bruno Lepri et al., "Fair, Transparent, and Accountable Algorithmic Decision-Making Processes," *Philosophy & Technology* 84, no. 3 (2017).

25. Richard Berk et al., "Fairness in Criminal Justice Risk Assessments: The State of the Art," *Sociological Methods & Research* (2018).

26. "Unfairness by Algorithm: Distilling the Harms of Automated Decision-Making," Future of Privacy Forum, December 2017, https://fpf.org/wp-content/uploads/2017/12/FPF-Automated-Decision-Making

-Harms-and-Mitigation-Charts.pdf. For a treatment of representational harms to individuals and society, see Kate Crawford, "The Trouble with Bias," keynote presentation at the Neural Information Processing Systems Conference, Long Beach, CA, 2017, https://www.youtube.com/watch?v=fMym_BKWQzk.

27. Meghan E. Irons, "Caught in a Dragnet," *Boston Globe,* July 17, 2011, http://archive.boston.com/news/local/massachusetts/articles/2011/07/17/man_sues_registry_after_license_mistakenly_revoked/.

28. Sapna Maheshwari, "On YouTube Kids, Startling Videos Slip Past Filters," *New York Times,* November 4, 2017, https://www.nytimes.com/2017/11/04/business/media/youtube-kids-paw-patrol.html?_r=0.

29. Diakopoulos, "Sex, Violence, and Autocomplete Algorithms."

30. Simon Scott, "With a Hurricane Approaching Florida, Airline Algorithms Show No Sympathy," NPR, September 9, 2017, https://www.npr.org/2017/09/09/548853940/with-a-hurricane-approaching-florida-airline-algorithms-show-no-sympathy.

31. "Sydney Siege Sees Uber Raise Prices before Backtracking," BBC, December 2014, http://www.bbc.com/news/technology-30478008.

32. Michal Kosinski, David Stillwell, and Thore Graepel, "Private Traits and Attributes Are Predictable from Digital Records of Human Behavior," *Proceedings of the National Academies of Sciences* 110, no. 15 (2013).

33. Kate Crawford and Jason Schultz, "Big Data and Due Process: Toward a Framework to Redress Predictive Privacy Harms," *Boston College Law Review* 55, no. 1 (2014).

34. Kashmir Hill, "How Facebook Outs Sex Workers," Gizmodo, October 2017, https://gizmodo.com/how-facebook-outs-sex-workers-1818861596.

35. Kashmir Hill, "How Facebook Figures Out Everyone You've Ever Met," Gizmodo, November 2017, https://gizmodo.com/how-facebook-figures-out-everyone-youve-ever-met-1819822691.

36. Ryan McNeill and Janet Roberts, "Exclusive: Readying for Sandy, NJ Transit Erred in Modeling Storm," Reuters, January 11, 2013, http://www.reuters.com/article/us-storm-sandy-newjerseytransit/exclusive-readying-for-sandy-nj-transit-erred-in-modeling-storm-idUSBRE90B00I20130112.

37. Friedman and Nissenbaum, "Bias in Computer Systems." See also the notion of "transfer context bias" in David Danks and Alex John London, "Algorithmic Bias in Autonomous Systems," presented at the International Joint Conference on Artificial Intelligence, Melbourne, Australia, 2017.

38. "Machine Bias with Jeff Larson," Data Stories Podcast, October 2016, http://datastori.es/85-machine-bias-with-jeff-larson/.

39. Daniel Trielli and Nicholas Diakopoulos, "How to Report on Algorithms Even If You're Not a Data Whiz," *Columbia Journalism Review,* May 2017, https://www.cjr.org/tow_center/algorithms-reporting -algorithmtips.php.

40. Eldad Eilam, *Reversing: Secrets of Reverse Engineering* (Indianapolis: Wiley, 2005).

41. Lennart Ljung, "System Identification," in *Signal Analysis and Prediction,* ed. Ales Procházka et al. (Boston, MA: Birkhäuser, 1998).

42. Bucher, *If . . . Then: Algorithmic Power and Politics.*

43. S. Michael Gaddis, "An Introduction to Audit Studies in the Social Sciences," in *Audit Studies: Behind the Scenes with Theory, Method, and Nuance,* ed. S. Michael Gaddis (Cham, Switzerland: Springer, 2017).

44. Christian Sandvig et al., "Auditing Algorithms: Research Methods for Detecting Discrimination on Internet Platforms," presented at the International Communication Association Preconference on Data and Discrimination Converting Critical Concerns into Productive Inquiry, Seattle, WA, 2014.

45. Jennifer Valentino-DeVries, Jeremy Singer-Vine, and Ashkan Soltani, "Websites Vary Prices, Deals Based on Users' Information," *Wall Street Journal,* December 24, 2012, https://www.wsj.com/articles/SB10 001424127887323772045781893918138815534.

46. Kashmir Hill and Surya Mattu, "Keep Track of Who Facebook Thinks You Know with This Nifty Tool," Gizmodo, January 2018, https://gizmodo.com/keep-track-of-who-facebook-thinks-you-know -with-this-ni-1819422352.

47. In early 2018 Algorithm Watch launched an initiative to gather data donations that would enable an audit of the Schufa credit score in Germany; see https://www.startnext.com/openschufa, accessed October 26, 2018.

48. Jeremy B. Merrill, "Why Facebook Showed You That Ad for the Candidate You Hate," *New York Times,* November 8, 2016, https://www .nytimes.com/2016/11/08/us/politics/facebook-ads-campaign.html; Julia Angwin, Surya Mattu, and Terry Parris Jr., "Facebook Doesn't Tell Users Everything It Really Knows About Them," ProPublica, December 2016, https://www.propublica.org/article/facebook-doesnt-tell-users -everything-it-really-knows-about-them. For information on Algorithm Watch's Google audit, see "Datenspende," Algorithm Watch, 2017, https://datenspende.algorithmwatch.org/en/index.html.

49. Bucher, *If . . . Then: Algorithmic Power and Politics.*

50. Katie Notopoulos, "How I Cracked Facebook's New Algorithm and Tortured My Friends," *BuzzFeed News,* February 2018, https://www.buzzfeed.com/katienotopoulos/how-i-cracked-facebooks-new-algorithm-and-tortured-my.

51. Sandvig et al., "Auditing Algorithms."

52. Danielle Citron, "Technological Due Process," *Washington University Law Review* 85 (2017). For a recent example, see Colin Lecher, "What Happens When an Algorithms Cuts your Health Care," *Verge,* March 21, 2018, https://www.theverge.com/2018/3/21/17144260/healthcare-medicaid-algorithm-arkansas-cerebral-palsy.

53. Brendt Mittelstadt, "Auditing for Transparency in Content Personalization Systems," *International Journal of Communication,* 10 (2016).

54. Lauren Kirchner, "ProPublica Seeks Source Code for New York City's Disputed DNA Software," ProPublica, September 2017, https://www.propublica.org/article/propublica-seeks-source-code-for-new-york-city-disputed-dna-software.

55. Shefali Patil, Ferdinand Vieider, and Philip Tetlock, "Process versus Outcome Accountability," in *The Oxford Handbook of Public Accountability,* ed. Mark Bovens, Robert. E. Goodin, and Thomas Schillemans (Oxford: Oxford University Press, 2014); Karen Yeung, "Algorithmic Regulation: A Critical Interrogation," *Regulation & Governance* (2017).

56. Crawford and Schultz, "Big Data and Due Process."

57. Carolina Alves de Lima Salge and Nicholas Berente, "Is That Social Bot Behaving Unethically?" *Communications of the ACM* 60, no. 9 (2017).

58. Sentiments like this motivated our development of Algorithmtips.org, a website that seeks to lower the cost of finding newsworthy leads about the use of algorithms in government by providing an easily searchable database. See Daniel Trielli, Jennifer Stark, and Nicholas Diakopoulos, "Algorithm Tips: A Resource for Algorithmic Accountability in Government," presented at the Computation+Journalism Symposium, Evanston, IL, October, 2017; and see the Algorithm Tips site online at http://algorithmtips.org/, accessed October 26, 2018.

59. Nicholas Diakopoulos and Michael Koliska, "Algorithmic Transparency in the News Media," *Digital Journalism* 5, no. 7 (2017).

60. Albert Meijer, Mark Bovens, and Thomas Schillemans, "Transparency," in *The Oxford Handbook of Public Accountability,* ed. Mark Bovens, Robert. E. Goodin, and Thomas Schillemans (Oxford: Oxford University Press, 2014).

61. Nicholas Diakopoulos et al., "I Vote For—How Search Informs Our Choice of Candidate," in *Digital Dominance: Implications and*

Risks, ed. Martin Moore and Damian Tambini (Oxford: Oxford University Press, 2018).

62. Gaddis, "An Introduction to Audit Studies in the Social Sciences"

63. Nicholas Diakopoulos, "Accountability in Algorithmic Decision Making," *Communications of the ACM 59*, no. 2 (2016).

64. Diakopoulos et al., "I Vote For—How Search Informs Our Choice of Candidate."

65. Walt Hickey, "Be Suspicious of Online Movie Ratings, Especially Fandango's," FiveThirtyEight, October 2015, https://fivethirtyeight.com/features/fandango-movies-ratings/.

66. Julia Angwin and Surya Mattu, "Amazon Says It Puts Customers First. But Its Pricing Algorithm Doesn't," ProPublica, September 2016, https://www.propublica.org/article/amazon-says-it-puts-customers-first-but-its-pricing-algorithm-doesnt.

67. Reubin Binns, "Algorithmic Accountability and Public Reason," *Philosophy & Technology* (2017).

68. Universal Declaration of Human Rights, 1948, United Nations, http://www.un.org/en/universal-declaration-human-rights/. For an additional treatment of how AI could more broadly impact on human rights see: Mark Latonero, *Governing Artificial Intelligence: Upholding Human Rights & Dignity* (New York: Data & Society, 2018).

69. Two federal agencies, the Department of the Treasury (DoT) and the Social Security Administration, explicitly claim that software or source code are not "agency records"—meaning that they are not subject to public records requests. The guidance from DoT in the Code of Federal Regulations states unequivocally that "proprietary (or copyrighted) software is not an agency record." See Code of Federal Regulations § 1.1 General, United States, https://www.law.cornell.edu/cfr/text/31/1.1.

70. Nicholas Diakopoulos, "We Need to Know the Algorithms the Government Uses to Make Important Decisions about Us," *Conversation,* May 2016, https://theconversation.com/we-need-to-know-the-algorithms-the-government-uses-to-make-important-decisions-about-us-57869.

71. For the specific language we used in our requests see: http://algorithmtips.org/resources/, accessed October 27, 2018.

72. Katherine Fink, "Opening the Government's Black Boxes: Freedom of Information and Algorithmic Accountability," *Information, Communication, & Society* 21, no. 10 (2018).

73. Robert Brauneis and Ellen Goodman, "Algorithmic Transparency for the Smart City," *Yale Journal of Law & Technology* 20 (2018).

74. Esha Bhandari and Rachel Goodman, "Data Journalism and the Computer Fraud and Abuse Act: Tips for Moving Forward in an Uncertain Landscape," presented at the Computation + Journalism Symposium, Evanston, IL, 2017.

75. Tarleton Gillespie, "The Relevance of Algorithms," in *Media Technologies: Essays on Communication, Materiality, and Society*, ed. Tarleton Gillespie, Pablo Boczkowski, and Kirstin Foot (Cambridge, MA: MIT Press, 2014).

76. Gillespie, "The Relevance of Algorithms"; Mike Ananny, "Toward an Ethics of Algorithms," *Science, Technology & Human Values* 41, no. 1 (2015).

77. Susanne Fengler and Stephan Russ-Mohl, "The (Behavioral) Economics of Media Accountability," in *Journalists and Media Accountability: An International Study of News People in the Digital Age*, ed. Susanne Fengler et al. (New York: Peter Lang, 2014).

78. Michael Ananny and Kate Crawford, "Seeing without Knowing: Limitations of the Transparency Ideal and Its Application to Algorithmic Accountability," *New Media & Society* 20, no. 3 (2018).

79. Kelly McBride and Tom Rosenstiel, *The New Ethics of Journalism: Principles for the 21st Century* (Thousand Oaks, CA: CQ Press, 2013).

80. Mark Deuze, "What Is Journalism?: Professional Identity and Ideology of Journalists Reconsidered," *Journalism* 6, no. 4 (2015).

81. Maartje ter Hoeve et al., "Do News Consumers Want Explanations for Personalized News Rankings?" presented at the Fairness, Accountability, and Transparency in Recommender Systems (FATREC) Workshop, Como, Italy, 2017.

82. Stephen J. A. Ward, "The Magical Concept of Transparency," in *Ethics for Digital Journalists: Emerging Best Practices*, ed. Laurie Zion and David Craig (New York: Routledge, 2015).

83. Jenna Burrell, "How the Machine 'Thinks': Understanding Opacity in Machine Learning Algorithms," *Big Data & Society* 3, no. 1 (2016).

84. Diakopoulos and Koliska, "Algorithmic Transparency in the News Media."

85. Tal Montal and Zvi Reich, "I, Robot. You, Journalist. Who Is the Author?" *Digital Journalism* 5, no. 7 (2017).

86. Ward, "The Magical Concept of Transparency."

87. For an extensive accounting of factors influencing journalistic responsibility, see Denis McQuail, *Journalism and Society* (London: Sage, 2013).

88. For a list of dozens of Github repositories maintained by newsrooms, see https://github.com/silva-shih/open-journalism, accessed October 26, 2018. For examples of specific repositories that support editorial projects, see Jennifer Stark and Nicholas Diakopoulos, "Towards Editorial Transparency in Computational Journalism," presented at Computation + Journalism Symposium, Palo Alto, CA, 2016; Ryann Grochowski Jones and Charles Ornstein, "Matching Industry Payments to Medicare Prescribing Patterns: An Analysis," ProPublica, March 2016, https://static.propublica.org/projects/d4d/20160317-matching-industry -payments.pdf?22.

89. Stuart Myles, "How Can We Make Algorithmic News More Transparent?," presented at the Algorithms, Automation, and News Conference, Munich, Germany, 2018.

90. Nicholas Diakopoulos, "Enabling Accountability of Algorithmic Media: Transparency as a Constructive and Critical Lens," in *Transparent Data Mining for Big and Small Data,* ed. Tania Cerquitelli, Daniele Quercia, and Frank Pasquale (Cham, Switzerland: Springer International, 2017).

91. Nicholas Diakopoulos, "BuzzFeed's Pro Tennis Investigation Displays Ethical Dilemmas of Data Journalism," *Columbia Journalism Review,* November 2016, https://www.cjr.org/tow_center/transparency _algorithms_buzzfeed.php.

92. Tamar Charney, Michael Oreskes, and Thomas Hjelm, "The Secret Sauce behind NPR One: An Editorially Responsible Algorithm," NPR, December 21, 2016, https://www.npr.org/sections/npr-extra/2016/12 /21/505315422/secret-sauce-npr-one-algorithm.

CONCLUSION: THE FUTURE OF ALGORITHMIC NEWS MEDIA

1. Nicholas Diakopoulos, "There Are a Lot of Rote Tasks a Good AI Interviewer Could Do for You," *Columbia Journalism Review,* June 2018, https://www.cjr.org/tow_center/artificial-intelligence-reporting -interviews.php.

2. Astrid Gynnild and Turo Uskali, eds., *Responsible Drone Journalism* (New York: Routledge, 2018).

3. Pietro Passarelli, "An Open Source Tool for Enabling Faster, Easier Editing of Video Interviews," *Product* (blog), *Vox,* November 22, 2016, https://product.voxmedia.com/2016/11/22/13669486/faster-video -editing.

4. Lucas Graves, "Understanding the Promise and Limits of Automated Fact-Checking" (Oxford, UK: Reuters Institute for the Study of

Journalism, 2018), https://reutersinstitute.politics.ox.ac.uk/our-research/understanding-promise-and-limits-automated-fact-checking.

5. For details on how to apply user research methods in practice, see Kathy Baxter, Catherine Courage, and Kelly Caine, *Understanding Your Users: A Practical Guide to User Research Methods,* 2nd ed. (Waltham, MA: Morgan Kaufman, 2015). For examples of the user centered design process applied to automated journalism, see Hanna Zoon, "Designing for Automated Journalism in the Netherlands: First Steps and No Way Back," presented at the Algorithms, Automation, and News Conference, Munich, Germany, 2018, https://hannazoon.files.wordpress.com/2018/05/abstract-design-for-automated-journalism-in-nl-zoon-van-dongen-alves-lino.pdf.

6. See also Nikki Usher, *Interactive Journalism: Hackers, Data, and Code* (Urbana: University of Illinois Press, 2016).

7. Philip Meyer, *Precision Journalism: A Reporter's Introduction to Social Science Methods,* 4th ed. (Lanham, MD: Rowman & Littlefield, 2002).

8. Charles Berret and Cheryl Phillips, "Teaching Data and Computational Journalism" (New York: Columbia Journalism School, 2016), https://journalism.columbia.edu/system/files/content/teaching_data_and_computational_journalism.pdf.

9. Bahareh R. Heravi, "3WS of Data Journalism Education," *Journalism Practice* (2018).

10. For a critique of price, see Felix Salmon's contribution to Bill Grueskin, Felix Salmon, and Alexandria Neason, "Do We Need J-Schools?," *Columbia Journalism Review,* Spring/Summer 2018, https://www.cjr.org/special_report/do-we-need-j-schools.php/.

11. For a treatment of several worrisome scenarios see: Robert Chesney and Danielle Keats Citron, "Deep Fakes: A Looming Challenge for Privacy, Democracy, and National Security," *California Law Review* 107 (2019).

12. For an overview of media forensic techniques, see Hany Farid, *Photo Forensics* (Cambridge, MA: MIT Press, 2016).

13. V. Conotter, E. Bodnari, G. Boato, and H. Farid, "Physiologically-Based Detection of Computer Generated Faces in Video," presented at the International Conference on Image Processing (ICIP), Paris, France, 2014.

14. For a list of digital forensics tools, see Bellingcat's Digital Toolkit, https://docs.google.com/document/d/1BfLPJpRtyq4RFtHJoNpvWQjmGnyVkfE2HYoICKOGguA/edit, accessed October 27, 2018.

15. See Media Forensics (MediFor), Defense Advanced Research Projects Agency (DARPA), https://www.darpa.mil/program/media-forensics; Media Forensics Challenge 2018, National Institute of Standards and Technology (NIST), https://www.nist.gov/itl/iad/mig/media-forensics -challenge-2018; InVID—In Video Veritas, http://www.invid-project.eu /, accessed October 27, 2018.

16. Such guides are beginning to be developed and standardized. See First Draft, Resources, https://firstdraftnews.org/en/education/curriculum -resources/, accessed October 27, 2018; see also Alfred Hermida, "Filtering Fact from Fiction: A Verification Framework for Social Media," in *Ethics for Digital Journalists: Emerging Best Practices,* ed. Lawrie Zion and David Craig (New York: Routledge, 2015).

ACKNOWLEDGMENTS

The ideas in this book have been simmering for a while, some since as far back as 2006. As I've worked through the material over the years, and particularly in 2017 and 2018 as I wrote this book, I've gotten a lot of help along the way. Colleagues, friends and family, mentors, teachers, students, and editors have all played important roles in shaping the project.

As a computer scientist trained at the Georgia Institute of Technology, I never thought I would actually *write* a book. It's not something that computer scientists typically do. But here we are. Although I had been thinking about it off and on, it wasn't until 2016 that I jumped in wholeheartedly Sarah Oates deserves special thanks for encouraging me, as does Ben Shneiderman, who brought me into the fold on his own book project and showed me it wouldn't be so daunting. And it was Irfan Essa, who sidled up to my desk in 2006 and remarked something like, "I just got back from CNN and we started talking about this idea of *computational journalism*. We should talk about what that might mean." Without that spark I probably never would have started down the path that led to this book. Thanks, Irfan. Over the years there were others who encouraged me too, in both big and small ways, and I'm appreciative.

On the specific development of this book I'm particularly thankful for early help from Karin Assmann, a research assistant who identified resources, interview candidates, and other leads for the book. Speaking of interviewees, they also deserve a special acknowledgment since this book never would have happened without their generosity in spending their time talking to me. I'm also thankful to the scholars and students who offered valuable feedback on various draft versions of chapters, including Peng Ao, Scott Cambo, Diego Gómez-Zará, Hanlin Li, Carl-

Gustav Linden, Wiebke Loosen, Jacob Nelson, Chelsea Peterson-Salahuddin, Cornelius Puschmann, Jan Schmidt, Daniel Trielli Paiva da Silva, Nikki Usher, Nicholas Vincent, and Yixue Wang. And I'm indebted to my editor, Jeff Dean, who taught me a thing or two about writing a book as a crossover. Finally, the peer reviewers of this book had a number of insightful comments that really pushed me to make the book better. Thank you!

I've been lucky to have the intellectual support of many fine institutions over the years. Leaders at both the Tow Center for Digital Journalism at Columbia University and the Tow-Knight Center for Entrepreneurial Journalism at CUNY were early believers in the value of thinking critically and constructively about the role of computation in the news media. I learned a lot during the fellowships I spent at both places. I am also grateful to the University of Bergen in Norway, which saw something in my work perhaps before even I had fully grasped it. A particular thanks goes to Dag Elgesem there for beginning an intellectual exchange with the Nordic countries that is impressed in this book. And thanks to Astrid Gynnild for both continuing that exchange and helping to financially support some of my time writing the book in the context of her VisMedia project. I've also been lucky to have some of the research featured in the book financially supported by institutions including the Knight Foundation and the National Science Foundation. I'm grateful to the University of Maryland, College Park, for hosting me as I began this book and to Northwestern University for supporting me as I finished the book—the vibrancy of the campus community dedicated to computational journalism at NU is inspiring and nourishing every day.

I couldn't have written this text without the support of my family and friends. My father was a longtime visual journalist and editor. Having grown up in a household where there was a newspaper on the kitchen table every morning and where family dinner conversation frequently steered toward issues in the news, perhaps it's no surprise that I was primed to care about journalism. At home now I'm grateful for the support of Risa Chubinsky, who has over the years been a reader, critic, and sounding board for ideas while also helping provide a balance in life. And I have to thank Minerva (Minny), my thirteen-pound Siberian forest cat, for "big hugs" before (and often interjected between) intense bouts of writing.

INDEX

2016 presidential election: automatically generated article about, 99; evaluation of debates of, 87; fact-checking, 69, 70, 71; forecasting of results of, 107; predictive models about, 64–65; tweets about, 169, 171

abstracting, invention of automated, 17–18

abstraction, 32–33

accountability journalism, 157

actor network theory (ANT), 36

@actual_ransom bot, 157

adaptability, journalistic practice of, 29

Aftenposten, 195, 196, 200

algorithmic accountability: automation of, 231–32; characteristics of, 209, 239; ethical implications and, 258n37; external auditing of, 224; in government sector, 226, 229–30; information deficits and, 224–25; information disclosure and, 235–36; journalistic transparency and, 234–35, 236; in private sector, 226, 230; purpose of, 209; types of, 223–24

algorithmic accountability reporting: auditing techniques application, 218–19, 222; code inspection approach to, 221–22, 222; crowdsourcing approach to, 219–20, 222, 232; definition of, 207; of discrimination and unfairness, 210, 211; driving forces of, 210; examples of, 232–33; of human misuse of algorithms, 215–16, 300n17; human resources and, 232–33; of inaccurate predictions and classifications, 211–12; journalistic skills required for, 232; methods of, 217, 222; phenomenological approach to, 220–21, 222; reverse-engineering approaches to, 217–18, 222; types of stories in, 215, 216; use contexts in, 222; of violations of laws and social norms, 213–14

312

algorithmic decision-making, 11,
206, 209, 215
algorithmic media literacy, 248,
249, 250
algorithmic news media, 4–7, 11,
234–39, 240, 241–42, 248
algorithms: attention-mediated,
182; audits of, 218, 224, 230;
for claims assessment, 72; for
content optimization, 185;
control of, 200–201; in decision
making, 17, 19, 20–22, 225;
definition of, 16; design of, 29;
of dynamic pricing, 213–14;
editorial values and, 195–96,
197; eyewitness classification,
67; filtering, 212, 213; investigations into, 208; journalistic
work and, 8–9, 11, 26–27, 28,
207, 241; judgments of, 18;
legal access to, 228–30; limitations of, 4, 31, 194; machine-
learning, 18, 44; mistakes and
biases of, 206, 211–12; in news
distribution, role of, 10; in
news production, role of, 3–4,
12, 26, 28, 29; newsworthy,
208; output measuring, 223;
people and, 15–16, 37, 240,
300n17; positive and negative
effects of, 251–52; public
records requests for, 229–30;
setting of outcome expectations
for, 225–28; trending, 182;
updating of, 230–31; values
and, 28, 29, 240–41; in workflow design, 39. *See also* curation algorithms
algorithms beat, 207, 208, 209
Amazon's ranking algorithm,
227

AnecbotalNYT bot, 145–46, *146*,
147
Angwin, Julia, 233
anonymous sources, 158, 159
Application Programming
Interfaces (APIs), 190
argumentation, 137, 138, 139
Arria Studio tool, 132
Arthur, Rob, 232
artificial intelligence (AI):
advances of, 242; critique of,
243; definition of, 16; journalism and, 244; limitations
of, 243; prediction about,
127–28; problems of design,
243; training of, 243
Asher, Jeff, 232
Associated Press (AP): automated
content production, 1–2, 3, 9,
105, 109, 110; automation
editor position, 136–37; content
labelling practice, 236; transparency of, 237; use of data
mining technique, 52
association decisions, 20, 21, *21*,
206, 247
asylum seekers to Germany: data
analysis, *49*
Atlanta Journal Constitution:
data classification practice, 43,
57, 89; "Doctors & Sex Abuse"
story, 79, 91; Legislative
Navigator App, 63, 93
audience analytics tools, 184
automated content: adoption of,
107–8, 109; algorithmic
objectivity of, 118; business
impacts of, 114–16; coverage
bias of, 119; dependency on
data, 117–19; impact on content visibility, 116; limitations